Exchange Your Worries for God's Perfect Peace

Jack and Judy Hartman

Lamplight Ministries, Inc.
Dunedin, FL 34698-2921

ISBN 0-915445-09-3

Library of Congress Control Number: 2003092887

DEDICATION

We dedicate this book to Reverend Ebenezer Moses, the founder of India Gospel Fellowship in Salem, India. We honor you, Eb, for creating a home for and personally nurturing more than one thousand homeless children in your orphanage, for feeding the poor, for creating the Shepherd's Council of India where you provide mentoring and leadership for more than four thousand pastors, for founding and operating a Bible school and for your evangelical crusades with India Gospel Fellowship where you preach the gospel in power. We are deeply blessed to serve together with you to reach multitudes of people who have not yet come to know our loving Father through the Gospel of Jesus Christ. We love you, Eb, and your dear wife, Helen, and your daughter, Jessica. We are blessed to be your spiritual "Mum" and Dad.

FOREWORD

For many years my wife edited my books. When we stopped writing books to devote five years of our lives to writing ten sets of Scripture Meditation Cards, Judy contributed so much that she rightfully was listed as the co-author of these Scripture cards.

When we started writing books again, I assumed that Judy would merely edit the books as she had done previously. However, Judy made so many changes on each draft of our next book that she changed the book significantly. Judy's repeated suggestions caused me to make extensive changes. I concluded at that time that she legitimately should be listed as the co-author of that book. The same situation has occurred in this book.

I have not removed several first person references that I used in writing my portion of the book, but I want to emphasize that Judy definitely is the co-author of this book. I am indebted to Judy for hearing God and for all of the constructive rewriting she has done. Thank you, my dear wife. I believe the readers of this book also will thank you as they read the following pages.

Jack Hartman

I first started using this version of the Bible when I bought a paperback version of *The Amplified New Testament* many years ago because of the inscription on the cover. This inscription said, "...the best study Testament on the market. It is a *magnificent* translation. I use it constantly." (Dr. Billy Graham)

As I read about the history of this version of the Bible, I found that a group of qualified Hebrew and Greek scholars had spent a total of more than 20,000 hours amplifying the Bible. They believed that traditional word-by-word translations often failed to reveal the shades of meaning that are part of the Hebrew and Greek words.

After many years of extensive Bible study I have found that *The Amplified Bible* reveals many spiritual truths that I cannot find in other versions of the Bible. Because of this marvelous amplification, we now use this version of the Bible exclusively in all of our books and Scripture Meditation Cards.

If you are not familiar with this translation of the Bible, please be patient with the brackets and parentheses. They are used to indicate what has been added in the amplification. The brackets contain words that clarify the meaning. The parentheses contain additional phrases included in the original language. I don't want to bury you under a mass of parentheses and brackets, but I have found that *The Amplified Bible* is filled with specific and practical information that I believe will help *you* to overcome worry and to receive the magnificent peace our Father has made available to each of His beloved children.

TABLE OF CONTENTS

Introduction

When we ask Jesus Christ to be our Savior, we receive provision from God that enables us to be set free from worry, anxiety and fear for the rest of our lives. No one in heaven is worried, anxious or fearful. However, we must *learn* how to overcome worry, anxiety and fear while we are here on earth. We also can learn how to receive peace with God, the peace of God and the peaceful relationships with other people that were made available to us at Calvary.

Jesus knew that we would be tempted to worry. He instructed us to *guard* our hearts so that they would not be heavy. Jesus said, "...be on your guard, lest your hearts be overburdened and depressed (weighed down) with...worldly worries and cares pertaining to [the business of] this life..." (Luke 21:34).

This passage of Scripture tells us many things we should be on guard against – the three dots in the middle of this verse indicate that I have focused only on the instructions that Jesus gave us to guard against worldly worries and cares. When we guard against something, we are very careful that whatever we are guarding against does not happen to us. Jesus wants us to be very careful that we do not allow worried thoughts about the problems of life to get into our minds and our hearts.

Most Bible scholars believe that we live in the last days before Jesus Christ returns. The Bible tells us that we will face difficult problems during the last days. We already have faced and we now are facing the possibility of future acts of terror that have shaken the world. We face difficult times in the months and years ahead of us. If there ever was a time to learn how to overcome worry and fear, we live in this time. "...understand this, that in the last days will come (set in) perilous times of great stress and trouble [hard to deal with and hard to bear]" (II Timothy 3:1).

We do not have to learn how to worry. We inherited the tendency to worry from our ancestors Adam and Eve. This tendency to worry has been increased by the many stressful conditions that exist in the world today.

Imagine yourself driving by a hotel with a big sign out in front that said, "Learn How to Worry – 7:30 p.m. Tonight." Wouldn't that sign look ridiculous to you? You probably would think, "I don't need a training course to tell me how to worry. I already know how to worry."

Let's look again at this imaginary sign in front of the hotel and add one word to it. Imagine that this sign said, "Learn How to Overcome Worry – 7:30 p.m. Tonight." This sign would interest many people who want to learn how to overcome worry. Many people would like to learn how to overcome worry, but they do not know what to do to stop worrying.

Our Father knew that we would be tempted to be worried and anxious. The Word of God is filled with hundreds of specific instructions that tell us exactly what our Father wants us to do to exchange our worries for His perfect peace. As you study the Scripture references in this book, you will learn exactly what our Father wants us to do to overcome worry and anxiety.

In this book you will see the word "problems" used many times. This word is predominant in these chapters because many people worry about the problems they face now or anticipated problems they believe they might face in the future. Christians should understand that what the world looks at as problems actually are *opportunities* for the Lord to create His character in us. We must learn how to see every problem as an opportunity to trust the Lord more completely.

In the first twenty-eight chapters of this book you will learn how to give these problems to the Lord instead of worrying about them. You will learn how to trust the Lord so that you will let go of these problems, give them to Him and leave them with Him. In the final twenty chapters of this book we will change our emphasis from overcoming worry to peace. You will learn how to be at peace with God, how to receive the peace of God and how to keep the peace of God when other people treat you in such a way that you are tempted to give up this peace.

The peace of God cannot be purchased with any amount of money. The peace of God is available free of charge to every person who has asked Jesus Christ to be his or her Savior. Jesus has paid the full price that enables each of us to receive His wonderful peace.

We now are ready to proceed together to study the holy Scriptures to learn exactly what our Father has instructed us to do to overcome worry and fear. We then will learn exactly what our Father has instructed us to do to receive evidence of His wonderful peace.

Chapter 1

Our Father Does Not Want His Children to Worry

Some people are chronic worriers – they always are worried about something. Some people are not worriers – they never worry about anything. Many of us are between these two extremes – we don't worry continually, but we do worry when we face a severe challenge that seems to have no solution.

People who have not asked Jesus Christ to be their Savior have good reason to worry about the future. They must attempt to solve the difficult problems in their lives with their limited human abilities. They do not have the ability to give their problems to the Lord. "…you had no hope (no promise); you were in the world without God" (Ephesians 2:12).

This book is written for Christian believers who have asked Jesus Christ to be their Savior. Please read Chapter 29 and Chapter 30 now if you have never asked Jesus Christ to be your Savior and if you would like to trust Him completely. Also, please read the Appendix at the end of the book. These two chapters and the Appendix are filled with specific promises and instructions from the Word of God that will enable *you* to trust God for your eternal salvation, to overcome the tendency to worry and to receive God's perfect peace.

Unbelievers do not know how to rely upon a loving Father Who has promised to meet every need of His children. They do not study God's wonderful Book of Instructions that is filled with thousands of instructions from heaven. They do not understand that the Bible is filled with several thousand promises from Almighty God. They do not know God's promises and they do not have faith in the absolute reliability of every promise from God. They do not know how to trust the Holy Spirit Who lives in the hearts of all Christians. The Holy Spirit will guide us and help us.

Unfortunately, some Christians make these same mistakes. Although we have access to a personal relationship with our loving Father, to His instructions to us and to all of the promises He has given us, some Christians fail to live in the glorious inheritance that has been provided for them by Jesus Christ. These Christians know that they will live eternally in heaven, but they trust primarily in themselves and in other people to solve the problems they face.

Some believers worry constantly about difficult problems in their lives that seem to have no solution. Some Christians are worried, depressed and distraught because they constantly look to external sources for a solution to the problems they face. Instead of being worried, anxious and fearful, Christians have been given the opportunity to turn to God with absolute faith in Him.

Our Father has repeatedly told us that He does not want us to be afraid. I once heard the late Dr. Finis Dake say that he had counted 366 times in the Word of God where God says that we should not be afraid. Whenever we are worried or fearful, our worry and our fear indicate that our trust in God is weak.

I believe that our Father uses repetition in His Word as a means of emphasis. When our Father tells us 366 times that we should not be afraid, we can be absolutely certain that *He does not want us to be afraid of anything.*

In addition to telling us so many times that we should not be afraid, the Word of God also repeatedly tells us that we should not be worried or anxious. The following three Scripture references come from Jesus Christ's Sermon on the Mount:

"...stop being perpetually uneasy (anxious and worried) about your life..." (Matthew 6:25).

"...do not worry and be anxious..." (Matthew 6:31).

"...do not worry or be anxious about tomorrow..." (Matthew 6:34).

Once again we see that the Word of God provides emphasis through repetition. We will study each of these three passages of Scripture in detail in subsequent chapters. For now I want to emphasize that Jesus definitely does *not* want us to be worried or anxious.

Jesus gave a similar message to His disciples on the last night before He was betrayed. He said, "Do not let your hearts be troubled (distressed, agitated)..." (John 14:1). We also will study this passage of Scripture in detail in a subsequent chapter.

As we begin this book I want to point out the repeated emphasis in the Word of God that tells us that our Father definitely does *not* want us to be worried, anxious or afraid. Jesus has set us free from worry, anxiety and fear. "My desire is to have you free from all anxiety and distressing care..." (I Corinthians 7:32).

Our Father has instructed us to fill our minds and our hearts with His Word throughout every day of our lives (see Joshua 1:8,

Psalm 1:2-3, II Corinthians 4:16 and Ephesians 4:23). Unfortunately, many of God's children disobey these specific instructions from God. They do not renew their minds in the Word of God each day. They do not meditate on the Word of God throughout the day and night.

Christians who do not fill their minds and their hearts with the Word of God cannot believe the promises of God. How can we believe our Father's promises if we do not even know what He has promised? Can you honestly say that *your mind* and *your heart* are filled to overflowing with many of God's wonderful promises?

We will continually draw closer to God if we obey our Father's instructions to constantly fill our minds and our hearts with His Word. As we come to know our Father more and more intimately, we will be *absolutely certain* that He always will do exactly what He promises to do.

When we are worried or afraid, we show that we are not living by absolute faith in God and we are not obeying the specific instructions He has given us in the Bible. Our Father is not pleased when His children do not trust Him. "...the just shall live by faith...if he draws back and shrinks in fear, My soul has no delight or pleasure in him" (Hebrews 10:38).

If you are a parent, how would you feel if your children disobeyed your specific instructions? How would you feel if your children were constantly worried or afraid because they had not learned what you said you would do for them or because they did not believe you would do what you promised to do?

Our heavenly Father is no different. He has provided *everything* that any of His children will ever need. He has given us the Bible that is filled to overflowing with thousands of specific instructions that tell us exactly how He wants us to live our lives. He has given us thousands of promises that tell us exactly how we can live in victory if we know and believe His magnificent promises.

The English word "worry" comes from the Greek word "merimnous." This word is a combination of two words – "merim" which means "to divide" and "nous" which means "mind." Christians who worry have divided minds. Their minds go back and forth from worrying to faith in God and back to worrying again.

Our Father wants us to be single-minded. We will not be double-minded if we obey our Father's instructions to continually fill our minds and our hearts with His Word. We will not worry if we focus continually on the many promises from heaven that are contained in the Word of God.

Instead of being double-minded, our Father instructs us to come to Him in prayer with *absolute certainty* that He *will* answer our prayers. "…it must be in faith that he asks with no wavering (no hesitating, no doubting). For the one who wavers (hesitates, doubts) is like the billowing surge out at sea that is blown hither and thither and tossed by the wind. For truly, let not such a person imagine that he will receive anything [he asks for] from the Lord, [for being as he is] a man of two minds (hesitating, dubious, irresolute), [he is] unstable and unreliable and uncertain about everything [he thinks, feels, decides]" (James 1:6-8).

Our Father wants us to turn to Him continually with absolute faith in Him. He does not want us to go back and forth from worry and fear to faith in Him and then back to worry and fear again. Our Father has told us that He will not answer our prayers if we are double-minded. Christians who are worried and fearful block themselves from receiving the answer to their prayers that their loving Father has promised to give His children who have unwavering faith in Him.

Christians who worry often are engaged in a constant "tug of war" between faith in God and worry and anxiety about the problems they face. They are confused. They want to believe God, but they are worried about what they think might happen to them. They do not have the single-minded unwavering faith in God that our loving Father wants us to have.

Our Father created us to be single-minded and unwavering in our faith in Him. Satan wants us to worry. Satan and his demons do everything they can to put thoughts into our minds that will cause us to worry.

I have just mentioned for the first time about Satan and his demons and how they will attempt to influence us. You will find similar references throughout this book. I am aware that some readers of this book do not believe that Satan exists. I know that other readers who believe that Satan exists do not believe that Satan and his demons can put thoughts into their minds.

Satan wants us to think that he and his demons do not exist. Satan does not want us to believe that he and his demons can put thoughts into our minds. Satan's effectiveness is significantly increased in the lives of people who think this way.

There is no question that Satan exists. *Strong's Exhaustive Concordance* gives 52 separate instances where the word "Satan" is used in the Bible. Satan also is mentioned in the Bible many other times using such terms as "adversary," "devil," "Prince of the Power of the Air," "Ruler of Darkness" and "wicked one."

The Bible tells of the influence of Satan who is referred to as "the serpent" on Adam and Eve (see Genesis 3:1-24). We read many times about Satan in the Books of Matthew, Mark, Luke and John that describe the earthly ministry of Jesus Christ. There is no question that Satan existed when the Bible was written. Satan and his demons still are very active in the world today. Satan and his demons haven't gone anywhere. They are spirit beings who do not die.

We live in the last days before Jesus Christ returns. During these last days we can clearly see a distinct movement of Satan and an even greater movement of the Holy Spirit. Anyone who does not believe in the influence of Satan needs only to look at the content of many books in our libraries and book stores, the content of many "R" movies, the "sleeze" that easily can be found on the Internet and the wave of immorality that is sweeping the world today.

Anyone who does not believe that Satan can attempt to enter our minds needs to read about Judas Iscariot, a beloved disciple of Jesus Christ who betrayed Jesus. The Bible says that, "...Satan having already put the thought of betraying Jesus in the heart of Judas Iscariot..." (John 13:2).

We know that Satan and his demons exist. We know that Satan and his demons can attempt to influence us by putting thoughts into our minds. We also must know that Jesus Christ has given us a total victory over Satan and his demons (see Luke 10:19).

Our Father has provided us with the power of the Holy Spirit to enable us to *reject* thoughts from Satan and his demons. Our minds should be focused upon the Word of God. Our hearts should be filled with God's promises. We must not allow the circumstances in our lives or events that we think might take place in the future to overcome our absolute trust in Almighty God.

Whenever we open our mouths to speak words of concern about things we are worried about, we clearly indicate to Satan and his demons that we do not trust God. We verify to them that the thoughts they have tried to put into our minds have obtained a foothold. When we speak worried and fearful thoughts, we might as well turn to Satan and say, "Satan, come right in. Sit down. Make yourself at home."

Worry and fear give the devil a foothold in our lives that our Father absolutely does not want him to obtain. Our Father wants our minds and our hearts to be so filled with His promises that we absolutely will refuse to allow any thoughts from Satan to get into our minds and, from there, to drop down into our hearts. "Leave no [such] room or foothold for the devil [give no opportunity to Him]" (Ephesians 4:27).

This passage of Scripture refers to not allowing Satan to get into our minds with thoughts that tempt us to be angry. I believe that this passage of Scripture also indicates that we should not give Satan *any* opportunity whatsoever to get a foothold in any area of our lives.

Worry is a thief. Worry robs us of the peace and joy that are available to us when we believe wholeheartedly in God's promises, when we know that God lives in our hearts and when we trust God completely. One of Satan's primary goals is to *steal* the blessings that Jesus Christ provided for us at Calvary. Jesus said, "The thief comes only in order to steal and kill and destroy..." (John 10:10).

Worry and fear indicate that we do not believe totally, completely and absolutely in the victory Jesus Christ has won for us. We should refuse to worry about anything. We give Satan a foothold in our lives whenever we worry. "...fret not yourself – it tends only to evildoing" (Psalm 37:8).

The word "fret" means the same as the word "worry." We give Satan a foothold whenever we fret. Our fretting reacts to what Satan wants us to do instead of reacting to what our loving Father has promised to do.

Whenever we are tempted to worry, we immediately should turn away from whatever we are tempted to worry about to focus on God. We should be like the psalmist who said, "Why are you cast down, O my inner self? And why should you moan over me and be disquieted within me? Hope in God and wait expectantly for Him…" (Psalm 42:11).

We cannot stop Satan and his demons from attempting to put thoughts into our minds, but we can refuse to allow these thoughts to get a foothold in our minds. We cannot stop difficult problems from occurring in our lives, but we can refuse to focus on these problems.

We should make the quality decision throughout every day of our lives to focus constantly on God. Our Father wants us to continually fill our minds and our hearts with His Word so that we will have hope in Him because we trust Him completely while we wait patiently and faithfully for Him to do what we know He has promised to do.

The first chapter of this book has one purpose - to tell every person who reads this chapter that *our loving Father absolutely does not want us to be worried or afraid.* Now that we have established this foundation, we are ready to move forward in subsequent chapters to learn *how* to overcome worry and fear. We also will learn exactly what the holy Scriptures tell us to do to experience absolute peace from God throughout every day of our lives regardless of the problems we face.

Chapter 2

Our Father Promises to Meet Every One of Our Needs

I would like to begin this chapter by asking you a question that will help you to overcome the habit of worrying. The question is, "Would you ever worry about anything if you are *absolutely certain* that your loving Father will meet *every* need you have now and *every* need you will have in the future?"

As you read the next two chapters you will see that your loving Father repeatedly promises that He *will* meet every one of your needs. Because of the sacrifice of Jesus Christ at Calvary, our Father *already has done* everything He ever will do to provide for every one of our needs throughout our lives.

Will we pay the price to learn God's promises to supply every one of our needs? Will we believe God's promises wholeheartedly? Will we refuse to worry about anything because we know that every promise in the Bible is absolutely reliable? "…it is impossible for God ever to prove false or deceive us…" (Hebrews 6:18).

Our loving Father already has met the greatest need any of us will have. Our Father sent His beloved Son to earth to pay the price for our sins so that we will be able to live with Him in the glory of heaven throughout eternity. If God has met the greatest of all needs, can't we believe that He also has made provision to meet every other need throughout our lives on earth? "He who did not withhold or spare [even] His own Son but gave Him up for us all, will He not also with Him freely and graciously give us all [other] things?" (Romans 8:32).

The first part of this passage of Scripture applies to our eternal salvation. The last part applies to all of the needs that any of us will have at any time throughout our lives. Please personalize this statement. You are part of the word "us." Put in your name both times that this passage of Scripture says "us." Highlight or underline the words "all other things." You can be absolutely certain that these all-inclusive words apply to whatever *you* need right now and whatever *you* will need at any time in the future.

You will see from this passage of Scripture and from the other promises from God in these two chapters that our loving Father definitely has promised to meet all of our needs. You will *never* worry about *anything* if you learn the promises in the next two chapters, if you believe these promises from God wholeheartedly and if you live them every day of your life.

The last words that Jesus Christ said before He died on the cross at Calvary were "…It is finished!…" (John 19:30). Jesus said these words because He had accomplished everything He came to earth to accomplish. Our Father wants each of us to live with absolute faith in the finished work of our Lord Jesus Christ. We can trust Jesus for our eternal salvation. We also can be certain that the finished work of Jesus Christ includes every one of our needs being met throughout our lives on earth.

The finished work of Jesus Christ actually includes more than our needs being met. Jesus told us exactly why He came to earth when He said, "...I came that they may have and enjoy life, and have it in abundance (to the full, till it overflows)" (John 10:10).

The finished work of Jesus Christ includes an enjoyable life for each of us. The finished work of Jesus Christ includes an abundant life for each of us. Do you believe that Jesus told the truth when He spoke these words? *Why* would any of us ever worry about anything if we believe this statement? We can and should enjoy life fully and trust God to meet our needs absolutely, regardless of any temporary circumstances we may face.

Jesus Christ won a total, complete and absolute victory on the cross at Calvary. He gave us a marvelous promise guaranteeing that we will live an abundant life *if* we believe in Him. We can be certain that the victorious Jesus Christ actually lives inside of us. "...Do you not yourselves realize and know [thoroughly by an ever-increasing experience] that Jesus Christ is in you...?" (II Corinthians 13:5).

Many of God's children are striving, straining, worrying, struggling and pleading with God to give them things that *already have been provided for them.* We need to know who we are in Christ. We need to know that Jesus Christ lives in our hearts. We need to know exactly what our Father has provided through Jesus Christ. We need to trust completely in our absolute certainty of God's provision instead of worrying about things that already have been provided for us.

Jesus meant exactly what He said when He said, "It is finished". We have been redeemed by the blood of the Lamb. We can be absolutely certain that Jesus has provided all of His beloved brothers and sisters with everything we will need here on earth and throughout eternity.

Jesus Christ is our Provider. He also is our Shepherd (see John 10:14). Shepherds lead their sheep. Shepherds provide for all of the needs of their sheep. We can be absolutely assured that our wonderful Shepherd has made full provision for each of us throughout our lives.

Our Father wants us to be certain that He has made provision for every one of our needs just as beloved little children here on earth have absolute trust that their human parents will provide everything they need. If loving parents here on earth provide for the needs of their children, can't we believe that our loving heavenly Father has provided for everything we will need?

In the area of finances, our Father has given us specific instructions to follow to be certain that all of our financial needs are met. God instructs us to sow financial seeds to receive the harvest of financial blessings He has provided for us.

Our Father has instructed us to tithe ten percent of our income to Him (see Malachi 3:8-11). He instructs us to give freely of financial offerings over and above our tithes. Our Father will give us a harvest based upon the seeds we sow (see Luke 6:38 and II Corinthians 9:6-8). For detailed information pertaining to financial principles, please see our book, *Trust God for Your Finances,* and our Scripture Meditation Cards and cassette tape that each are titled *Financial Instructions from God.*

As we give into the kingdom of God, we are investing in what I call the Bank of Heaven. As we live our lives by giving everything to God, we will experience all of our needs being met. "…God will liberally supply (fill to the full) your every need according to His riches in glory in Christ Jesus" (Philippians 4:19).

In this passage of Scripture Paul is thanking the believers at Philippi for their gifts to him. He also is explaining to us today that God will be very pleased if we give sacrificial offerings as He directs us. As we faithfully give these offerings, we set into motion God's principle of sowing and reaping.

If you ever are tempted to worry about anything, focus on Philippians 4:19. Meditate constantly on this promise. This promise does not just say that God will supply all of our needs. Philippians 4:19 says that God will *liberally* supply *our every need through Jesus Christ.* God supplies these needs when we give freely into His kingdom (see Philippians 4:16-18).

Personalize this promise. Put your name in this promise where the word "your" is used. Focus continually on the word "every." Sow financial seeds into the kingdom of God. Sow additional seeds for prosperity by continually meditating on the Word of God (see Joshua 1:8 and Psalm 1:2-3). Know that your loving Father has promised to provide for every one of your needs through Jesus Christ. Refuse to worry about anything because of your absolute certainty that God already has provided for your every need.

Refuse to waver in your faith in God regardless of the circumstances in your life. This promise does not say that God will supply every one of our needs if the Dow Jones Average is above a certain level. God does not say that He will provide for all of our needs as long as the economy is doing well. External conditions can only have the degree of control over us that we allow them to have. God's promises are much greater and much more powerful than *any* circumstances we will face.

Our Father wants His Word to be the rock-solid foundation for our lives. He wants us to have such unwavering faith in Him that we never will allow circumstances of any kind to pull us down. Our Father has promised to meet all of our needs. We can be assured that our Father will do exactly what

He says He will do *if* we do not block ourselves from receiving His blessings through doubt and unbelief and if we give freely of our tithes and offerings.

Only a small percentage of God's children live according to God's principles that we have read about in this chapter. They have not tested these principles. They are not close enough to God to trust Him completely to do exactly what He says He will do. "For His divine power has bestowed upon us all things that [are requisite and suited] to life and godliness through the [full, personal] knowledge of Him Who called us by and to His own glory and excellence (virtue)" (II Peter 1:3).

Know that your Father has "bestowed upon *you* all things." The word "bestow" means to give someone a present or a gift. Know that God has given *you* the gift of "all things that are requisite and suited to life and godliness."

The word "requisite" has the same root as the word "required." You would be scripturally accurate if you said that God has provided you with everything that will be required during your life. How do we receive this wonderful gift from God? We are told that we will receive everything we will need *if* we know God intimately and trust Him completely.

How do we get this wonderful personal knowledge of God? This question is answered in the next verse of Scripture. "By means of these He has bestowed on us His precious and exceedingly great promises, so that through them you may escape [by flight] from the moral decay (rottenness and corruption) that is in the world because of covetousness (lust and greed), and become sharers (partakers) of the divine nature" (II Peter 1:4).

We could meditate on this passage of Scripture for a long time. For the purpose of what we are talking about here, I want to merely say that we will receive the full personal knowledge of God that we need if we know and believe that our loving Father has made provision to supply all of our needs through His promises.

We can walk in victory over the decay and corruption in the world if we will obey our Father's instructions to meditate continually on His wonderful promises. We are told that we actually will be able to *partake of the nature of God* if we obey these instructions. God's promises will come alive on the inside of us if we do what our Father has told us to do by renewing our minds in His Word every day of our lives and by meditating throughout the day and night on the holy Scriptures. If we faithfully obey these instructions, we will be able to trust God completely regardless of the circumstances we face.

We can be absolutely certain that our loving Father through His beloved Son, Jesus Christ, has provided for every need we ever will have throughout our lives. God's provision provides for all of our financial needs, our physical needs, our emotional needs and our spiritual needs.

Our Father gives us His peace when we are tempted to be agitated by the circumstances in our lives (see John 14:27). Our Father gives us His strength when we are weak and cannot go any further (see II Corinthians 12:9-10). Our Father has made provision for us to partake of His wisdom so that we can transcend the limitations of human wisdom (see James 1:5).

Chapter 3

Trust God for Everything You Need

By His grace and His mercy, God sometimes meets the needs of people even when they do not have faith in Him. When the Israelites were in the wilderness they grumbled, griped and complained, but God still provided for them. "You gave them bread from heaven for their hunger and brought water for them out of the rock for their thirst..." (Nehemiah 9:15)

You might want to read the entire ninth chapter of Nehemiah. I only have commented on the basic needs of food and water. This chapter gives many other illustrations of God's provision for the Israelites as they wandered through the wilderness. If God made all of this provision for the Israelites who grumbled and complained because they did not believe in Him, can you believe that He will supply all of *your* needs if you have deep and unwavering faith in Him?

We see another example of the provision of the Lord when Jesus Christ sent His disciples out to minister with no money and no provision of any kind. Jesus wanted to show His disciples that He would provide everything they needed even though they had no visible means of support. Jesus said, "...When I sent you out with no purse or [provision] bag or sandals, did you lack anything? They answered, Nothing!" (Luke 22:35).

This same principle applies to each of us today. The Word of God is filled with specific promises from God telling us that all of our needs have been provided for. *What more do we need? Why would we ever worry about anything if we truly believe* all of these wonderful promises from heaven we are reading about?

Our Father wants us to trust Him completely. He does not want us to worry about anything. "…they who seek (inquire of and require) the Lord [by right of their need and on the authority of His Word], none of them shall lack any beneficial thing" (Psalm 34:10).

Our Father wants us to seek Him whenever we have a need. If we have absolute faith in God, we will not lack anything that we need. The word "none" in this passage of Scripture includes *you.* Our Father will not withhold anything from any of His children who do their very best to live their lives according to the instructions He has given us in His marvelous Book of Instructions. "…No good thing will He withhold from those who walk uprightly" (Psalm 84:11).

Many of us bring problems upon ourselves because we fail to continually study and meditate on the Word of God so that we will *do* what our Father has instructed us to do to – "walk uprightly." Our Father promises to bless every one of His children who fear Him, revere Him, worship Him and obey His instructions. "Blessed (happy, fortunate, to be envied) is everyone who fears, reveres, and worships the Lord, who walks in His ways and lives according to His commandments" (Psalm 128:1).

Please highlight or underline the word "everyone" in this passage of Scripture. We all should fear God and revere Him. When we fear and revere God, we always hold God in absolute awe. Every aspect of our lives should revolve around Him. Our Father promises to bless us when we worship Him continually and obey the specific instructions He has given to us.

Our Father wants us to lean on Him with absolute faith that He will answer our prayers. We must not miss out on the blessings our Father has provided for us because we do not know or do not have complete faith in God and His Word. "...the message they heard did not benefit them, because it was not mixed with faith (with the leaning of the entire personality on God in absolute trust and confidence in His power, wisdom and goodness)..." (Hebrews 4:2).

Some Christians hear promises from God and fail to receive manifestation of these promises. They do not receive what their Father has promised to give them because they do not have absolute faith in God's promises. They do not trust God enough to "lean" upon Him, trusting Him completely to do exactly what He says He will do.

In these two chapters you have seen numerous promises that God will supply everything you need. Our Father is omniscient – He has all knowledge. He knows every one of the needs of every one of His children. He knows exactly what *you* need.

Our Father has repeatedly assured us that He has made full provision for every one of our needs. All of our needs will be met if we live in harmony with our Father's love, if we know our Father intimately, if we love Him with all of our hearts and if we trust Him completely.

Our Father does not want our faith in Him to waver when we face a crisis situation. He wants our hearts to sing with joy because we know exactly what He has promised to do and because we have absolute faith that He will do what He promises to do.

If you would like more specific instructions on how to continually fill your mind and your heart with God's Word, I recommend our book and our two cassette tapes that are titled *How to Study the Bible*. This book and these two tapes are filled with specific and exact instructions that explain a proven method of Bible study and meditation that will enable you to increase your faith in God continually.

We should praise our Father and thank Him continually before we receive the wonderful blessings He has promised to us. "May blessing (praise, laudation, and eulogy) be to the God and Father of our Lord Jesus Christ (the Messiah) Who has blessed us in Christ with every spiritual (given by the Holy Spirit) blessing in the heavenly realm!" (Ephesians 1:3).

When we praise God boldly and continually in the face of the problems in our lives, our praise releases our faith in God. God has provided wonderful blessings for us because of Jesus Christ. We receive these blessings by surrendering to God.

We must not allow words of doubt and unbelief to come out of our mouths if we do not see God immediately supplying all of our needs. Instead, we should continually speak God's promises of provision back to Him. We should claim these promises by faith. We should praise our Father and thank Him continually for His marvelous provision.

Our Father created us to enjoy continual fellowship with Him. He gave us the Bible so that we could know Him intimately. Our recreated human spirit can speak to God Who is a Spirit throughout every day of our lives. Our nature will become more and more like God's nature as we spend more and more time with Him. We will begin to think as God thinks, speak as He speaks and act as He acts.

Record on 3 + 5

— 36 —

Victory comes when we look up from the written Word of God into the face of our Father, the Author. In His presence we will find all that we need instantly. We will behold the face of our Father Who loves us so much when we constantly study and meditate on the precious Bible He has given to us.

We must not give up. Our Father always does what He says He will do. He wants us to trust Him completely. He also wants us to trust His timing just as we trust Him in every other area. If our needs have not yet been met, the words that come out of our mouths should show that we are absolutely certain that our Father will meet every one of our needs in His way and in His good timing.

Whenever we face a crisis situation of any sort, our words and our actions should clearly indicate our absolute conviction that our Father already has made complete provision to supply everything we need. If we have paid the price of increasing our faith in God by continually filling our minds and our hearts with His promises, these promises will flow out of our mouths regardless of the circumstances we face. Jesus Christ said, "...out of the fullness (the overflow, the superabundance) of the heart the mouth speaks. The good man from his inner good treasure flings forth good things, and the evil man out of his inner evil storehouse flings forth evil things" (Matthew 12:34-35) True

We will store up an abundance of wonderful promises from God in our minds and in our hearts if we pay the price of studying and meditating on His Word throughout every day as our Father has instructed us to do. We will know that God's nature is developing within us so that we are ready to face any crisis situation. God's promises that fill our hearts abundantly will pour out of our mouths regardless of the circumstances we face.

Many people store up money so that they will have this money when they face a crisis situation. Our Father wants us to store up His Word in our hearts. He wants our security to come from His Word living in our hearts and from His indwelling presence.

The last two chapters have been filled with magnificent truth from the living, eternal Word of God telling us that our loving Father has made complete provision for every one of our needs. I hope these wonderful truths have encouraged you. I hope they will help you to stop worrying.

Some Christians in North America are somewhat complacent. Their security comes from external sources. If everything is going well in your life at this time, you might think that these are "nice" chapters and go on with your reading. Do not allow these chapters to get away from you.

Circumstances change. You should know and believe completely in God's provision if you come to a time in the future where you have a definite need in some area and you cannot see how this need will be met. The contents of these chapters that seem like a "nice to have" when everything is going well can and will become a "have to have" if the circumstances in your life change enough.

Chapter 4

Know That the Lord Lives in Your Heart

In the last two chapters we have seen that God has given us many promises to supply all of our needs. In the next two chapters we will see that God actually comes to live inside of us when we ask Jesus Christ to be our Savior. Our Father wants us to *know* that He is with us at all times. He wants us to trust Him completely.

Our Father has given each of us the antidote to worry, fear and discouragement. His name is Jesus Christ. He is the King of Kings and the Lord of Lords (see Revelation 17:14 and Revelation 19:16). Jesus lives on the inside of us. *Why* would we ever worry about anything if we are absolutely certain that the same Jesus Christ Who won a total victory at Calvary actually lives in our hearts?

Whenever we are tempted to worry, we should stop immediately. We should focus on the indwelling presence of our precious Lord instead of focusing on whatever we are tempted to worry about. We should say, "I will not worry about this situation. I know that You live inside of me, dear Jesus. You are with me at all times. You are all-powerful. You are in complete control. I will place all of my trust in You."

Some people allow worry and fear to consume them because they think that they are alone when they face difficult problems. Life can be very difficult when we walk alone. Our Father *never* meant for us to walk alone. He wants each of His children to know exactly what His Word says about His indwelling presence. Our Father wants us to be certain that He can help us and that He will help us.

God never takes time off. He is with us throughout every minute of every hour of every day of our lives. Jesus Christ was constantly aware of His Father's presence throughout His earthly ministry. When Jesus faced adversity, He was secure because He knew His Father was with Him. Jesus said, "...He Who sent Me is ever with Me; My Father has not left Me alone..." (John 8:29).

We should not give in to worry and fear because of our absolute certainty that our Father is always with us. "Fear not [there is nothing to fear], for I am with you; do not look around you in terror and be dismayed, for I am your God. I will strengthen and harden you to difficulties, yes, I will help you; yes, I will hold you up and retain you with My [victorious] right hand of rightness and justice" (Isaiah 41:10).

Why would we ever be worried or afraid of anything if we know our Father says that we should *not* be afraid of anything? If we have absolute faith in God's indwelling presence, we will not be terrified when we face difficult problems. We can be absolutely certain that God will give us the strength and the ability to do what has to be done. We should know that our loving Father has promised to help us. He has promised to hold us up.

We must not be afraid. We should be encouraged at all times because of our absolute certainty that Almighty God is with us wherever we go. "…Be strong, vigorous, and very courageous. Be not afraid, neither be dismayed, for the Lord your God is with you wherever you go" (Joshua 1:9).

Satan's demons try to get into our minds constantly with many different thoughts that they believe will cause us to be worried and afraid. We should not have any fear of Satan and his demons. They were defeated at Calvary by Jesus Christ. The same Jesus Christ Who defeated them lives inside of us. "…I will fear or dread no evil, for You are with me…" (Psalm 23:4).

In this chapter we have seen that the Word of God repeatedly tells us that the Lord is with us at all times. Please do not read these passages of Scripture and forget about them. Meditate on them continually. Do not just pay "mental assent" to the fact that the Lord is with you. *Know* that He is with *you* at all times.

We know that God lives inside of us. We now are ready to study several passages of Scripture that assure us that God never will leave us. Our Father wants us to be absolutely certain that He will be with us throughout every day of our lives.

When Moses was 120 years old, he knew that he could not continue to do the things he used to do. He spoke to Joshua who would replace him as the leader of the Israelites. Moses said, "Be strong, courageous, and firm; fear not nor be in terror before them, for it is the Lord your God Who goes with you; He will not fail you or forsake you" (Deuteronomy 31:6).

This promise of God that Moses spoke to Joshua applies to us today. We should not give in to fear or terror. We should be strong and courageous. We can stand firmly in place because we are absolutely certain that the Lord our God goes with us at all times. We have been assured that God will not fail us or forsake us.

Moses continued to encourage Joshua. He said, "It is the Lord Who goes before you; He will [march] with you; He will not fail you or let you go or forsake you; [let there be no cowardice or flinching, but] fear not, neither become broken [in spirit – depressed, dismayed, and unnerved with alarm]" (Deuteronomy 31:8).

Please personalize this promise. Know that this same promise of God that was given through Moses to Joshua applies to *you* today. Know that the Lord is with you at all times. You can be absolutely certain that He will never fail you or forsake you.

Refuse to be a coward. Do not flinch. Refuse to be alarmed by any problems you face. Refuse to give in to depression. Trust the Lord Who is with you at all times to bring you safely through every situation. Do not block His mighty power from working on your behalf because of ignorance of His promises or by doubt and unbelief in His power. You can be certain that your loving Father will never let you down.

God appeared to Joshua to encourage him after Moses died. This young man understandably had some concerns about his ability to carry on in Moses' footsteps as the leader of millions of Israelites. God reassured Joshua when He said, "…As I as with Moses, so I will be with you; I will not fail you or forsake you" (Joshua 1:5).

Because of our Savior Jesus Christ, you can be assured that the same God Who was with Moses and Joshua is with *you* today. You can be absolutely certain that He never will fail you. You can be absolutely certain that He never will forsake you.

We have been studying several passages of Scripture from the Old Testament. A similar promise is given to us in the New Testament. "...He [God] Himself has said, I will not in any way fail you nor give you up nor leave you without support. [I will] not, [I will] not, [I will] not in any degree leave you helpless nor forsake nor let [you] down (relax My hold on you)! [Assuredly not!]" (Hebrews 13:5).

Once again, our Father promises that He never will fail us. He promises that He never will leave us. He repeats the words "I will not" three times to emphasize that He absolutely will not leave us. Once again, He promises that He never will forsake us.

Please review the passages of Scripture in this chapter. See that several anointed men of God have told us that God will never forsake us. See for yourself that your Father has given you this promise in Deuteronomy 31:6, again in Deuteronomy 31:8, again in Joshua 1:5 and again in Hebrews 13:5.

God emphasizes through repetition. We have just seen that our Father has assured us on four different occasions that He never will forsake us. He has assured us that He will not leave us.

Our loving Father will never forget us. He knows exactly what each of His children is going through. Our Father has wonderful compassion for each of us. He said, "...Can a woman forget her nursing child, that she should not have compassion on the son of her womb? Yes, they may forget, yet I will not forget you" (Isaiah 49:15).

We cannot comprehend how a new mother could forget about the baby she had carried and birthed. However, as inconceivable as that might seem, our Father guarantees us that we can be absolutely assured that He never will forget any of His beloved children.

Meditate on this wonderful truth. Personalize it. Know that your loving Father never will forget you. Know that He is watching over you at all times wherever you go and whatever you do. He said, "…behold, I am with you and will keep (watch over you with care, take notice of) you wherever you may go…" (Genesis 28:15).

Our Father assures us again and again that He is with us at all times. He repeatedly promises to watch over us. He will protect us if we will trust Him completely instead of blocking ourselves from receiving His mighty power through doubt and unbelief (see Mark 6:1-6).

Little children on earth have faith in their human parents when they know that their parents love them. They are secure when their parents are with them. They are secure when they know their parents are carefully watching them wherever they go. Our loving heavenly Father wants each of us to have security that is far beyond any security on the human level.

Our Father wants us to place all of our trust and confidence in Him. He wants us to know that He loves us with a love that is much, much greater than we can possibly comprehend (see Ephesians 3:11-21). He wants us to know that we will be safe at all times if we will place all of our trust in Him, knowing that He lives in our hearts and that He always will take care of us. "…The beloved of the Lord shall dwell in safety by Him; He covers him all the day long, and makes His dwelling between his shoulders" (Deuteronomy 33:12).

I hope that this chapter has encouraged you as much as it has encouraged me. Meditate continually on these wonderful promises from God until they come alive deep down inside of your heart. Make the decision that you never will worry again or give in to fear. Know that Almighty God lives inside of you, that He never will leave you and that He will take care of you at all times.

Chapter 5

Trust the Lord to Bring You Safely through Every Trial

In the last chapter we saw several Scripture references pertaining to the indwelling presence of God. In this chapter we will look at some additional statements from the Word of God pertaining to God living in our hearts. We will begin with God's assurance to the Israelites when He told them that He would be with them in the midst of their worst problems. "When you pass through the waters, I will be with you, and through the rivers, they will not overwhelm you. When you walk through the fire, you will not be burned or scorched, nor will the flame kindle upon you. For I am the Lord your God, the Holy One of Israel, your Savior…" (Isaiah 43:2-3).

Please personalize this promise. Know that this promise that God made to the Israelites many years ago applies to *you* today. Our Father wants us to be absolutely certain that He is with us when we face difficult problems.

Please highlight or underline each of the three times the word "through" is used in this passage of Scripture. Our Father wants us to be encouraged because we trust Him completely to bring us safely *through* the problems we face, no matter how difficult these problems may seem to be.

If you are a Christian, you can be certain that the same God Who created you lives within you. Know that the Creator of every person in the entire universe lives in *your heart*. Refuse to be dismayed by any problem you face because you know that God is omnipotent. No problem is too difficult for Almighty God (see Matthew 19:26, Mark 10:27, Luke 1:37 and Luke 18:27).

Focus continually on the magnificent truths from heaven that are included in the last chapter and in this chapter. Meditate on these truths throughout the day and night. Open your mouth and speak these wonderful truths boldly. Personalize these truths as you speak. See for yourself how increasing faith in God will rise up on the inside of you as you continually meditate on these magnificent truths and boldly speak them with your mouth.

Some Christians dwell *far too much* on the seeming severity of the problems they face and *far too little* on the indwelling presence of Almighty God. They allow their problems to become "big, big problems" and they cause God to become, in their estimation, "little, little God."

Our Father wants us to do exactly the opposite. He wants us to meditate continually on the wonderful promises He has given to us. He wants our faith in Him to grow and mature so that we will look at the problems we face as He looks at them – as "little, little problems." He wants us to see Him as He truly is - "big, big God."

Our Father wants us to know how weak and inadequate we are without Him. He does not want us to stop there. He wants us to go from our weakness to His strength. He wants us to go from our inadequacy to His supremacy (see II Corinthians 12:9-10).

None of us will ever come across any problem in our lives that can even begin to tax His mighty power, strength and ability.

We make a big mistake if we focus on the circumstances in our lives instead of focusing continually on the presence of Almighty God Who lives in our hearts. Our Father wants us to be like the apostle Paul who said, "…I saw the Lord constantly before me, for He is at my right hand that I may not be shaken or overthrown or cast down [from my secure and happy state]" (Acts 2:25).

The amplification of this passage of Scripture speaks of a "secure and happy state." Many people look for security and happiness from external sources. We must understand that true security and happiness cannot come from any external source. We will be completely secure at all times if we are absolutely certain that Almighty God lives in our hearts. Our hearts will sing with joy regardless of the circumstances we face. "…the Lord said, My Presence shall go with you, and I will give you rest" (Exodus 33:14).

Ryan-work Michelle - motherhood

When we work according to our flesh, we tire. When we work God's way, we do not become weary. We rest because God refreshes us. "…he who has once entered [God's] rest also has ceased from [the weariness and pain] of human labors…" (Hebrews 4:10).

When we rest in the Lord, we are able to rest because we trust Him completely to carry all of our burdens. We must not struggle and strain. When we call upon the Lord, He is always there. "The Lord is near to all who call upon Him, to all who call upon Him sincerely and in truth" (Psalm 145:18).

The word "all" is used twice in this passage of Scripture. Know that this all-inclusive word includes *you*. If you are a Christian, you can be certain that the Lord is with you whenever you face difficult problems. "…we are the temple of the living God; even as God said, I will dwell in and with and among them and will walk in and with and among them, and I will be their God, and they shall be My people" (II Corinthians 6:16).

Know that your body is a temple where God makes His home. Constantly acknowledge His lordship and His indwelling presence. Open your mouth often to speak about God's indwelling presence. Refuse to allow anything or anyone to cause you to be worried or afraid.

If God lives in your heart, what difference does it make who is opposing you or how difficult any problem might seem to be from your limited human perspective? "…If God is for us, who [can be] against us? [Who can be our foe, if God is on our side?]" (Romans 8:31).

We can be absolutely certain that our foes are not at all formidable to the God of the universe Who lives in our hearts. *Why* would we ever be afraid of anyone if we are certain that the same God Who created every person lives inside of us? Almighty God in us is much greater and much more powerful than any problem or any foe.

In addition to meditating on the biblical truths in these two chapters, you also might want to purchase a set of our Scripture Meditation Cards that are titled *God is Always with You*. These 52 Scripture cards contain approximately eighty passages of Scripture. Many of the truths in these two chapters and many other facts from the holy Scriptures will help you to enjoy God's presence.

These Scripture Meditation Cards will fit easily into a pocket or a purse. You can carry these Scripture cards with you so that you will be able to meditate constantly on these wonderful promises from God.

We could not include everything that can be said on this subject into fifty-two 2 ½" by 3 ½" cards. I have recorded an eighty-five minute cassette tape to supplement these Scripture cards. This tape also is titled *God Is Always with You.* If you want to continually increase your awareness of God's indwelling presence, I suggest that you purchase both the Scripture cards and the cassette tape.

You can listen to the cassette tape when you are driving your car. You can fill your ears, your mind and your heart with scriptural truths pertaining to God's indwelling presence as you drive from one place to another. You can enjoy the presence of God.

Go back and read this chapter again. Study and meditate on these Scripture references. Carry our Scripture cards with you constantly. Meditate on them throughout the day and night. Listen to the cassette tape repeatedly.

We cannot get too many truths about the presence of God on the inside of us. The more we are able to get these truths from the holy Scriptures into our eyes and into our ears, the more our minds and our hearts will enjoy the presence of God continually.

Experience God's wonderful presence in your life. Know that Almighty God is *your constant companion.* You can be certain that you never are alone. Obey God's specific instructions in Joshua 1:8 and Psalm 1:2-3 to meditate throughout the day and night on His Word. See for yourself how this continual meditation will cause you to grow in your intimacy with God.

Trust completely in God Who lives inside of you. The wonderful scriptural truths that are contained in these two chapters and in our Scripture cards pertaining to God's indwelling presence will lead you directly to the throne of God Who loves you so much.

Let these truths speak to your heart. Highlight them. Underline them. Meditate on them constantly. Enjoy the indwelling presence of Almighty God instead of focusing on the problems you face. Your life will be transformed beyond comprehension if you have not been doing these things and if you now do them continually.

Thank you, dear Lord, for Your presence in our lives. We worship You. We praise You. We glorify You.

Chapter 6

The Word of God is More Powerful Than Any Problem

We have learned that our Father does not want us to worry. Our Father has made provision to meet all of our needs. He is with us throughout every day of our lives. We now are ready to learn additional facts from the holy Scriptures that will help us to deal with the circumstances in our lives.

We have very little control over many of the things that happen to us, but God has given each of us the ability to control *our reaction to* the things that happen to us. Whenever we face a crisis situation we have been given the ability to determine what our attitude will be.

We will be empowered and encouraged by the Word of God living on the inside of us if we have obeyed our Father's instructions to fill our minds and our hearts with His Word on a daily basis. We will react to the circumstances in our lives according to God's instructions and promises if we will open our mouths and praise Him continually instead of griping, grumbling and complaining. Our Father can and will solve the problems we face if we will remain quiet and calm because we trust Him completely.

I am not saying that we should ignore any problems we face. We should carefully evaluate each problem. I believe a problem that is well defined is half solved.

Once we know exactly what we are facing, we should refuse to focus on that problem. Some people continually dwell upon the problems they face. They think about these problems constantly. There is no place in God's Book of Instructions where we are instructed to dwell upon the problems we face.

Instead of focusing on circumstances, we should *focus on God*. The presence of God will dispel any fear. We should focus continually on His Word that should fill our eyes, our ears, our mouths, our minds and our hearts. Our Father will honor our faith in Him if we refuse to focus on the problems we face and, instead, focus continually on Him.

We should not talk about the problems we face. The more we talk about these problems, the more we give them an opportunity to affect us. We should never respond emotionally to the circumstances in our lives. The presence of God in us enables us to face every situation with boldness, power and victory. The Word of God in us is much greater than any evil force, any problem or any person that come against us.

If the circumstances in our lives tell us one thing and the Word of God tells us another thing, we should always believe what the Word of God says. We should praise the Lord continually. We should focus constantly on our Father's promises to us. "Bless (affectionately, gratefully praise) the Lord, O my soul, and forget not [one of] all His benefits..." (Psalm 103:2).

This passage of Scripture tells us that we bless the Lord when we affectionately and gratefully praise Him. Our Father is blessed whenever His beloved children praise Him. When we face difficult problems we are not naturally inclined to praise the Lord with gratitude, but that is exactly what we should do. After many experiences of God's faithfulness, praise will live on our lips.

Jesus Christ is our example in every area of our lives. Throughout His earthly ministry, Jesus was unruffled by the circumstances He faced. Jesus lived above the circumstances in His life.

Jesus didn't live above these circumstances because He was the Son of God. Throughout the gospels of Matthew, Mark, Luke and John we are repeatedly told that Jesus lived His earthly ministry as the Son of Man. Jesus chose to live in relation to His Father in heaven and not by His own divine power. He set His power aside to come to earth as a man.

Jesus was able to rise above the circumstances He faced because He trusted completely in His Father. He was able to walk in victory because He trusted completely in the Word of God which He knew very well.

Jesus remained calm, quiet and confident in the face of every situation because He was in constant communion with His Father. Jesus Christ lives inside of all Christians who have asked Him to be their Savior. We will not be worried about any problems we face if we have complete confidence in Him.

I am beginning my eighth decade of life on earth as I write this book. If I could go back and live my life over again, the one thing I would do above all else is to *not* react so much to problems that I now know I should not have reacted to. As I look back on many seeming crises during the past seven decades, I can see that the Lord has brought me safely through all of them. I could have done much better by facing these problems with absolute faith in God.

We must not allow ourselves to become discouraged or depressed by the circumstances in our lives. We should have unwavering faith that the Lord will bring us safely through these circumstances. "Arise [from the depression and prostration in which circumstances have kept you – rise to a new life]! Shine (be radiant with the glory of the Lord)…" (Isaiah 60:1).

Our Father does not want us to give in to the depression and frustration that many people experience as a result of the trials and tribulations in their lives. We each have been given the opportunity to experience a new life that is lived with absolute faith in our precious Lord. We always should shine radiantly with the glory of the Lord.

We must not make the mistake the Israelites made when they wandered needlessly through the wilderness because of their continual negative reaction to the trials they faced. "…the people became impatient (depressed, much discouraged), because [of the trials] of the way" (Numbers 21:4).

If we are impatient, depressed or discouraged because of the problems we face, we can be assured that we are not reacting the way the Word of God tells us to react to these problems. The carnal part of our human nature tends to react negatively to problems. We should be so close to our Father that we will face every challenge with absolute faith that He can and will lead us to the solution.

Too many of us are dominated by the circumstances in our lives. We do not understand that the Word of God is *much more powerful* than *any* circumstance we will face. When we are faced with bad news of any kind, we should always step out in faith based upon all of the good news that is contained in the Word of God.

The Word of God is filled with good news from heaven. We should have so much of this good news coming into our eyes and our ears that bad news of any kind will not be able to get a foothold in our lives. Our Father wants us to immerse ourselves in His Word. Only a small percentage of God's children faithfully obey these instructions. Christians who consistently "saturate" themselves in the Word of God throughout the day and night renew their minds and their hearts constantly with the supernatural power of the living Word of God.

This continual programming of our minds and our hearts is similar to the way a computer is programmed. These Christians have programmed so much of the Word of God into their eyes, their ears, their minds, their hearts and their mouths that the bad news of the problems they face *cannot* pull them down because they are filled to overflowing with the magnificent power of the good news of the Word of God.

We are constantly inundated with a continual flow of bad news from the news media. Take a careful look at the bad news in your daily newspaper today. Think about all of the bad news that is pouring out of the mouths of newscasters on radio and television. Realize that this constant flow of bad news that many people have grown accustomed to was not a part of the lives of our forefathers two or more generations ago. They did not have the proliferation of bad news from the news media that we have today.

We do not have to do anything to receive a constant flow of bad news. This bad news comes to us automatically from the news media, if we choose to listen to it. We each must make a continual choice whether we will focus on the bad news of the world or spend time focusing on the good news from God.

The bad news of the world comes from the outside in. The good news from heaven will come from the inside out if our lives are completely focused upon the indwelling presence of God and if our minds and our hearts are filled to overflowing with the good news of the Word of God.

All of God's children should have so much of God's Word stored up inside of themselves that God's good news will flow up from their hearts whenever they face bad news from the world. We each should have so much of the good news of God on the inside of us that this good news always will predominate and take authority over the bad news we receive when we read our newspapers and news magazines, listen to the radio, watch television or receive bad news from the Internet.

We should spend *much more time each day* focusing upon the good news of the Bible than we do focusing upon the bad news of the world. I am not saying that we should ignore what is taking place in the world. I read my newspaper carefully each day. I like to scan the headlines in the newspaper. This scanning enables me to pick and choose what I want to read without being inundated with all of the remaining bad news that is contained in that newspaper.

I believe we should be very careful what we listen to from our radios and our television sets. When we listen to this bad news, we cannot scan the headlines and pick and choose what we want to hear. We have to take in *all* of the bad news that is packaged in any news program we listen to. Jesus Christ said, "…Be careful what you are hearing…" (Mark 4:24).

We should be very selective about what we allow to come into our eyes and our ears. If the bad news in our lives is increasing on a personal, national or international basis, we should offset this proliferation of bad news by *increasing* the amount of time we spend each day "programming" the good news of God's Word into our eyes, our ears, our minds, our hearts and our mouths. The good news from heaven in the Word of God is infinitely more powerful than any bad news we will receive in the world, no matter how bad this news might seem to be.

The Bible is not just black ink printed on white paper (or red ink for the words of Jesus Christ). The Bible is the living Word of God. The Bible is God Himself speaking directly to each of us from heaven. The Word of God is spiritually alive. It is filled to overflowing with the power of Almighty God.

When we ask Jesus Christ to be our Savior, our Father enables us to continually learn great spiritual truths from His Word through the Holy Spirit. He gives us the opportunity to constantly increase our faith in Him by filling our minds and our hearts with His Word throughout every day of our lives. Jesus Christ said, "Whoever is of God listens to God. [Those who belong to God hear the words of God.]..." (John 8:47).

The supernatural power of the Word of God is available to all of God's children. Why should we fail to partake of this precious privilege? Vast new spiritual horizons have been made available to us. Spending precious time with the Lord should be our top priority.

Our hearts will overflow with joy as we begin to comprehend the magnificent power of the Word of God. We will have a constantly increasing desire to receive and believe more of God's promises and to learn and obey all of God's instructions. We will be like the psalmist who said, "Your testimonies are wonderful [far exceeding anything conceived by man]; therefore my [penitent] self keeps them [hearing, receiving, loving, and obeying them]" (Psalm 119:129).

The Word of God is absolutely wonderful. It is much greater than anything in the world. The amplification says that the psalmist was penitent. He was sorry he had sinned. He was determined to obey God's instructions as he continually heard, received, loved and obeyed these instructions from heaven.

The Word of God is more powerful than thermonuclear power or any other power on earth. Our Father has assured us that the power of His Word is more than sufficient to overcome every problem we will face. "...with God nothing is ever impossible and no word from God shall be without power or impossible of fulfillment" (Luke 1:37).

Our Father wants us to trust Him completely instead of trusting in ourselves to do what has to be done. He wants us to know that His Word is filled with His mighty power. "...we possess this precious treasure [the divine Light of the Gospel] in [frail, human] vessels of earth, that the grandeur and exceeding greatness of the power may be shown to be from God and not from ourselves" (II Corinthians 4:7).

Our Father has made it possible for His Light to live in our hearts. We will depend completely on God when our hearts are filled with the power of God from the Word of God. We will be able to receive manifestation of the supernatural power of God when our minds and our hearts are filled with the supernatural power of His living Word.

Satan wants us to be afraid of the bad news of the world. Our Father wants His children to react with unwavering faith to bad news because we trust Him completely. "...the [uncompromisingly] righteous (the upright, in right standing with God) shall be in everlasting remembrance. He shall not be afraid of evil tidings; his heart is firmly fixed, trusting (leaning on and being confident) in the Lord. His heart is established and steady, he will not be afraid…" (Psalm 112:6-8).

Our Father wants us to be "in everlasting remembrance" of His Word. He does not want us to react with worry or fear when we receive bad news from the world or when Satan's demons attempt to influence us negatively. Our Father wants our minds and our hearts to be so filled with His Word that we will trust Him completely. He wants us to lean on Him at all times with absolute trust and confidence in Him. He wants our hearts to be so solidly established in His Word that we will not be afraid of anything because we know that He has made complete provision for our safety.

When we hear bad news, we absolutely must not allow ourselves to become discouraged, worried and anxious. We must not be like the people the prophet Jeremiah spoke of who "…have heard bad news; they are fainthearted and wasting away; there is trouble and anxiety [like] on a [storm-tossed] sea which cannot rest" (Jeremiah 49:23).

We each make a choice when we face problems. Will we react with fear, worry and anxiety? Or, will we react with unwavering faith in Almighty God because our eyes, our ears, our minds, our hearts and our mouths are continually being filled with the supernatural power of God's living Word?

I hope that the powerful truths from God that are contained in this chapter have encouraged you. I pray that you will be motivated by these supernatural truths from heaven to fill your mind and your heart continually with God's Word so that you will react to the circumstances in your life with absolute faith in God. I pray that you will live in God's presence and operate in His power instead of reacting with worry, fear and anxiety to the circumstances in your life.

Chapter 7

Trust God with Single-Minded, Unwavering Faith

We block ourselves from receiving God's answer to our prayers if our minds go back and forth from faith to fear, worry, doubt and unbelief. The Bible says that wavering faith in God actually is an indication that we are not loyal to God because we do not trust Him. "…[realize that you have been disloyal] wavering individuals with divided interests, and purify your hearts [of your spiritual adultery]" (James 4:8).

This passage of Scripture tells us that we are not loyal to God if our faith in Him wavers and if we go back and forth from trusting Him to worrying and doubting Him. The amplification in this passage of Scripture tells us that we actually commit "spiritual adultery" whenever our faith in God wavers. We are unfaithful to our loving Father whenever we doubt Him.

I do not believe we can develop single-minded, unwavering faith in God unless we obey our Father's instructions to renew our minds daily in His Word and to meditate continually on His Word throughout the day and night. In several of our books, tapes and Scripture Meditation Cards, I have given specific and exact instructions on the system I use to continually fill my mind and my heart with the supernatural power of the living Word of God. If you will look in the back of this book, you will see a wide variety of study material that will help you to purify your mind and your heart so that you will not be disloyal to God by being double-minded.

The Bible tells us about many people who were single-minded in their unwavering faith in God when they faced seemingly overwhelming problems. When King Jehosophat was surrounded by a hostile army that seemed to be much too powerful for him to defeat, he refused to dwell upon this seemingly insurmountable problem. He said to God, "…we have no might to stand against this great company that is coming against us. We do not know what to do, but our eyes are upon You" (II Chronicles 20:12).

When we face difficult problems and we do not know what to do, we should keep our eyes focused on the Lord. We should be like the psalmist who said, "I have set the Lord continually before me; because He is at my right hand, I shall not be moved. Therefore my heart is glad and my glory [my inner self] rejoices; my body too shall rest and confidently dwell in safety" (Psalm 16:8-9).

We cannot think about two things at the same time. We cannot focus on the problems we face if we are focusing continually on the Lord. We will not be moved by the problems in our lives if we stay close to the Lord and focus on Him continually. Our hearts will sing with joy if they are filled to overflowing with the supernatural power of the living Word of God. We will rest in the Lord because we trust Him completely.

If we have obeyed God's instructions to draw close to Him throughout each day of our lives and to constantly fill our minds and our hearts with His Word, we will know that our Father has everything under control. We will know that we can do all things through the strength of Jesus Christ (see Philippians 4:13). We will know that God's strength is made perfect in our human weakness (see II Corinthians 12:9-10). Like the psalmist, we will focus continually on the Lord. "My eyes are ever toward the Lord..." (Psalm 25:15).

We make a big mistake if we allow the problems in our lives to seem to be more powerful than Almighty God. "Unto You do I lift up my eyes, O You Who are enthroned in heaven" (Psalm 123:1).

Whenever we face difficult problems, we should lift up our eyes toward heaven. We should be God-centered instead of being problem-oriented or self-oriented. "Let your eyes look right on [with fixed purpose], and let your gaze be straight before you. Consider well the path of your feet, and let all your ways be established and ordered aright. Turn not aside to the right hand or to the left; remove your foot from evil" (Proverbs 4:25-27).

We should look straight ahead at all times. We should center every aspect of our lives around God's indwelling presence because our minds and our hearts have been filled to overflowing with the magnificent truth of His Word.

Satan will try to distract us in any way he can. He does not want us to keep moving straight ahead. He wants us to turn to the right or turn to the left because of our concern about the problems we face. Our Father wants us to refuse to give in to the influence of Satan as we keep moving straight ahead with absolute and unwavering faith in Him.

When the prophet Isaiah prophesied about the crucifixion of Jesus Christ, he prophesied that Jesus never would waver in His faith in God because of His absolute certainty that God would help Him. "For the Lord God helps Me; therefore have I not been ashamed or confounded. Therefore have I set My face like a flint, and I know that I shall not be put to shame" (Isaiah 50:7).

A flint is a very hard rock. When this passage of Scripture was written, a flint was used to start a fire. Flint is so hard that the friction caused by striking the rock against something that is hard produces flame. When we are told to set our faces like a flint, we are told that our faith in the Lord should be rock-solid because we trust Him completely. *Awesome!!*

Isaiah told us exactly how to react to adversity. "Who is among you who [reverently] fears the Lord, who obeys the voice of His Servant, yet who walks in darkness and deep trouble and has no shining splendor [in his heart]? Let him rely on, trust in, and be confident in the name of the Lord, and let him lean upon and be supported by his God" (Isaiah 50:10).

The word "darkness" in the Bible refers to satanic influence that causes us to be separated from God. We should not "walk in darkness" when we are in trouble. Instead, we should fear God and obey Him.

Our hearts should be filled with the "shining splendor" of the Word of God. We should lean on God at all times because we trust Him completely. We should be like Moses who "...never flinched but held staunchly to his purpose and endured steadfastly as one who gazed on Him Who is invisible" (Hebrews 11:27).

This passage of Scripture refers to the attitude Moses had when King Pharaoh tried to kill him. We can see that Moses had an eternal perspective. He "held staunchly to His purpose and endured steadfastly."

We must not flinch when we face adversity. Instead of focusing on the problems we face, we are instructed to continually "gaze on Him Who is invisible." Even though we cannot see God with our natural eyesight, we should have a very close relationship with Him as a result of spending a considerable amount of precious time alone with Him each day. We will be able to endure without wavering if we focus continually on God instead of focusing on the problems we face.

Whatever we nourish will flourish in our lives. We nourish whatever we focus on continually. The Word of God is our spiritual food. Our faith in God will flourish and grow if we focus on God's promises continually because we constantly feed ourselves with the magnificent spiritual nutrition our Father has provided in His Word. On the other hand, if we continually dwell upon the problems we face, these problems will seem to be much worse.

If we allow our minds to dwell continually on problems, this decision will tear us up deep down inside of ourselves. Focusing continually on problems causes ulcers, high blood pressure and many other sicknesses. Continual worry will damage our health. Dr. Charles Mayo, the founder of the world-famous Mayo Clinic, once said, "Worry affects the circulation, the heart, the glands, the whole nervous system, and profoundly affects the health. I have never known a man who died from overwork, but many who died from doubt."

Most physicians agree that between fifty percent and seventy-five percent of their patients come to them with illnesses that have a mental and emotional origin instead of a physical origin. Many of the people who go to physicians go to these doctors because of concerns that are caused by worry, fear and anxiety. Many doctors would not be able to stay in business if all of the patients in their waiting rooms whose problems are caused by these negative emotions learned and applied God's instructions to overcome worry, fear and anxiety.

Worry can take years from our lives. Worry is a killer. Many chronic worriers die prematurely. Although these people might die of cancer, heart disease or some other illness, the truth is that excessive worrying often is the cause of premature death.

People who worry continually become despondent. Despondent people ultimately become sick. "All the days of the desponding and afflicted are made evil [by anxious thoughts and forebodings], but he who has a glad heart has a continual feast [regardless of circumstances]" (Proverbs 15:15).

People who are despondent open themselves to the evil influence of Satan. Their anxious thoughts cause them to become afflicted with physical illness that has its origin in continual anxiety. Christians who fill their hearts continually with the Word of God will have glad hearts. Their hearts will sing with joy regardless of the circumstances they face.

Many physicians have no answer for their anxious and overwrought patients except sedatives. The Word of God is our Father's prescription for us. God's prescription is much greater than any medicine the world can offer. Physical medicine usually is taken through our mouths or through a needle that penetrates our skin. Our spiritual medicine is taken through our eyes and our ears.

Our hearts will not be heavy if we continually partake of the spiritual medicine our Father has provided for us. Instead of allowing anxiety to cause us to be sick, we should have happy hearts that will make us well. "A happy heart is good medicine and a cheerful mind works healing, but a broken spirit dries up the bones" (Proverbs 17:22).

Our minds will be cheerful and our hearts will be happy if we continually fill our minds and our hearts with the supernatural healing power of the Word of God. We will be quiet and calm. This calmness will improve our health and enable us to live a long and full life. "A calm and undisturbed mind and heart are the life and health of the body..." (Proverbs 14:30).

Dwelling on our problems is easy. Turning these problems over and over in our minds does not require any fortitude. Visualizing the effects that problems can have upon us is easy. God's way is not the easy way.

Turning our backs on seemingly insurmountable problems to focus continually upon the Word of God is not easy. When we face a crisis, meditating throughout the day and night on the holy Scriptures is not easy. Our Father wants us to take the right way, not the easy way. The right way is to do what He has instructed us to do.

Attempting to influence us to take the easy way is one of Satan's most effective devices. Many of us have learned through bitter experience that taking the easy way ultimately becomes the hard way. We should be absolutely determined to do what the Word of God tells us to do. We must not give in to the temptations that Satan's demons try to put into our minds.

Whenever we are tempted to worry about anything, we should substitute God's thoughts for whatever we are tempted to worry about. As we meditate continually on God's precious promises and seek God with our whole hearts, we will learn to live in the presence of God. Whatever we are tempted to worry about will disappear from our minds. We will see the problems in our lives from God's perspective. We will realize that these problems actually are opportunities for us to draw closer to God and to trust Him even more.

Circumstances always change. We make a big mistake whenever we dwell on circumstances – either good circumstances or bad circumstances. We should focus constantly on the eternal Word of God that never changes instead of focusing on the temporary circumstances in our lives.

People who constantly react to the circumstances in their lives go through continual ups and downs. As they begin to comprehend the immense power of the Word of God, they will see the circumstances in their lives as they truly are – constantly changing and always subject to the eternal and unchanging Word of God.

We recommend our Scripture Meditation Cards to assist you in meditating on the Word of God. We have invested five years of our lives to produce ten comprehensive sets of Scripture Meditation Cards and the accompanying eighty-five minute cassette tape that goes with each set of cards. These Scripture cards and cassette tapes will help you to focus continually on the Word of God.

Please look at the list of Scripture Meditation Cards and cassette tapes in the back of this book. You will see that these Scripture cards can help you to overcome worry, to solve potential problems and to receive healing from the Lord. You can learn how to increase your faith in God and how to enjoy the wonderful peace our Father has provided for us. Continual meditation on the Word of God will cause the problems that seem to be so overwhelming to become insignificant as you look at them in the light of God's presence, God's power, God's Word and God's eternal purpose for your life.

Chapter 8

Our Hearts Should Sing with Joy

The Word of God does not instruct us to focus on the circumstances in our lives. Again and again we are told that we should be *so focused upon the Lord* that we will *not* be afraid of anyone or anything. "...Do not be afraid of the enemy; [earnestly] remember the Lord and imprint Him [on your minds]..." (Nehemiah 4:14).

Instead of being afraid, we are instructed to "earnestly remember the Lord." When we do something earnestly, we are very determined about whatever we are doing. We should make a determined effort at all times to focus on the Lord. We should "imprint" Him on our minds.

We imprint the Lord on our minds by continually filling our minds with His Word. We also should fill our hearts with truth from God's Word. I believe that we fill our *minds* with God's instructions and promises by *studying* the Word of God on a daily basis. I believe that we fill our *hearts* with the Word of God by *meditating* constantly on our Father's instructions and promises.

As we meditate continually on the Word of God, I believe that the holy Scriptures drop from our minds down into our hearts.

We keep our faith in God strong and unwavering by obeying our Father's instructions to renew our minds in His Word every day of our lives and to meditate throughout the day and night on the holy Scriptures.

Our Father wants our minds to be happy. He wants our hearts to be filled with joy. "...let all those who take refuge and put their trust in You rejoice; let them ever sing and shout for joy, because You make a covering over them and defend them..." (Psalm 5:11).

Complete trust in God makes our hearts sing with joy. When we trust God completely, we will sing and shout with delight regardless of the circumstances we face. When our hearts are filled with joy, we will be comforted by the Lord regardless of the circumstances we face. We will be like the apostle Paul who said, "...with all our tribulation and in spite of it, [I am filled with comfort] I am overflowing with joy" (II Corinthians 7:4).

Don't you love the words "overflowing with joy" in this passage of Scripture? We should never allow anyone or anything to steal the joy of the Lord from us. Jesus Christ said, "...your hearts will rejoice, and no one can take from you your joy (gladness, delight)" (John 16:22).

Jesus spoke these words to His disciples shortly before His crucifixion. Jesus told them that they should not allow the upcoming circumstances to steal their joy. He assured them that He would see them again.

This same principle applies to each of us today. Our hearts will sing with joy if we have a close personal relationship with Jesus Christ. "Without having seen Him, you love Him; though you do not [even] now see Him, you believe in Him and exult and thrill with inexpressible and glorious (triumphant, heavenly) joy" (I Peter 1:8).

We do not have to see Jesus Christ with our human eyesight to trust Him. We can know Jesus intimately and place all of our trust in Him without actually seeing Him. We will trust Jesus completely if we set aside a significant amount of time each day to draw close to Him.

As we grow and mature in the Lord, Jesus will become more and more real to us. We will be able to see Him through the eyes of the Holy Spirit. He will become much more real to us than anyone we can see with our physical eyesight.

When we have a close personal relationship with Jesus Christ, we will "exult and thrill with inexpressible and glorious triumph and heavenly joy." Deep down inside of ourselves we will be absolutely certain that everything is under control, regardless of how difficult the circumstances in our lives might seem to be. "...My trust and assured reliance and confident hope shall be fixed in Him..." (Hebrews 2:13).

Please highlight or underline the words "assured reliance" in this passage of Scripture. We can be absolutely assured that total reliance on Jesus Christ will not be in vain. Jesus should be so real to us that we always will rely on Him, no matter what we face.

If we can trust Jesus Christ for our eternal salvation, we also can trust Him to bring us safely through every problem we will face during our lives on earth. "...in [your] faith (in your strong and welcome conviction or belief that Jesus is the Messiah, through Whom we obtain eternal salvation in the kingdom of God) you stand firm" (II Corinthians 1:24).

Is Jesus Christ your personal Savior? Have you trusted Him completely to pay the price for your sins? Are you absolutely certain that you will live eternally in heaven? If you can answer these questions affirmatively, you also can "stand firm" on your faith in Jesus Christ throughout your life on earth.

If you are certain that you will live eternally in heaven, you also can be certain that Jesus Christ has a plan for your life (see Proverbs 19:21, Psalm 139:16 and Ephesians 2:10). You can be certain that He has made provision for all of your needs as you carry out your part in God's plan (see Psalm 57:2, Acts 5:38-39, Ephesians 3:20 and Hebrews 12:1-2).

We must not allow our faith in God to waver because of the circumstances we face. "Be alert and on your guard; stand firm in your faith (your conviction respecting man's relationship to God and divine things, keeping the trust and holy fervor born of faith and a part of it). Act like men and be courageous; grow in strength!" (I Corinthians 16:13).

This passage of Scripture tells us that we always should be alert. We should stand firmly upon our faith in God, no matter what we face. I like the words "holy fervor" in the amplification of this passage of Scripture. We will be "on fire" deep down inside of ourselves if we have obeyed our Father's instructions to constantly fill our minds and our hearts with His Word. We will be totally, completely and absolutely committed to God at all times.

This passage of Scripture concludes by telling us to behave as men and women of strong faith. We will be courageous because of the power vested in us by the Holy Spirit. Our awareness of and dependence upon God's strength will increase continually as our faith in God constantly increases.

We must persevere in our faith in the Lord no matter how difficult the problems we face might seem to us. We should persevere for as long as the Lord requires us to wait. "Wait and hope for and expect the Lord; be brave and of good courage and let your heart be stout and enduring. Yes, wait for and hope for and expect the Lord" (Psalm 27:14).

We must not give up hope. We can be absolutely certain that our wonderful Lord always will do exactly what He says He will do. We always should "wait and hope for and expect the Lord." Our hearts should be "stout and enduring."

God often uses repetition for the purpose of emphasis. Please note that this passage of Scripture begins with the words "Wait and hope for and expect the Lord" and ends with the words "wait for and hope for and expect the Lord." Our Father does not want us to *ever* give up hope.

We will not be shaken by the circumstances in our lives when we know that God lives inside of us and we are certain that He will bring us safely through our problems for His glory. We will be totally secure deep down inside of ourselves because all of our security comes from the indwelling presence of the Lord and not from external sources of security.

When we face seemingly impossible situations, our faith in God should not waver in the slightest. We should praise God and thank Him in the face of adversity. We should react to the problems we face with the same unwavering faith Abraham exhibited when he faced a seemingly impossible situation. "No unbelief or distrust made him waver (doubtingly question) concerning the promise of God, but he grew strong and was empowered by faith as he gave praise and glory to God, fully satisfied and assured that God was able and mighty to keep His word and to do what He had promised" (Romans 4:20-21).

We must not allow doubt or unbelief to get a foothold in our minds and in our hearts. We should never waver in our absolute faith in God's promises. We should open our mouths and praise the Lord continually. We should worship the Lord and glorify Him. This passage of Scripture tells us that our faith in God will grow stronger when we praise God and glorify Him in the face of our problems. The joy of the Lord is much greater than any circumstances in our lives.

My faith in God has soared as I have written the first eight chapters of this book. I hope that your faith has soared as you read these chapters.

We began the book by seeing that God repeatedly has told us that He does not want us to worry. Then we saw why God told us that we shouldn't worry. We learned about the complete provision our Father has made for every one of His children through Jesus Christ. After studying several promises from God about the provision He has made for us, we then studied several additional promises that assure us that God lives on the inside of us. We have learned that we should not worry about anything because God lives inside of us.

In the last three chapters we have seen that we absolutely must not dwell upon the problems we face. We have seen that our Father wants us to be single-minded and unwavering in our faith in Him. He does not want us to be double-minded, going back and forth continually between faith in Him and worry, doubt and unbelief. Our Father wants our hearts to sing with joy at all times.

We now are ready to learn what the Word of God says about giving our problems to the Lord and leaving them with Him. With the foundation that we have built in the first eight chapters of this book, we are ready to learn how to let go of our problems completely, absolutely refusing to take them back. We are ready to learn how to leave our problems with the Lord with absolute certainty that He can and will take care of us because we place all of our trust in Him.

We are ready to move from the realm of being centered upon ourselves to the glorious realm of living in God. We will see life from God's perspective instead of looking at everything from our limited human perspective. We will live to bring glory to God in every situation. We will feel the character of God being imprinted indelibly in our lives.

Chapter 9

Give All of Your Burdens to the Lord

When God created us, He knew that we would face many problems. Our Father tells us exactly what He wants us to do when we face difficult problems. He wants us to give our problems to Him.

Whenever we face a problem in a specific area, we turn to someone who has professional training in that particular area. God is the greatest professional of all. He wants us to come to Him with all of our difficult problems because we know that He can and will help us. Our Father wants us to follow the example of the psalmist David who said, "...when my heart is overwhelmed and fainting; lead me to the rock that is higher than I..." (Psalm 61:2).

Human parents here on earth should be pillars in their children's lives. Our heavenly Father wants to be the pillar in our lives. He does not want us to be overwhelmed by anything. He wants us to be like the psalmist who said, "...on You do I lean and in You do I trust. Cause me to know the way wherein I should walk, for I lift up my inner self to You" (Psalm 143:8).

Our Father wants us to trust Him so much that we will lean on Him. When we don't know what to do, our Father wants us to pray to Him saying something like the following. "Dear Father, I worship You. I praise You. You are Mighty God. You know that I am faced with the problem of (explain your problem). I need Your wisdom and direction. I ask You to direct my steps. I trust You completely. In the name of Jesus Christ, I thank You for divine wisdom and supernatural intervention, dear Father. I give You all of the praise and the honor and the glory."

We give our burdens to God by praying to Him with unwavering faith. Our Father wants our faith in Him to be so strong that we trust Him completely. When we complete our prayer of faith, we have *let go* of the burden. We know that God has the burden.

Some of us allow the prideful characteristics we inherited from our ancestor, Adam, to predominate in our lives. We want to be in charge. Some of us insist on attempting to do in our human mediocrity what only God can do in His excellence. We are wasting our efforts if we try to do what only God can do. "Except the Lord builds the house, they labor in vain who build it; except the Lord keeps the city, the watchman waits but in vain" (Psalm 127:1).

I have used the following poem in other books I have written. I will use this poem in this book because the message that is taught by this poem explains very clearly what some of us attempt to do when we should be trusting completely in our Father.

The man who led me to the Lord wrote this poem. He gave me permission to use this poem on the condition that I would not use his name. Please do not read the following poem quickly. Please study it carefully. Ask yourself as you read exactly how much of the instruction this poem gives applies to you:

Father and Son

Dad and his bulldozer went to dig a huge hole,
His small son came to help, tho' not on the payroll.
The son brought his little shovel and his sand pail,
He had good equipment, but on the wrong scale.
Dad was proud to see his loving-hearted son,
Coming to help him get this job done.

Dad moved several tons of dirt with every pass of the blade,
His son filled his bucket diligently over in the shade.
Soon it was time to move the dirt where the lad worked so hard.
"Son, it's time to move away from that part of the yard"
"Oh, Dad, not now! Just let me finish this bucket,
I am doing so well!
See how much work I've done for you, can't you tell?
Let me do this part over here, and you do the rest,
You know that I love you and am doing my best."

Dad was a kind parent who loved his son,
But he knew he had to move him to get this job done.
His son was valuable, precious, but in the way
So this is what his dad to him did say.
"Come up on the bulldozer seat and work with me,
We'll move a mountain of dirt, and together we'll be."

So, together father and son worked that mountain-moving
machine,
Digging deep and wide, making this new ravine.
He learned that by teaming up with Dad
he could do impossible things,

Enjoying the accomplishment and fellowship
that partnership brings.
He learned that working together this day,
He could do miraculous things in an exciting way!

Dad had several choices to ponder here.
One, he could wait for the son on his own to get clear,
Two, he could move him away to let him watch Dad
the job complete,
Three, he could bring him up with Dad on the dozer seat.
When you are helping your child in growth with security
You let these choices depend upon the child's maturity.

What kind of child are you, my friend?
Do you have to do it "on your own" clear to the end?
Or are you open to really learn your Father's way?
Are you just a spectator who only listens to what He may say?
Or are you standing in the way while God waits for you to see,
That you could listen and obey and the mountain-mover be?

How many times do we tell our heavenly Father to wait
Until we fail?
To let us try to clear the way with our little sand pail,
Trying to help Him in our own strength and potentiality
When His instruction of love and wisdom changes our reality
From working in the natural,
to working where flow eternal fountains.
So instead of filling buckets, we move big mountains!

Somewhere we got the idea that we have to do it of ourselves,
And leave His gifts and power and wisdom to do it on our
shelves,

Working with our own resources, diligently and strong,
We do a lot humanly but we do it wrong.
God would show us, and He does, when we will yield,
How to do it all in Him, by faith revealed.

You are free to choose whatever way you think you should,
But He'd rather that you choose His way if you would.
Are you listening to God, speaking to you true,
Or does He have to just listen to you?

Some of us are like the child in this poem. We strive diligently, attempting to do things we are unable to do. We will not hesitate to give our problems to our Father if we can even begin to comprehend that He has a job to be done and that we can partner with Him to accomplish His plan and purpose.

When we face difficult problems, our Father allows each of us to decide what we will do. If we insist on trying to solve these problems ourselves, He will let us. He wants us to choose to give our problems to Him instead of struggling and straining in a vain attempt to solve them by ourselves. "Commit your way to the Lord [roll and repose each care of your load on Him]; trust (lean on, rely on, and be confident) also in Him and He will bring it to pass" (Psalm 37:5).

When we commit something to someone else, we give whatever we are committing to that person for safekeeping. We trust that person to take good care of whatever we give to him or to her. Our Father wants us to "roll" our heavy burdens onto Him. We are instructed to "repose" our cares upon Him. The word "repose" means to rest. We repose ourselves on a bed when we are tired.

Our Father wants us to trust Him completely. He wants us to lean on Him by giving all of our burdens to Him because of our complete trust and confidence in Him. He wants us to have absolute faith that He means what He says when He says He will bring it to pass. Our Father gives us similar instructions in the Book of Proverbs. "Roll your works upon the Lord [commit and trust them wholly to Him; He will cause your thoughts to become agreeable to His will, and] so shall your plans be established and succeed" (Proverbs 16:3)

This passage of Scripture refers to seeking God's will for our lives instead of pursuing selfish desires. Once again, we are told to "roll" what we are trying to do upon the Lord because we trust Him completely. If we obey this instruction, we are told that the Lord will cause our thoughts to come into alignment with His will. Our plans will succeed because our plans and God's plan will be one and the same. To know God's will and purpose, we must know His Word, the Bible.

We must understand the word "wholly" in this passage of Scripture. Our Father wants us to give *all* of our burdens to Him. We are given similar instructions in the New Testament. "Casting the whole of your care [all your anxieties, all your worries, all your concerns, once and for all] on Him, for He cares for you affectionately and cares about you watchfully" (I Peter 5:7).

Before we discuss the word "casting," please highlight or underline the word "whole" and also the four times the word "all" is used in this passage of Scripture. This repetition emphasizes that our Father wants us to give *all* of our burdens to Him.

Our Father tells us to "cast" all of our burdens on Him. This word actually means to "throw" these burdens to Him. Visualize a fisherman casting a line into the water. The fisherman throws that line far away from himself. The lead sinker on his line causes the line to go far away from him when he casts it.

When we throw something, we let go of it. Our Father wants us to let go of our burdens completely. The amplification of this passage of Scripture tells us to "cast *all* your anxieties, *all* your worries, *all* your concerns, *once and for all* on Him."

Whenever we are tempted to be worried, anxious and concerned about anything, we are instructed to give *all* of these potential burdens to God. Our Father wants us to trust Him completely because we know how much He loves us, cares for us and watches over us.

We cannot cast all of our burdens on the Lord if we are proud. In the following paragraph I will repeat the passage of Scripture we have just studied, but I have included an additional portion of Scripture that precedes I Peter 5:7 so that we can see exactly *how* to cast our problems on the Lord:

"...Clothe (apron) yourselves, all of you, with humilty [as the garb of a servant, so that its covering cannot possibly be stripped from you, with freedom from pride and arrogance] toward one another. For God sets Himself against the proud (the insolent, the overbearing, the disdainful, the presumptuous, the boastful) — [and He opposes, frustrates, and defeats them], but gives grace (favor, blessing) to the humble. Therefore humble yourselves [demote, lower yourselves in your own estimation] under the mighty hand of God, that in due time He may exalt you, casting the whole of your care [all your anxieties, all your worries, all your concerns, once and for all] on Him, for He cares for you affectionately and cares about you watchfully" (I Peter 5:5-7).

When we look at this passage of Scripture in its entirety we can see exactly what our Father wants us to do when we cast our cares upon Him. We are instructed to "clothe" ourselves with humility. When we put on clothing, we cover ourselves. Our Father wants us to cover ourselves with humility to the degree that we cannot possibly be stripped of this humility by pride and arrogance.

This passage of Scripture continues with a remarkable statement. We are told that "God sets Himself against the proud." We must understand that *Almighty God will come against us if we are proud.* How could any of us ever want our Father Who loves us so much to have to come against us? That is exactly what God will do if we are proud.

What does God do when He comes against us? The amplification of this passage of Scripture tells us that He will "frustrate" us. Can you imagine your loving Father actually causing you to be frustrated? We are told that He will "defeat" us. Can you imagine your loving Father actually defeating you? There is no question how our Father will treat us if we are proud. Some of us continually have to learn this lesson the hard way.

We then are told that our Father will give us grace if we are humble. Our Father will give us blessings we have not earned and do not deserve if we are humble before Him and before one another.

We are told that our Father wants us to "lower ourselves in our own estimation." Our Father does not want us to attempt to be on the throne of our lives. He does not want us to be proud. He wants us to be humble. He wants us to know how inadequate we are apart from Him. He wants us to know how complete we are in Him. He wants us to cast our cares upon Him with total humility. He does not want us to fail to give our burdens to Him because we are so proud and stubborn that we think we are little gods ourselves.

Our Father wants us to humbly admit our inadequacy apart from Him. When we humble ourselves before God, we yield ourselves to Him. We submit ourselves to His control. We admit our total dependence upon Him.

We are instructed to humble ourselves under the mighty hand of God. We must acknowledge the sovereignty of God. We must acknowledge that He is Almighty God and that He can and will handle all of the burdens we give to Him.

We also are told that God will "exalt" us. When God exalts us, He lifts us up. He promises to exalt us "in due time." Our Father's timing is very different from our timing. When we give our problems to Him, we should trust completely in His timing just as we trust Him in every other area.

Our Father gives us similar instructions in the Book of Psalms where we also are instructed to "cast" our burdens on Him. "Cast your burden on the Lord [releasing the weight of it] and He will sustain you; He will never allow the [consistently] righteous to be moved (made to slip, fall, or fail)" (Psalm 55:22).

The amplification of this passage of Scripture instructs us to "release the weight" of our burdens. We must not hold on to our burdens. We should give them to the Lord completely. We are promised that the Lord *will* sustain us *if* we let go of our burdens completely and trust Him to take care of them for us. Our Father will carry our burdens for us if we release them and give them totally, completely and absolutely to Him. He will not allow us to "slip, fall or fail."

In this chapter we have read again and again that our loving Father instructs us to give our burdens to Him. Psalm 37:5, Psalm 55:23, Proverbs 16:3 and I Peter 5:5-7 instruct us to release all of our burdens and give them to the Lord. Many people know that they should give their burdens to the Lord, but they do not know how. In the next chapter we will look into the Word of God for additional instructions that tell us *how* to give our burdens to the Lord.

Chapter 10

Trust the Lord Completely

Over the years I have heard people say something like, "I know I am supposed to give my problems to the Lord. I want to give my problems to Him, but I don't know how to let go of them."

We only will trust the Lord depending upon how close we are to Him, how well we know what His Word says He will do and how deeply we believe He actually will do exactly what He says He will do. The Lord has assured us that He knows what to do with our burdens if we will give them to Him. ". the Lord knows how to rescue the godly out of temptations and trials…" (II Peter 2:9).

We must not attempt to do what only the Lord can do. He is completely trustworthy. "…Believe in the Lord Jesus Christ [give yourself up to Him, take yourself out of your own keeping and entrust yourself into His keeping]…" (Acts 16:31).

These words were spoken by the apostle Paul when Paul and Silas were in a prison. Instead of being distraught, Paul and Silas prayed and praised God. Suddenly, a mighty earthquake shook the prison. The locked doors were opened by the force of the earthquake and the prisoners were set free.

The jailer who was in charge of Paul and Silas was very distraught. He contemplated killing himself because all of his prisoners were escaping. Paul urged the jailer not to kill himself. The jailer fell down because the power of God caused him to fall.

The jailer asked Paul and Silas what he should do in order to be saved. The words that we just read in Acts 16:31 apply to eternal salvation. The jailer and his entire family came to know Jesus Christ as their Savior. The jailer and his family trusted God for eternal salvation. I believe that Acts 16:31 also applies to every day of our lives after we are saved. Jesus wants us to trust Him completely throughout our lives on earth just as we trust completely that we will live eternally with Him in heaven.

We must have absolute faith in our Lord Jesus Christ. We need to "take ourselves out of our own keeping and entrust ourselves into His keeping" to take care of our heavy burdens just as we trust Him completely for our eternal salvation.

Jesus wants us to put our lives into His hands. He wants us to be like the apostle Paul who said, "...I know (perceive, have knowledge of, and am acquainted with) Him Whom I have believed (adhered to and trusted in and relied on), and I am [positively] persuaded that He is able to guard and keep that which has been entrusted to me and which I have committed [to Him] until that day" (II Timothy 1:12).

Paul said that he believed in the Lord. The amplification tells us that he trusted the Lord completely and relied on Him totally. Paul said he was "positively persuaded" that the Lord would take care of anything He had committed to him. The key to absolute trust in the Lord can be found in the first part of this passage of Scripture.

Before Paul tells us about his faith in the Lord, he tells us that he *knows* the Lord. He speaks of his personal acquaintance with the Lord. Here on earth we only place our complete trust in people who are close to us. This same principle applies in the spiritual realm. If we really want to trust the Lord, we only will place all of our trust in Him if we have consistently spent precious time alone with Him on a daily basis, constantly drawing closer to Him.

Some of us think that we trust the Lord. The moment of truth always comes when we face a severe problem. Will we be afraid to let go and give this burden to the Lord? Unfortunately, the answer is "yes" for some Christians.

Some of us are afraid to let go because we do not have a close personal relationship with the Lord. We have not spent enough time drawing close to Him so that we will trust Him completely when everything in our lives seems to be falling apart.

If you want to be able to trust the Lord with the difficult problems in your life, make the decision now that you will spend quality time alone with Him. Draw closer to Him on a daily basis through prayer, through praise and worship, through studying and meditating on His Word and through being quiet before Him as you progressively come to know Him more intimately. Refuse to allow any appointment on your daily appointment schedule to come ahead of your daily time with the Lord.

Our Father must grieve when He sees so many of His children struggling and straining, trying to accomplish their goals as little gods who ignore their Father. Human beings cannot totally comprehend the majesty of Almighty God. His grandeur is so great that we only can begin to describe it with the limitations of our human vocabulary. We would not hesitate to let go of our problems if we could comprehend how mighty and powerful and majestic He is. We would trust Him with simple childlike faith.

I believe that learning to trust the Lord is similar to learning how to swim. When people are learning to swim, they need to dare to let go and trust the water to hold them up. We need to dare to let go and trust the Lord to hold us up. We must not thrash, splash and sink as we laboriously try to solve problems apart from God.

Please visualize a group of people trying to learn how to swim. Some of the students fight the water. They don't "let go" and trust the water to hold them up. Good swimmers trust the water. They glide along almost effortlessly. They are not afraid of the water. Instead, they know that the water is their ally. They relax and allow the water to hold them up.

This same principle applies to our faith in God. Once swimmers let go, they learn that the water will hold them up. Once we learn that God will hold us up, we no longer thrash, splash and sink because our faith is in the solid rock, Jesus Christ.

Our loving Father wants to take care of us even more than loving parents here on earth want to take care of their children. Infants place all of their trust in their parents. They are helpless. They sense how much their parents love them. They are secure in their parents' love.

We can be absolutely secure in our Father's love. We can trust our Father completely to bring us safely through every problem. Little children who trust their father are not afraid to jump into their fathers' arms. They have complete confidence. They know that their father will catch them. They are willing to let go completely as they leap toward their father.

This same principle applies to our heavenly Father. We must trust Him enough to let go as we literally jump into His arms, trusting Him to hold us up. We can be certain that God's arms are there to catch us. Our heavenly Father will catch us and hold us up if we trust Him completely. "The eternal God is your refuge and dwelling place, and underneath are the everlasting arms..." (Deuteronomy 33:27).

We will trust the everlasting arms of Almighty God *if* He is our "refuge and dwelling place." The key to trusting in the everlasting arms of God is to have a close relationship with Him. Then, we will not hesitate for a moment to trust Him completely because we know Him intimately.

We must not allow our doubt and unbelief to cause us to limit the God Who knows no limits. He promises to help us when we are in trouble if we will trust Him. "The Lord is good, a Strength and Stronghold in the day of trouble; He knows (recognizes, has knowledge of, and understands) those who take refuge and trust in Him" (Nahum 1:7).

Our precious Lord is good. When we are in trouble, He will give us the strength we have to have. He will carry all of our burdens if we will just stay close to Him and trust Him completely. "Blessed (happy, fortunate, to be envied) is the man whose strength is in You..." (Psalm 84:5).

If we have a close personal relationship with Jesus Christ, we will be able to draw upon His strength, His power and His ability. His strength is more than sufficient. "...be strong in the Lord [be empowered through your union with Him]; draw your strength from Him [that strength which His boundless might provides]" (Ephesians 6:10).

We are told that we are able to receive the Lord's strength "through our union with Him." We will be able to trust in, rely upon and receive the mighty strength of the Lord if we have set aside quiet time on a daily basis to draw close to Him as He has instructed us to do. We only will place all of our trust in the Lord if we know Him intimately.

I hope that the truth from the Word of God in this chapter has encouraged you as much as it has encouraged me. Now that we have learned that we should give our burdens to the Lord and that we should trust Him completely, we are ready to look into the Word of God to learn how to *leave* our burdens with the Lord for as long as He requires us to wait.

Chapter 11

Leave Your Burdens with the Lord

In the last chapter we studied I Peter 5:7 which tells us to cast all of our anxieties, all of our worries and all our concerns on the Lord. In this chapter we will focus on four words in this passage of Scripture that are especially significant. These words are "once and for all."

Our Father does not want us to give our burdens to Him for a few days or a few weeks and then take them back because nothing seems to be happening. Our Father wants us to give our burdens to Him and to *leave our burdens with Him.*

Some of us give our burdens to God and take them back a few days later. Then we give the same burdens to Him again and take them back again a few days or a few weeks later. Some of us repeat this process several times. When we take the burdens back, we actually are saying that we do not believe God will take care of these burdens for us.

When we lay our burdens at the feet of the Lord, we need to *throw them away* just as we would throw away old clothes that are worn out and unusable. We never should take up our burdens again once we have given them to the Lord. These burdens now belong to Him, not to us.

We should refuse to worry or fret about the situation. We should listen to God for His wisdom and instruction. We should have complete faith that He will guide us (see our book *God's Wisdom is Available To You*).

On many occasions nothing seems to be happening over a period of weeks and months after we have given our burdens to the Lord. Sometimes we are tempted to become frustrated. We are tempted to take the burdens back. This moment is our moment of truth. Do we trust the Lord or don't we? We should say, "I have given this problem to You, Lord. You have it. I will not take it back. I refuse to worry. I trust You completely."

True faith in God requires complete abandonment. If we really trust the Lord, we will release all that we are and all that we have to Him. If we die to ourselves daily and surrender more of ourselves to God, we will realize that what seems to be our problems are not ours at all. These burdens belong to God.

If we truly surrender to the Lord, every issue in our lives becomes *His responsibility*. We should stop trying to figure things out when we have given our burdens to the Lord. We should not speculate about how we believe He will solve these problems. We often will find that He will solve these problems in a much different way than we could even contemplate.

We cannot "figure out" how God will do anything. Human logic and understanding cannot begin to comprehend how God will move in His divine wisdom and power (see Proverbs 3:5-6). We should always give our burdens to our Father with simple childlike trust.

We will walk with absolute faith in the victory that Jesus Christ won for us at Calvary if we can learn how to surrender our lives to Him and to trust Him completely. We will gladly release the weight of the burdens we were tempted to carry. We will experience the wonderful peace, joy and freedom He has made available to each of us who have unwavering faith in Him.

God always will do His part. *Will we do our part?* God's part is to lead us, reveal His plan to us and to direct us. Our part is to surrender our lives to God because we trust Him completely.

Many of us are able to give our burdens to the Lord. Some of us have a difficult time leaving these burdens with Him when absolutely nothing seems to be happening. We know that we are doing nothing. We think that we absolutely have to do something.

We cannot make a bigger mistake than to take our burdens back from Almighty God. Our intervention often stops God from doing what He was about to do if we had kept on trusting Him for as long as He required us to wait.

If we really have surrendered our lives to God, we should act exactly the way we would act if the problems already had been solved. Many times we think we have turned our burdens over to the Lord, but anyone who closely observes our words and our actions could see that we really have not abandoned these problems.

We must understand that God's ways are very different from our ways. "…My thoughts are not your thoughts, neither are your ways My ways, says the Lord. For as the heavens are higher than the earth, so are My ways higher than your ways and My thoughts than your thoughts" (Isaiah 55:8-9).

God has ways to solve problems that we cannot even begin to comprehend. We should give Him a free hand to take care of everything in His infinite wisdom. *God cannot fail.* We need to release our faith when we give our burdens to Him. We must not try to fight battles we cannot possibly win. "...the battle is not yours, but God's" (II Chronicles 20:15).

Some Christians give up too soon because their faith in God is a shallow faith instead of a deeply-rooted faith. Our faith in God would be much more deeply rooted if we had obeyed His instructions to draw close to Him on a daily basis before we face difficult problems. Jesus spoke of people who "...have no real root in themselves, and so they endure for a little while; then when trouble or persecution arises on account of the Word, they immediately are offended (become displeased, indignant, resentful) and they stumble and fall away" (Mark 4:17).

Our Father wants our faith in Him to be deeply rooted because we have obeyed His instructions to constantly immerse ourselves in His Word. If you are faced with difficult problems and if you have not prepared as you should have prepared, make up your mind that you will immediately immerse yourself in the Word of God throughout the day and night. Make the decision that you will focus continually on the Word of God instead of focusing on the problems you face.

God gave each of us freedom of choice when He created us. We all would be mere robots if God did not give us freedom to choose. God respects our right to choose. We are completely free to give our burdens to Him whenever we want to give them to Him. We are free to take these burdens back from Him.

When we face difficult situations, we are given an opportunity to choose between being frustrated by the problems we face or being calm because we trust God completely. Some of us react to the problems we face the way that some people who are drowning react. Sometimes people who are drowning are so afraid that they pull a person who is trying to save them under the water with them.

If people who are drowning want to be saved, they must trust completely in the person who is trying to rescue them. This analogy is applicable to what we should do when we face difficult problems. We should relax and let go completely. We should place all of our trust in God. We should willingly give up our God-given right to control our lives.

In this chapter we have laid the foundation for letting go of our burdens and leaving them with the Lord. In the next chapter we will explore additional facts from the holy Scriptures that will give us more information on what we should do to give our burdens to the Lord and leave them with Him.

Chapter 12

See Every Problem as a Magnificent Opportunity

We must know that Satan and his demons will not be silent when we have given our burdens to the Lord. Satan wants us to be problem-centered. He does not want us to understand that the problems in our lives actually are magnificent opportunities for us to trust the Lord to complete His plan and purpose in our lives.

The last thing that Satan and his demons want is for us to give our burdens to the Lord and to leave with Him. They know what will happen if we place all of our trust in the Lord and if we persevere in our faith in Him. Satan and his demons will do everything they can to attempt to influence us to stop trusting the Lord so that we will take our burdens back from Him.

Satan and his demons will do everything they can to increase our doubt and unbelief. They want us to be worried, anxious and afraid. They will hammer away at us continually by attempting to put worried and anxious thoughts into our minds.

Satan and his demons do not want us to focus on the Word of God and on the indwelling presence of God. They try to influence us to focus on the circumstances. They attempt to persuade us to be discouraged if our circumstances have become worse since we gave our burdens to the Lord. They will do everything they can to persuade us that we have not done the right thing in giving our problems to the Lord and leaving them with Him.

When Satan and his demons come at us hard, we need to come back at them just as hard. We cannot fight spiritual battles in the natural realm with our fists, with knives or with guns (See II Corinthians 10:3-4).

We fight spiritual battles with our mouths. We need to open our mouths and boldly speak the Word of God. We need to open our mouths and continually release words of absolute and unwavering faith in God as we boldly speak God's promises whenever Satan's demons attempt to weaken our faith in God. The Word of God is our spiritual sword (see Ephesians 6:17).

We cannot afford to dwell upon the thoughts Satan's demons try to put into our minds. We should actively and aggressively resist these thoughts in the name of our Lord Jesus Christ. We should boldly tell Satan and his demons that we *will not* under any circumstances take back any burden we have given to the Lord.

Instead of dwelling upon the thoughts that Satan's demons attempt to put into our minds, we should turn to specific promises from our loving Father and focus continually on these promises. We should continue focusing on these promises until we receive the wonderful, quiet inner assurance from the Lord that He has everything under control regardless of what the circumstances seem to indicate.

We come out from under God's protection if we allow the thoughts from Satan's demons to influence us to worry and cause us to attempt to take things into our own hands. Our words and our actions show God and Satan and his demons that we no longer are trusting God with unwavering and persevering faith. We will open ourselves to increasing influence from Satan and his demons if we make this very poor decision.

Our loving Father knows exactly what we are going through. He knows that many of us have difficulty trusting Him when we have given our burdens to Him and nothing seems to be happening. We have seen that God is always with us in the midst of our battles. We are not alone.

We should focus continually on God's promises that say that He is always with us and that He will help us if we have deep and unwavering faith in Him. We should focus continually on His indwelling presence (see our Scripture Meditation Cards, *God is Always with You*). Our Father wants our faith in Him to grow and mature to the point where we will have a smile on our face and a song in our heart regardless of the circumstances in our lives.

When we learn how to leave our burdens with God, His peace that is deep down inside of us will be manifested in us. His peace will fill our hearts. In the last half of this book we will look into God's Word to study numerous promises and instructions pertaining to the peace of God. For now, know that the peace of God lives on the inside of you. Know that this peace will be released in you and through you if you will focus on knowing God intimately instead of focusing on the problems you face and the appearance that nothing seems to be happening to solve these problems.

The very best thing we can do when we face difficult problems is to take our attention off these problems and focus this attention upon the Word of God. Our minds cannot think about two things at the same time. We will *not* be able to worry about the problems we face as long as we continually fill our eyes, our ears, our minds, our hearts and our mouths with the supernatural power of God's Word.

God knew that we would face difficult circumstances in our lives. Many years ago He made provision to help us during these difficult times. "...whatever was thus written in former days was written for our instruction, that by [our steadfast and patient] endurance and the encouragement [drawn] from the Scriptures we might hold fast to and cherish hope" (Romans 15:4).

These words that were written in the Bible long ago apply to eternal salvation. I believe these instructions also apply to the problems we face after we are saved. Our Father has given us the Bible to give us the instructions we need to live our lives the way He wants us to live them. This passage of Scripture tells us that we should endure steadfastly and patiently by drawing from His Word the encouragement we need.

The word "encouragement" begins with the prefix "en" which means "in." When we are faced with difficult problems, our Father wants us to continually put courage *into* ourselves by meditating constantly on His promises. The word "discouragement" begins with the prefix "dis" which means "lack of." When we are tempted to have a lack of courage because of the difficult problems we face, we should encourage ourselves by obeying our Father's instructions to meditate continually on His Word so that we will be able to "hold fast to and cherish hope."

Whenever we are tempted to give up, we should turn away from whatever is tempting us to give up hope. We should focus instead on God's magnificent promises. Our Father wants us to hold tightly onto Him. He wants us to cherish Him.

Our Father does not want us to talk about the problems we face after we have given these burdens to Him. *Why* would we talk about these problems if we truly have given them to God? Our

Father wants us to speak continually of our deep and unwavering faith in Him. "...let us seize and hold fast and retain without wavering the hope we cherish and confess and our acknowledgement of it, for He Who promised is reliable (sure) and faithful to His word" (Hebrews 10:23).

We can be absolutely certain that our Father always will do exactly what His Word says He will do. Our Father tells us to "seize" our hope. Our Father does not want our faith in Him to waver. When we seize something, we hold tightly onto it. We refuse to let go.

Our Father wants us to "cherish" the hope we have in Him. When we cherish something, we love whatever we cherish. We talk continually about whatever we cherish. Our Father wants us to constantly acknowledge our faith in Him. He is completely reliable. He wants us to be absolutely certain that He is faithful to His Word.

Our Father wants His Word to "explode" deep down inside of us as a result of our continual focus upon filling our eyes, our ears, our minds, our hearts and our mouths with the supernatural power of His living Word. Our Father wants us to "know that we know that we know" that everything is under His control and that He will bring us safely through the problems we face.

The words that we speak when we face a crisis situation should always reflect our absolute certainty that our Father will bring us through the crisis as a vessel forged in the fire and purified. Our praise and our thanksgiving while we face difficult circumstances should show our absolute and unwavering faith in Almighty God. Our Father wants us to praise His name throughout the day and throughout the night. "From the rising of the sun to the going down of it and from east to west, the name of the Lord is to be praised!" (Psalm 113:3).

We will find that the joy of the Lord will rise up on the inside of us if we resist the urge to feel sorry for ourselves because of what we are going through. Instead, we should praise the Lord continually and thank Him continually. The heavy burdens that Satan attempts to put on us will be lifted when we praise the Lord continually. Satan and his demons cannot remain in the presence of God. We come into God's presence when we praise Him and thank Him continually (see Psalm 100:4).

God will make something beautiful out of the problems in our lives when we give our burdens to Him and praise Him continually. God made something beautiful out of our lives when we were saved. He will continue to make our lives beautiful if we continue to trust Him to bring us through the problems we face just as we trusted completely in Him for our eternal salvation when we asked Jesus Christ to be our Savior. No matter how difficult our problems might seem to us, we must believe deep down in our hearts that our Father can and will solve these problems if we will commit them completely to Him and trust Him without reservation.

Whenever we face difficult problems, we should turn away from these problems. We should focus instead on the tremendous price that Jesus Christ paid for us. "Just think of Him Who endured from sinners such grievous opposition and bitter hostility against Himself [reckon up and consider it all in comparison with your trials], so that you may not grow weary or exhausted, losing heart and relaxing and fainting in your minds" (Hebrews 12:3).

If you are a Christian, you can be assured that the same Jesus Christ Who went through such an ordeal in the Garden of Gethsemane and on the cross at Calvary lives inside of *you*. Instead of focusing on the problems we face, we should focus continually upon the indwelling presence of Jesus Christ. We should thank Him again and again for His sacrifice.

We will be able to endure just as Jesus endured if we focus continually upon Jesus and upon promises in the Word of God. When we are tempted to focus on the trials and tribulations we face, we are instructed to compare our situation with what Jesus went through. We will "not grow weary or exhausted" if we focus continually on Jesus. We will not "lose heart" and give up.

Our Father wants us to persevere because we have unwavering faith in Him. The Bible speaks of "...those who through faith (by their leaning of the entire personality on God in Christ in absolute trust and confidence in His power, wisdom, and goodness) and by practice of patient endurance and waiting are [now] inheriting the promises" (Hebrews 6:12).

Our Father wants us to have so much faith in Him that we will *lean on Him* with absolute trust and confidence in Him. If we lean on someone, we allow the person we are leaning upon to support us and to hold us up. Our Father wants us to lean our "entire personality on Him" with absolute faith in "His power, wisdom and goodness."

let Jesus Drive,!

Our Father often requires us to be very patient while we wait for Him to bring us safely out on the other side of the problems we face. His Word assures us that we will "inherit the promises" He has given us *if we add patience to our faith* so that we will be able to wait with absolute confidence in Him for as long as He requires us to wait.

If we do not see anything happening, our Father wants us to be calm, quiet and patient deep down inside of ourselves. "...if we hope for what is still unseen by us, we wait for it with patience and composure" (Romans 8:25).

This passage of Scripture refers to eternal salvation. I believe it also refers to trusting God patiently during our lives on earth when we cannot see any apparent solution to the problems we face.

Our Father instructs us to wait with "patience and composure" if we hope to receive something from Him that we cannot see. We must not be impatient and try to take matters into our own hands. Our Father wants us to be calm, quiet and confident deep down inside of ourselves as we wait patiently for Him.

Anyone who has studied the Book of Job knows that Job endured and was blessed abundantly as a result of his endurance. Our Father will bless us as He blessed Job if we will persevere with faith in Him for as long as He wants us to persevere. "...we call those blessed (happy) who were steadfast [who endured]. You have heard of the endurance of Job, and you have seen the Lord's [purpose and how He richly blessed him in the] end, inasmuch as the Lord is full of pity and compassion and tenderness and mercy" (James 5:11).

Job refused to give in to the problems he faced. Job honored God. He endured. The Lord blessed Job abundantly. Our Father "is full of pity and compassion and tenderness and mercy." He knows exactly what every one of His children is going through.

Sometimes people live with heavy burdens for many years without losing their peace. These people are not bitter, resentful, frustrated or anxious. They have learned to trust the Lord completely to bring them through whatever they are called upon to face.

Our precious Lord is faithful. He is completely reliable. We must not give up. We can be absolutely assured that He has the victory. Please see our book *Never, Never Give Up* for many additional passages of Scripture that tell us exactly how to persevere in our faith in God.

Chapter 13

Discouragement Is a Luxury That We Cannot Afford

We must not allow ourselves to become discouraged while we patiently wait for God to honor our faith in Him. My friend, Charlie Jones, says that discouragement is a luxury that we cannot afford. I believe that Charlie has the right word to describe discouragement. Many people who wouldn't think of spending large amounts of money on something they could not possibly afford are partaking of the *luxury* of discouragement that none of us can afford.

The price of discouragement is very high. Discouragement denies the instructions in the Word of God which do not ever tell us that we should be discouraged. Instead of being discouraged, we should be *encouraged* by our continual awareness of God's indwelling presence and by our continual meditation on the magnificent truth He has given us in the holy Scriptures.

I believe that our lives can be compared to a "spiritual bank account." We will make constant "deposits" of faith and courage into our minds and into our hearts if we obey our Father's instructions to continually study and meditate on His Word. When we face difficult circumstances and we need to make "withdrawals" from our "spiritual bank account," we must have more than enough faith in God on deposit to cover the "withdrawals" that are created by having to face difficult problems in our lives.

Satan wants us to be discouraged. He wants to rob us of the faith in God that is available to each of God's children. Our Father wants us to continually put courage into ourselves. He wants our faith in Him to increase constantly because we have obeyed His instructions to fill our minds and our hearts with His Word, to draw closer to Him, to worship Him constantly and to pray continually.

I believe that many people who are easily discouraged also are easily elated. People who often allow their emotions to go "way up" almost inevitably will find themselves getting "way down" when they face severe problems.

Our Father wants us to be steady and consistent. He does not want our emotions to go "way up" easily or to go "way down" quickly (See Philippians 4:11-13). We should not allow the circumstances of life to cause us to be easily elated. We should not be easily discouraged. Our lives should be focused continually upon the indwelling presence of God and on His Word in our hearts instead of being focused on the circumstances we face.

Emotional maturity is developed by consistently setting aside quiet time to be alone each day with the Lord as we fellowship with Him, pray to Him and worship Him. Emotional maturity is developed by constantly studying and meditating on the Word of God as we continually fill our eyes, our ears, our minds, our hearts and our mouths with its supernatural power.

Our Father wants us to encourage ourselves constantly instead of allowing the circumstances in our lives to cause us to be discouraged. We will encourage ourselves if we "saturate" ourselves in the Word of God each day. We will learn the character of God and His plan for our lives as we spend time in the Bible consistently. We will be constantly encouraged if we live in the presence of God.

John Wesley, the founder of the Methodist church, once said that he had never had a period of discouragement, depression, doubt or unhappiness that lasted longer than thirty minutes. He refused to allow discouragement to take root and grow in his mind and in his heart.

We may get discouraged temporarily, but we need to identify this discouragement and cast it out before it gets a foothold. Someone once said, "Discouragement is like a baby — the more you nurse it, the bigger it grows."

Thomas Edison was a very successful inventor who performed thousands of experiments past the point where other inventors gave up. He once said, "I never allow myself to become discouraged under any circumstances." Abraham Lincoln, one of the greatest presidents of the United States, once said, "Let no feeling of discouragement prey upon you and in the end you are sure to succeed."

Discouragement has no value. Discouragement has never caused a problem to be solved. Discouragement has never brought about a victory. Instead, discouragement stops us from walking in the victory Jesus Christ won for us.

We must not give in to the god of discouragement (Satan). We should walk constantly with the God of victory (Jesus Christ). We can trust Jesus completely, regardless of the circumstances we face. We should be like the apostle Paul who said, "I have been crucified with Christ [in Him I have shared His crucifixion]; it is no longer I who live, but Christ (the Messiah) lives in me; and the life I now live in the body I live by faith in (by adherence to and reliance on and complete trust in) the Son of God, Who loved me and gave Himself up for me" (Galatians 2:20).

We will "crucify" our God-given right to control our lives if we truly have yielded control of our lives. We will not be discouraged if we continually yield control of our lives to Jesus Christ Who lives in our hearts. If we have so much faith in Jesus that we yield control of our lives to Him, we will live for Jesus and not for ourselves. Discouragement cannot get a foothold in our minds and in our hearts if Jesus Christ truly is the Lord of our lives.

Jesus knows exactly how to bring us through every crisis we face. Will we refuse to give in to the luxury of discouragement because of our absolute, unwavering faith in Jesus Christ? If we allow ourselves to remain discouraged over a period of time, I believe this discouragement indicates that we are more problem-centered then Christ-centered.

Discouragement that continues over a period of time leads to depression. A virtual epidemic of depression has occurred in the United States in recent years. Many people who are depressed take antidepressants and other medication. This medication does nothing to solve the problem of depression. Medication only makes depression more bearable by masking the symptoms of depression. Our Father has provided all of the medicine we ever will need to overcome depression (see Proverbs 17:22).

Our Father wants us to constantly fill our hearts with the spiritual medicine of His Word. Whenever we face difficult circumstances in our lives, we should turn away from these circumstances and turn toward the Lord. We must not give in to discouragement and depression. "...be not grieved and depressed, for the joy of the Lord is your strength and stronghold" (Nehemiah 8:10).

Christians can overcome depression through the supernatural joy of the Lord that is available to us through faith in God. Our Father does not want us to be grieved and depressed. Instead of being depressed, we should rejoice in the Lord whenever we face difficult circumstances.

So True

Our hearts will sing with joy if we have obeyed our Father's instructions to constantly fill our minds and our hearts with His living Word. Our hearts will sing with joy if we truly have yielded control of our lives to the Holy Spirit (see Galatians 5:22).

Our faith in the power of God on the inside of us should be much greater than the power of any circumstances. We must not allow circumstances to rule our lives. People who allow circumstances to rule their lives inevitably become discouraged and depressed.

Our Father has told us exactly what He wants us to do to overcome discouragement. "…we do not become discouraged (utterly spiritless, exhausted, and wearied out through fear). Though our outer man is [progressively] decaying and wasting away, yet our inner self is being [progressively] renewed day after day" (II Corinthians 4:16).

The amplification of the word "discouraged" in this passage of Scripture explains that people who are discouraged are "utterly spiritless, exhausted and wearied out through fear." People who are discouraged have allowed a satanic spirit of fear to obtain a foothold in their minds and in their hearts. This satanic oppression ultimately will bring them to the point where they are exhausted by the struggle with the problems they face. Their faith in God is weak or non-existent. They have become weary because of the cumulative effect the spirit of fear has upon them.

This passage of Scripture goes on to explain that our "outer man" (our body) is "progressively decaying and wasting away."

Chronic illness can cause many people to become discouraged. Our Father wants us to offset the discouragement that comes from the circumstances in our lives and from our bodies continually decaying and wasting away by constantly renewing "our inner selves progressively" day after day, week after week, month after month and year after year. I believe that we can offset many of the effects of the aging process by faithfully obeying our Father's instructions to constantly renew our minds in His Word.

There is no discouragement in heaven. The Word of God comes to us from heaven. We will not give in to the temptation to become discouraged if we obey our Father's instructions to constantly fill our minds and our hearts with His Word. Instead of being discouraged, we will be encouraged continually because God's Word will fill our minds and our hearts. "The strong spirit of a man sustains him in bodily pain or trouble…" (Proverbs 18:14).

We need to have a "strong spirit" when we face problems. A strong spirit can be developed consistently on a daily basis over a period of time through the supernatural power of the living Word of God. Christians who allow themselves to become discouraged and depressed have not obeyed their Father's instructions to renew their minds continually in His Word. "…be constantly renewed in the spirit of your mind [having a fresh mental and spiritual attitude]…" (Ephesians 4:23).

Please highlight or underline the word "constantly" in this passage of Scripture. We saw in II Corinthians 4:16 that we should renew our minds "day after day." This passage of Scripture tells us that we should renew our minds *constantly*. We must understand the vital importance of obeying our Father's instructions to continually fill our minds and our hearts with His Word so that we always will have "a fresh mental and spiritual attitude." We will constantly be refreshed and our minds will not be weary if we obey our Father's instructions to renew our minds continually in His Word.

Christians who fail to renew their minds in the Word of God on a daily basis and Christians who disobey God's instructions to meditate on His Word throughout the day and night often do not pay an immediate penalty for their transgressions. They usually pay this penalty in the future when they face difficult problems. They reach deep down inside of themselves and nothing is there. They have not paid the price of building themselves up spiritually. They can become discouraged and ultimately they can become depressed as a result.

In the next chapter we will look into the Word of God to see what it says about pride and the problems we ultimately will experience as a result of pride. Proud people think that they have to solve their problems themselves. Humble Christians know that they do not have all of the answers. They trust the Lord completely.

Chapter 14

The Relationship between Pride and Worry

Some Christians think that they trust God but, when they suddenly are faced with a very severe problem, they find much to their dismay that their faith in God is not as strong as they thought it was. Many of us actually trust more in ourselves, in other people and in external sources of security than we trust in God. We may not know or admit this truth. We can see how much faith in God we really have when our backs are against the wall and everything that can go wrong seems to be going wrong.

Some of us panic when we face a crisis situation. We find that we are paralyzed with worry, anxiety and fear. The circumstances we face seem to be much more powerful than the Word of God in our hearts and God Who lives in our hearts.

Many of us want to be in control of our lives because we feel secure when we face situations we know we can handle with our human abilities and with worldly sources of security. I believe that worry and fear are able to obtain a foothold in our lives when we face problems we know we cannot control.

God gave us a healthy fear to protect us from danger. However, a negative emotion of fear does not come from God. This negative fear often has a spiritual source. This negative fear often is influenced by Satan and his demons. "…God did not give us a spirit of timidity (of cowardice, of craven and cringing and fawning fear), but [He has given us a spirit] of power and of love and of calm and well-balanced mind and discipline and self-control" (II Timothy 1:7).

This passage of Scripture says that God has given each of us "a *spirit* of power and love and a calm and well-balanced mind, discipline and self-control." Please highlight or underline the word "spirit." *Know* that God's power resides in *you*. Our Father wants us to be secure in our knowledge that He loves us with a love that is much greater than we can possibly comprehend. He wants us to trust Him so much that we are able to control our emotions to remain calm in the face of a crisis.

When Satan tries to get at us through a spirit of fear, we cannot combat his attacks with our human abilities. We can only overcome a spirit of fear to the degree that God truly is in control of our lives. If we are in control of our lives, we provide Satan with an opportunity to constantly hammer away at us by attempting to put thoughts of discouragement, worry, anxiety and fear into our minds.

We live in power and boldness when we yield control of our lives to the Holy Spirit because we trust Him completely. Nothing can harm us or intimidate us. We belong to God. He is our Protector, our Director and our Leader. We stand tall because God lives inside of us.

We cannot stand tall in selfish pride. We stand tall because we are ambassadors of the Lord Jesus Christ, strong and mighty. We realize that Satan cannot harm us because we know that Satan was totally defeated by Jesus Christ (see Luke 10:19). Satan only can do what we allow him to do by any ignorance we have of the authority we have been given over him that can stop him from obtaining a foothold in our lives.

Our Father does not want us to be proud people who always attempt to control our lives. He wants each of His children to be loving, humble and trusting. True humility allows God to move in our lives. Pride allows Satan to move in our lives.

We are proud if we think we can solve our problems ourselves. We must humble ourselves before God and trust Him completely. We ultimately will pay a severe penalty if we fail to realize the difference between living according to the flesh and living according to the Spirit. All of this ties together. We have learned that we cannot cast our cares on God if we are proud. We have learned that we only can give our burdens to God and leave them with Him if we are humble.

The Bible tells us that Satan fell because of pride. Humility and childlike trust release the power of God in our lives. Pride blocks us from receiving the power of God. Pride gives a foothold to Satan and his demons.

Jesus was humble. We should follow His example. "Let this same attitude and purpose and [humble] mind be in you which was in Christ Jesus: [Let Him be your example in humility:] Who, although being essentially one with God and in the form of God [possessing the fullness of the attributes which make God God], did not think this equality with God was a thing to be eagerly grasped or retained, but stripped Himself [of all privileges and rightful dignity], so as to assume the guise of a servant (slave), in that He became like men and was born a human being. And after He had appeared in human form, He abased and humbled Himself [still further] and carried His obedience to the extreme of death, even the death of the cross!" (Philippians 2:5-8).

Our Father wants each of us to be humble just as Jesus was humble. Even though Jesus was "one with God and in the form of God," *He was not proud.* Instead, Jesus voluntarily "stripped Himself of all privileges and rightful dignity."

Jesus Christ, Who was one with God, came to this earth as a human being. Jesus came to earth as a servant. The amplification of the word "servant" tells us that He actually came to earth as a *slave.* Throughout His earthly ministry, Jesus was the epitome of humility right up until the most humble act of all time – the Son of God willingly died on a cross to pay for the sins of all mankind.

The holy Scriptures tell us that the greatest Man Who ever walked the face of this earth was exceedingly humble. Jesus said, "…the Son is able to do nothing of Himself…" (John 5:19).

Jesus always looked to His Father for the direction He knew He had to have. Jesus did not try to do anything apart from His Father. He said, "…I do nothing of Myself (of My own accord or on My own authority)…" (John 8:28).

We should be humble at all times just as Jesus always was humble. Jesus said, "…I am gentle (meek) and humble (lowly) in heart…" (Matthew 11:29).

✗ Humility does not come to us naturally. Pride comes to us naturally. We inherit pride from our ancestor, Adam. Satan continually tries to influence us to be proud just as he was able to influence Adam and Eve because of pride.

We can see how pride can cause a fall by learning about Satan's background. At one time Satan was an archangel in heaven named Lucifer. He was very close to God. However, Lucifer became proud.

He fell from being Lucifer in heaven to being Satan here on earth. We should be very careful that we do not "...[develop a beclouded and stupid state of mind] as the result of pride [be blinded by conceit, and] fall into the condemnation that the devil [once] did" (I Timothy 3:6).

The amplification of this passage of Scripture tells us that pride causes our minds to be "stupid." We are told that our thinking will be cloudy if we allow pride to get a foothold in our minds. We will be spiritually blind. We will not be able to see and understand spiritual truths from God's perspective. If we are proud, we can be assured that we are headed for trouble. "Pride goes before destruction, and a haughty spirit before a fall" (Proverbs 16:18).

We actually sin against God when we trust in our human abilities instead of trusting Him. "...let anyone who thinks he stands [who feels sure that he has a steadfast mind and is standing firm], take heed lest he fall [into sin]" (I Corinthians 10:12).

Please highlight or underline the word "anyone" in this passage of Scripture. Know that God is talking to _you_. We will "fall into sin" if we think we have what it takes to solve all of the difficult problems we will face in our lives. We sin whenever the selfish, prideful part of our nature controls our lives.

Please review the scriptural contents of this chapter. Personalize these instructions from God. Ask yourself if you are making the mistake of thinking you should act apart from Jesus Christ. Ask yourself how deeply rooted your faith in God is. Can you really trust God if the bottom falls out in your life?

When you face difficult circumstances, you can be certain that Satan's demons will try to fill your mind with thoughts of worry, anxiety and fear. Know that your loving Father wants you to continually deepen and widen the roots of your faith in Him so that you actually laugh at these thoughts (see Job 5:22). You can command these thoughts to be gone in the name of Jesus Christ which is much more powerful than any thoughts that Satan's demons can attempt to put into our minds (See Mark 16:17, John 14:14 and Philippians 2:9-11).

We have seen that pride inevitably leads to problems. In the next several chapters we will learn many more spiritual truths from the Bible about the insidious trap of pride and the significant problems we ultimately will experience if we are proud.

Chapter 15

Our Father Does Not Want Us to Be Self-confident

As we learn more and more from the Word of God about pride, we will see that many of us do not understand how proud we actually are. Some people who think they are living righteous lives have a lot of pride hidden inside of themselves.

I believe that one of the most important prayers we can pray each day is to ask the Lord to show us whenever we say or do something that is caused by pride. I believe we should ask the Lord to help us to get rid of all pride, no matter what is required to accomplish this goal. The Lord has continued to reveal pride in my life. I will say or do something that has its roots in pride only to have the still, small voice of the Lord tell me that what I had just said or done was caused by pride.

Pride is like a termite. We can't see pride, but it often is there inside of ourselves. A definite relationship exists between pride and self-confidence. There is *no* place in the Bible where we are told that we should be self-confident. I learned this lesson the hard way before I became a Christian. I have continued to learn this hard lesson many times since I have been a Christian.

When I was a child I had a very poor self-image because of severe personal problems that existed within my family. Because my self-image was so poor, I was voted the most bashful person in my high school graduating class. I received this negative notoriety when I was eighteen years old. My poor self-image became even worse.

By the grace of God, I was able to go to college. I paid a good portion of my college expenses by working after my classes and on vacations. I was the first person in my family to receive a college degree.

I was enrolled in the Reserve Officers Training Corps while I was in college. I entered the army as an officer shortly after graduating from college. I was in charge of many enlisted men during the two years I was an army officer. I also taught many classes to audiences of several hundred soldiers. My poor self-image began to change.

After I was discharged from the army I went into the financial services industry as a salesman. I succeeded to the point where I was able to head my own agency at the age of twenty-eight. Our agency covered a relatively rural area in New Hampshire, Vermont and part of Massachusetts. Even though we were located in a sparsely populated area, we received national recognition for our sales achievements.

As a result of our accomplishments, I was asked to give many speeches in the United States and Canada. I gave several of these speeches on the subjects of positive thinking and self-confidence. I had read hundreds of books on these subjects and I considered myself to be an expert in these areas.

I wrote two books on sales management. I also was invited to go to a recording studio in New York City where I made a recording on sales that was quite successful. The same man who a few years earlier was voted most bashful in his class had become very proud, although I did not realize it at that time. All of the standing ovations from all of the audiences I spoke to and all of the congratulatory letters and telephone calls on our sales achievements, my books and my recording definitely went to my head.

I did not have any self-confidence when I was a child. I became extremely self-confident as I began to achieve some success in the business world. I thought I had all of the answers. I was really caught up with myself. I did not understand how proud I had become. I did not know that I was riding for a fall.

Everything began to fall apart approximately fifteen years after I started building this business. We had achieved much of our growth through the leverage of borrowed money. I borrowed liberally and extended credit liberally to our sales representatives. I knew I was in deep trouble when our sales decreased and my debt load increased. Violating God's financial principles which I did not know at the time also took a great toll on my health.

The same man who had built the large agency, given all of the speeches, written two books and made a recording was on the verge of business failure, bankruptcy and a nervous breakdown. I could not find any solution to my problems. Pride had caused me to fall just as pride caused Satan to fall. Fortunately, Jesus Christ was there to save me when I fell.

At the age of forty-three, when my problems began to look as if they could not be solved, a friend of mine led me to Jesus Christ. After I committed my life to Christ my friend told me that the *only* way I ever would get out of the mess I was in was to immerse myself in the holy Bible. He told me that the Bible was the Word of God. He told me that every word in the Bible is inspired by God (see II Timothy 3:16).

I studied and meditated on the Word of God continually. By God's grace, our business did not go bankrupt. Instead, the business miraculously rebounded and became very successful – this time in the Lord's way, not my way. I kept my word to every creditor and paid each one back. Today, even though I live in Florida, I still participate actively in this firm by giving counsel to many of the sales representatives and management personnel through a weekly telephone appointment schedule.

Northeast Planning Associates now has almost one hundred sales representatives and employees. This firm is headed by Ed Hiers, a humble and committed Christian. I recruited Ed thirty years ago when he was twenty-two years old. Neither of us knew Jesus Christ at that time.

Northeast Planning Associates is solidly anchored upon scriptural principles. We have two prayer meetings every week and a voluntary Bible study class every week. All of the good things that have happened to this firm over the years have happened because of the grace of God. I thank the Lord that He showed Ed and me how to move our firm onto the solid foundation of godly principles.

I am very grateful that God is rescuing me from pride. God often uses the adversity we face to cause us to know Him more intimately. I can say what the psalmist said when he said, "It is good for me that I have been afflicted, that I might learn Your statutes. The law from Your mouth is better to me than thousands of gold and silver pieces" (Psalm 119:71-72).

The best thing that ever happened to me was receiving Jesus Christ as my Savior. I learned then how utterly dependent I am upon God. I have filled my eyes, my ears, my mind, my heart and my mouth with the Word of God consistently over the past twenty-nine years except for one season of adversity that numbed me, but did not numb my faith in God.

I still have to fight against pride, but the situation is much different now. Because I have been so proud, I now recognize my pride, selfishness, self-reliance and self-confidence more clearly. I often repent for my prideful words and actions.

I believe that we live in the last days before Jesus Christ returns. The Bible teaches us that many people will be proud and selfish at this time. "…people will be lovers of self and [utterly] self-centered, lovers of money and aroused by an inordinate [greedy] desire for wealth, proud and arrogant and contemptuous boasters…" (II Timothy 3:2).

Our Father wants us to be God-centered. He does not want us to be self-centered. Our Father wants us to be aware of the pitfalls of pride. We must understand that pride is a terrible thing. Satan's demons continually attempt to influence us to be proud in every way they can. They want us to fall just as they fell because of their pride.

A direct relationship exists between pride and self-confidence. Self-confidence has been exalted in our generation. Many books have been written about self-confidence, a positive self-image and many other words that are anchored upon the word "self." Some Christians even teach about the importance of self-confidence.

I believe that all teaching on self-confidence is unscriptural. We must understand that the Bible repeatedly tells us that we should *not* be self-confident. We should not make the mistake of trying to increase our self-confidence.

A fine line exists between self-confidence that is based upon pride in self and self-love that is based upon absolute faith in Jesus Christ. If we do not know how very special each one of is to

God, we cannot love ourselves as the Word of God instructs us to do (see Leviticus 19:18 and Matthew 19:13). If we do not love ourselves, we cannot love anyone else, even God.

When we learn all of the rights and privileges that are ours as sons and daughters of the Most High God, we will be filled with joy. We will love the person that we are, not in a prideful way but because we are partaking of the nature of God. We will comprehend God's plan and purpose and our part in it. We must know the Bible to learn where we are in the plan of God.

Some Christians are deceived into thinking that self-confidence is good. The Word of God teaches us to place our trust in the Lord instead of depending upon ourselves. We should "...put no confidence or dependence [on what we are] in the flesh and on outward privileges and physical advantages and external appearances..." (Philippians 3:3).

Anyone who thinks that self-confidence is a biblical trait should carefully study this passage of Scripture. We are clearly told that we should not have confidence in ourselves. Our Father does not want us to trust in ourselves. He also does not want us to place our faith in other human beings ahead of our faith in Him. "It is better to trust and take refuge in the Lord than to put confidence in man" (Psalm 118:8).

Any person who thinks that self-confidence is an asset should meditate carefully on the following passage of Scripture. This passage of Scripture tells us exactly what self-confident people are. "He who leans on, trusts in, and is confident of his own mind and heart is a [self-confident] fool..." (Proverbs 28:26).

If you would like to clearly see that God does not want us to be self-confident, please take some time to go through the Book of Proverbs in *The Amplified Bible*, if you have this version of the

Bible. I heartedly recommend that you purchase *The Amplified Bible* if you do not own one. See how many times the amplification shows that people who are self-confident are *fools*. I believe you will be surprised at the number of times the words "self-confident" and "fool" are linked in the Book of Proverbs.

Our Father warns every one of His children against thinking more highly of themselves than they should. We should take the following warning from God to heart. "...I warn everyone among you not to estimate and think of himself more highly than he ought [not to have an exaggerated opinion of his own importance]..." (Romans 12:3).

Please highlight or underline the words "everyone among you." You can be sure that your Father is talking to directly to *you* when He gives you these instructions. We must not make the mistake of exalting ourselves.

The apostle Paul was blessed with many abilities and talents. He learned how to go from the extreme pride that drove him when he was Saul of Tarsus to be the humble man of God he was after he became the beloved apostle Paul. We must understand the big mistake we make if we trust in our human abilities apart from God. "Cease to trust in [weak, frail and dying] man, whose breath is in his nostrils [for so short a time]; in what sense can he be counted as having intrinsic worth?" (Isaiah 2:22).

Why would we ever trust in ourselves when we can trust Almighty God? This passage of Scripture tells us that "frail and dying" human beings do not have "intrinsic worth." The word "intrinsic" means something that comes from within. Because we are born with a sin nature, we do not have anything in our flesh that is of any value to God. When we become Christians, God takes up residence inside of us so that we can trust Him throughout every day of our lives instead of trusting ourselves.

Self-confident people block themselves from receiving God's blessings. Our Father is looking for dependence, not independence. *The same self-confidence that often is perceived to be such an asset in the natural realm actually is a liability in the spiritual realm.* Anyone who has carefully studied the Scripture references in this chapter will know that our Father does not want us to be self-confident.

Our Father wants us to be humble. He wants us to understand that humility is not weakness. Humility requires great strength of character. Pride is weakness. Pride comes from weakness of character.

The best thing that can happen to a self-confident achiever is to face a situation that he or she is helpless to solve. If you are facing this situation and you have not asked Jesus Christ to be your Savior, I pray that you will reach out to Jesus Christ as I did when I faced a seemingly impossible situation. God will answer with salvation through His Son and through the indwelling presence of the Holy Spirit. Our loving Father can and will take your weakness and turn it into glory for His kingdom.

We never will be completely rid of pride. We always should realize how vulnerable we are to pride. If we think we are humble, we probably are not humble. Humble people do not think about being humble. True humility comes from our gratitude to God for Who He is and what He has done for us.

This chapter is filled with facts from the Word of God telling us that we make a big mistake if we place too much confidence in ourselves instead of trusting the Lord. In the next chapter we will look carefully into the Word of God to see the relationship that exists between humility and trusting the Lord.

Chapter 16

Experience God's Strength in Your Weakness

As our ministry has developed over the years, we often have observed the simple, humble childlike trust in God that is held by many Christians in Third World countries. These people know nothing of the worldly sources of security that are taken for granted by many people who live in more prosperous countries. Many of the people in Third World countries face severe problems on an ongoing basis. They do not look to themselves or to external sources for security. They can easily grasp the necessity of depending totally upon God.

We have learned that our Father does not want us to be self-confident. Our Father wants us to be completely dependent upon Him. "Not that we are fit (qualified and sufficient in ability) of ourselves to form personal judgments or to claim or count anything as coming from us, but our power and ability and sufficiency are from God" (II Corinthians 3:5).

Our Father wants us to turn to Him with absolute faith for the power, ability and sufficiency we need. He wants us to surrender all that we are to Him. He wants us to become so immersed in

Him that He shines through us for others to see. Jesus Christ said, "...Whoever lives in Me and I in him bears much (abundant) fruit. However, apart from Me [cut off from vital union with Me] you can do nothing" (John 15:5).

Let's look at the last part of this passage of Scripture first. Please highlight or underline the words "you" and "nothing." Jesus Christ tells each of us that we cannot do anything with eternal value if we are severed from His mighty power.

Jesus tells us that a close personal relationship with Him is *vitally important.* We only can produce abundant fruit of eternal significance if we live in Jesus Christ and He lives in us. Every aspect of our lives should spring from the indwelling presence of Jesus Christ Who can and will do great things in us and through us if we yield to Him and place all of our trust in Him.

When the apostle Paul turned to the Lord with full realization of his personal weakness, the Lord said, "...My grace (My favor and loving-kindness and mercy) is enough for you [sufficient against any danger and enables you to bear the trouble manfully]; for My strength and power are made perfect (fulfilled and completed) and show themselves most effective in [your] weakness. Therefore, I will all the more gladly glory in my weaknesses and infirmities, that the strength and power of Christ (the Messiah) may rest (yes, may pitch a tent over and dwell) upon me!" (II Corinthians 12:9).

This passage of Scripture sums up everything we have talked about so far in this chapter. Because of the grace of God we have been provided with the strength we need to face *any* danger we may encounter. Our Father has provided us with all of the strength we will need to live in victory if we have complete faith in Him.

How are the strength and power of God perfected in our lives? We only can experience the completeness of God's strength if we admit our weakness. God's strength and power are manifested in our weakness. This passage of Scripture tells us that we actually should "glory" in our human weakness. We should rejoice in our weakness.

God's ways certainly are different from the ways of the world, aren't they? We only can experience the mighty strength and power of our Lord Jesus Christ if we know and admit how weak we are. Paul said, "So for the sake of Christ, I am well pleased and take pleasure in infirmities, insults, hardships, persecutions, perplexities and distresses; for when I am weak [in human strength], then am I [truly] strong (able, powerful in divine strength)" (II Corinthians 12:10).

This passage of Scripture tells us that we actually should be *pleased* when we face difficult problems for the sake of the Gospel. We are told that we should be pleased when people insult us and persecute us, when we are faced with hardships and when we are tempted to be distressed because we serve Jesus Christ. If we obey these instructions from God, we will be strengthened by Jesus Christ.

In our culture some people "put on a mask." Some of us are so concerned about what other people think of us that we try to "act cool" and portray an attitude of confidence when we actually are worried and afraid. When we act in this way, we block God from operating through us. We should be like the apostle Paul who said, "...I know that nothing good dwells within me, that is, in my flesh..." (Romans 7:18).

Instead of thinking that we have to trust completely in ourselves, we should humbly turn to the Word of God each day. God says, "...this is the man to whom I will look and have regard: he who is humble and of a broken or wounded spirit, and who trembles at My word and reveres My commands" (Isaiah 66:2).

The first part of this passage of Scripture explains the vital importance of being humble and broken. Some people can come to this state of brokenness because they are able to surrender all that they are to God without a devastating experience. Some of us have to be broken by severe adversity before we can come to a place of brokenness before God. We may lose all of the worldly possessions that were so important to us.

If we truly are humble before God, we will turn to the Word of God to obtain the instructions from heaven that we vitally need. Our Father tells us that He wants us to actually "tremble" before the magnificence and splendor of His Word. We should be in absolute awe of the supernatural power of the living Word of God. Our Father wants us to "revere" the magnificent instructions and promises He has given to us. He wants us to constantly immerse ourselves in His Word.

I felt that I was totally defeated just before I became a Christian. I could not see any solution to the problems I faced. The man who led me to Jesus Christ told me that I could not possibly solve these problems unless I "saturated" myself in the Word of God. He told me that every word in the Bible is inspired by Almighty God. "Every Scripture is God-breathed (given by His inspiration)..." (II Timothy 3:16).

I was determined to obey the instructions that this precious brother gave me. In my desperation, I believed in my heart that the only way out of the problems I faced was to continually immerse myself in the Word of God. I did not know then that Christians who continually meditate on the Word of God will come to know God personally.

The Bible is the Book with God in it. God and His Word are one and the same. We should approach the Word of God with absolute reverence and awe throughout every day of our lives because we actually are approaching God Himself whenever we turn to His Word. *True*

How can we be certain that God and His Word are the same? "…the Word was God Himself" (John 1:1). We are told that Jesus Christ is the Word of God. "…the Word (Christ) became flesh…" (John 1:14). In the Book of Revelation Jesus is referred to as the Word of God. "…the title by which He is called is the Word of God" (Revelation 19:13).

The Word of God will personally introduce us to Jesus Christ. If we continually fill our minds and our hearts with the Word of God, Jesus will reveal Himself to us. Jesus told a group of Jewish people who criticized Him that the Word of God they studied so intently actually testified about Him. Jesus said, "…these [very Scriptures] testify about Me!…" (John 5:39).

We must understand that our loving Father speaks to us through His Word. The Word of God is a spiritual bridge that connects heaven and earth. Can you name *anything else on earth* that comes from heaven that we actually can see with our eyes and hear with our ears? The Word of God is spiritually alive. The Word of God is filled with the power of Almighty God. "…the Word that God speaks is alive and full of power…" (Hebrews 4:12).

We must understand that the Word of God is more powerful than thermonuclear power or any other power here on earth that seems to be extremely potent from our limited human perspective. Nothing in this world can even remotely compare to the supernatural power of the living and eternal Word of God.

Many people cannot comprehend how words that are printed on paper actually are *much greater and much more powerful* than the very real and very potent problems they face. The Bible is the living Word of God. The Bible comes to us from heaven. The Bible is God Himself speaking directly to us.

We have seen that our Father wants us to approach His Word with absolute awe and reverence. He wants us to know that His Word is filled to overflowing with His mighty power. The apostle Paul said, "…when you received the message of God [which you heard] from us, you welcomed it not as the word of [mere] men, but as it truly is, the Word of God, which is effectually at work in you who believe [exercising its superhuman power in those who adhere to and trust in and rely on it]" (I Thessalonians 2:13).

In this passage of Scripture Paul is discussing with the church at Thessalonica the persecution they suffered because of their support of Jesus Christ. Paul commended the Thessalonians because they did not look at the inspired message of God he gave to them as words that came from human beings. The Thessalonians understood that Paul was anointed by God when he spoke to them.

This same spiritual principle applies to the anointed Word of God that we have available to us in written form today. We will receive "superhuman power" from God if we continually fill our minds and our hearts with His Word. The supernatural power of Almighty God can and will work in us and through us if we do our very best at all times to obey the specific instructions He has given us and if we place complete trust and reliance upon Him.

Our Father wants each of us to learn how to get His Word up off the printed pages of the Bible into our minds. He then wants us to learn how to get His Word to drop from our minds down into our hearts. He then wants His Word to flow continually out of our mouths. Our Father wants every aspect of our lives to revolve around our absolute commitment to faithfully obey all of His instructions and to trust completely in the absolute reliability of all of His promises.

We must understand that we make a big mistake if we fail to obey our Father's instructions to continually study and meditate on His Word. Christians who do not faithfully obey these instructions are unaware of the mighty power of the holy Scriptures. Jesus said, "...You are wrong because you know neither the Scriptures nor God's power" (Matthew 22:29).

Jesus spoke these words to a group of Sadducees who questioned Him. He told these Sadducees that they were wrong because they did not understand the Scriptures or the power of God. We must not make this mistake.

We will be guarded by the supernatural power of God throughout every day of our lives if our minds and our hearts are filled with the Word of God. The Word of God will guide us throughout the night when we sleep. The Word of God will guide us when we wake up in the morning. "When you go, they [the words of your parents' God] shall lead you; when you sleep, they shall keep you; and when you waken, they shall talk with you" (Proverbs 6:22).

We must understand that our Father has provided everything we will need through the sacrifice of Jesus Christ Who died on a cross at Calvary. Jesus Christ and the Word of God are the same. The Word of God is alive with the power of Almighty God. The Word of God is filled with supernatural power to enable each of us to carry out God's will for our lives. If we can even begin to comprehend the immensity of the power of the Word of God, we will eagerly saturate ourselves in this wonderful, magnificent and powerful Book from heaven throughout the day and night, every day of our lives.

Lamplight Ministries is dedicated to providing the Word of God in a way that can be easily understood by Christians who sincerely desire to grow and mature in the Lord. You will see a complete listing of all of our books and Scripture Meditation Cards in the back of this book. Each of these publications is filled with the Word of God. We hope that the thousands of hours of hard work we have put into these publications will help you to turn the problems in your life into glorious opportunities to know God more intimately and to experience His power by constantly studying and meditating on His Word.

Chapter 17

Trust the Lord with Childlike Trust

Proud and self-centered people have a difficult time trusting the Lord. Jesus Christ must increase in importance to many of us if we sincerely desire to place all of our trust and confidence in Him. Selfish goals must decrease. The power of God will only increase in our lives as we yield ourselves to Him. "He must increase, but I must decrease. [He must grow more prominent; I must grow less so.]" (John 3:30).

These words that John the Baptist spoke pertaining to Jesus Christ apply to each of us today. Instead of exalting ourselves, we should lift up Jesus Christ. If we continually try to lift ourselves up, we will be brought down. If we humble ourselves before God and before one another, we will be lifted up and honored before God. Jesus said, "Whoever exalts himself [with haughtiness and empty pride] shall be humbled (brought low), and whoever humbles himself [whoever has a modest opinion of himself and behaves accordingly] shall be raised to honor" (Matthew 23:12).

Our Father does not want us to have an exalted opinion of ourselves. Proud people inevitably will be brought down. The only question is when they will be brought down, not if they will be brought down.

I have found that the times I am the most confident are the times I feel the most humble and dependent upon God. Our Father wants us to realize that great things are done *through us, not by us.* He wants us to willingly yield control of our lives to Him because we trust Him completely to do in us and through us what our human wisdom and abilities cannot possibly accomplish.

We see this wonderful attitude of humility throughout the earthly ministry of Jesus Christ. If we carefully study the four gospels of Matthew, Mark, Luke and John, we will see again and again the tremendous faith that Jesus Christ had in His Father. This careful study also will reveal the wonderful humility, love and compassion of Jesus Christ.

We have seen that humility and trusting God go together. We have seen that Satan and pride go together. Satan does not want us to live simple, trusting lives. He wants us to live confusing, complicated lives. The Bible explains the relationship between confusion, pride and Satan. "…wherever there is jealousy (envy) and contention (rivalry and selfish ambition), there will also be confusion (unrest, disharmony, rebellion) and all sorts of evil and vile practices)" (James 3:16).

This passage of Scripture tells us that jealousy and a contentious nature come from pride. Confusion often comes from pride. We give Satan a foothold whenever we are proud. Pride opens spiritual channels to "all sorts of evil and vile practices."

Satan wants us to be confused. He wants our lives to seem to be incredibly complicated. Our Father does not want us to be confused. He wants us to simplify our lives. Every aspect of our lives will come into order if He is the core of our being and if our lives are centered completely around Him. God "...is not a God of confusion and disorder but of peace and order..." (I Corinthians 14:33).

These two passages of Scripture show us that confusion and disorder often come from Satan. Our Father wants us to live an ordered life of spirit, soul and body because we trust Him completely. He wants us to be like the psalmist who said, "In You, O Lord, do I put my trust and confidently take refuge; let me never be put to shame or confusion!" (Psalm 71:1).

The psalmist knew how to turn away from the confusion that Satan tries to bring into our lives. He knew that we need to trust the Lord completely, placing all of our confidence in Him. The psalmist speaks of the Lord being our refuge. When the Lord is our refuge, we enter into His presence where Satan cannot get at us to confuse us.

Our lives can seem to be very complicated if we make the mistake of looking at life from a worldly perspective. Our Father does not want us to look at our lives from a worldly perspective. He wants us to learn to look at our lives from His heavenly perspective.

Our lives will *not* be complicated and confusing if we faithfully obey our Father's instructions to renew our minds daily in His Word, to meditate constantly on the holy Scriptures and to yield control of our lives to the Holy Spirit Who lives in our hearts. A complicated life is a life that is lived from the outside in based upon a worldly perspective. A simple life is a life that is lived from the inside out based upon absolute trust in the indwelling presence of God and minds and hearts that are filled to overflowing with the supernatural power of the living Word of God.

Some people worry constantly because their lives seem to be so incredibly complex. Their minds are overactive because they attempt to solve every problem they face with their limited human intelligence and understanding. Our lives can become incredibly complicated when we are in control of our lives. Our lives will not be complicated if the Holy Spirit is in control of our lives. God never complicates things. He keeps everything simple.

Our Father is looking for simple childlike trust from each of us. We must understand that He is our Father and we are His children. Little children here on earth turn to their parents with simple trust. Our Father wants us to always turn to Him with absolute trust.

Jesus Christ told us that we cannot enter into the kingdom of heaven unless we have simple childlike trust. He said, "…Truly I say to you, unless you become like little children [trusting, lowly, loving, forgiving], you can never enter the kingdom of heaven [at all]" (Matthew 18:3).

When we ask Jesus to be our Savior, He becomes our Savior through simple childlike faith. We have absolute faith that He has paid the price for all of our sins and that He has provided us with eternal life in the magnificence and splendor of heaven. Our eternal life begins the moment we first believe. The same simple childlike trust that we exhibit when we become Christians should remain intact throughout the remainder of our lives on earth.

God's plan is for children to be brought up in Christian homes. These children should learn to trust God by continually observing the way their parents trust God. This absolute trust in the Lord from the time they are very young gives these children a foundation for the remainder of their lives. They will be like the psalmist who said, "…You are my hope; O Lord God, You are my trust from my youth and the source of my confidence. Upon You have I leaned and relied from birth; You are He Who took me from my mother's womb and You have been my benefactor from that day. My praise is continually of You" (Psalm 71:5-6).

I did not become a Christian until I was 43 years old. I soon learned that I had to undo many bad habits and inaccurate beliefs that were caused from living more than four decades in the world as an unbeliever. Today I enjoy observing our Christian grandchildren who are guided and instructed by their loving Christian parents.

I often think how blessed these young children are to have so much trust in the Lord when they are so young. Their simple childlike trust in the Lord will provide them with a marvelous foundation for the rest of their lives. Trust in the Lord is the richest legacy parents can leave their children.

Those of us who did not have the opportunity to develop this simple childlike trust as a result of being taught by Christian parents need to learn how to develop this childlike trust as adults. We have to undo the programming we have automatically received from the ways of the world. We can develop this childlike trust by constantly filling our minds and our hearts with the Word of God, by spending quiet time alone with God each day, by worshipping God daily and by regularly gathering with other believers to grow in Christ together.

Our Father's promises will come alive inside of us as we saturate ourselves more and more in His Word. We will come to know our Father more intimately as we continue this process. The misconceptions that we previously held will be revealed to us over a period of weeks, months and years. We will draw closer to the Lord. Our trust in Him will increase continually.

Most little children are happy and carefree. They laugh and play. They are natural and uninhibited. They live free, spontaneous and uncomplicated lives. Childlike trust does not include any "if's" and "but's." Little children trust completely in their parents. We need to trust our heavenly Father completely.

Childlike trust takes God at His Word. Our Father wants our minds and our hearts to be filled to overflowing with His Word. Whenever we face difficult problems, He wants us to spontaneously turn to His living Word in our hearts instead of allowing the problems we face to seem to be bigger than He is.

Spiritual maturity and childlike trust go together. The less spiritual maturity we have, the less childlike our trust in God will be. The more spiritual maturity we have, the more childlike trust we will have.

Our Father does not want us to be moved by the circumstances in our lives. He does not want us to be moved by our emotions. He wants us to react to every circumstance with calm, quiet, childlike trust in Him that does not waver in the slightest. "…blessed (happy, fortunate, and to be envied) are all those who seek refuge and put their trust in Him!" (Psalm 2:12).

Please highlight or underline the word "all" in this passage of Scripture. This word includes *you*. Your Father promises to bless you if you will seek refuge in Him and trust Him completely.

In this chapter we have seen several Scripture references that explain the blessings our Father will give us if we refuse to worry and, instead, approach every challenge we face with simple childlike trust in Him. In the next chapter we will learn many facts from the Word of God that clearly instruct us to turn away from the limitations of human logic and understanding because we trust completely in the Lord with all of our hearts.

Chapter 18

Human Logic Often Is Insufficient

Now that we have seen what the Bible says about childlike trust in the Lord, we need to compare what we have learned with what the Bible says about attempting to solve all of our problems with our limited human logic and understanding. We can try to figure everything out ourselves or we can trust God. "Lean on, trust in, and be confident in the Lord with all your heart and mind and do not rely on your own insight or understanding. In all your ways know, recognize, and acknowledge Him, and He will direct and make straight and plain your paths. Be not wise in your own eyes; reverently fear and worship the Lord and turn [entirely] away from evil. It shall be health to your nerves and sinews, and marrow and moistening to your bones" (Proverbs 3:5-8).

This passage of Scripture begins by telling us that we should *lean* entirely upon the Lord. We are instructed to place *all* of our trust and confidence in the Lord. These instructions are consistent with what we learned in the last chapter about having continual childlike trust in the Lord.

Please highlight or underline the words *"do not rely on your own insight or understanding."* We must learn that we all will face difficult challenges that cannot possibly be solved with the limitations of our human insight and understanding.

We then are told that we should acknowledge the Lord in *every* area of our lives. Our lives should flow from the indwelling presence of the Lord. We should be conscious of His presence throughout every day of our lives. We should trust Him completely. We are told that the Lord will show us exactly what paths He wants us to follow. He will guide us as we go down these paths.

I believe that this verse is one of the most important passages of Scripture in the entire Bible. We will see the plan of God unfold if we will turn away from trusting ourselves and place all of our trust in the Lord. Unfortunately, too many of us make the mistake of attempting to solve our problems with our limited human understanding.

We then are told that we should *not* be "wise in our own eyes." We do not have to rely on the limitations of our human wisdom to solve the problems we face (see our book *God's Wisdom is Available to You*). Instead, we are instructed to fear the Lord with reverence and awe and to worship Him constantly.

If we obey these instructions, we will be able to turn away from the evil influence of Satan and his demons. Satan *cannot* get a foothold in the minds and hearts of God's children who trust God completely, acknowledge Him in every area of their lives and rely totally on Him to provide the guidance they need. Satan is completely ineffective in the lives of Christians who fear God with reverent awe, worship Him constantly and turn completely away from reliance upon the limitations of their human understanding.

This passage of Scripture promises us that we will have healthy nerves if we obey these instructions. We will not have a nervous breakdown. We will not be depressed or discouraged. We will be calm, quiet and confident because the Lord is in charge of our lives. This passage of Scripture then tells us that our muscles and our bones will be healthy if we obey these specific instructions from Almighty God. We can see that trusting in God is a key to optimum health.

Please do not take this passage of Scripture lightly. The instructions in Proverbs 3:5-8 are profound. God's promises in this passage of Scripture are filled with His supernatural power. I urge you to spend a significant amount of time studying Proverbs 3:5-8, meditating on it and personalizing it. Your life will be changed tremendously if you will consistently live your life in complete obedience to these magnificent instructions from God.

Abraham Lincoln was one of the greatest presidents in the history of the United States. President Lincoln was blessed by his Bible study. He gave us specific advice on how to study the Bible. President Lincoln said, "I am profitably engaged in the Bible. Take all of this book upon reason that you can and the rest by faith, and you will live a better man."

This great Christian leader told us that we should learn everything we can about the Bible from our human logic and reason. We should trust God completely in any areas of our Bible study that are difficult for us to believe. We can trust the Holy Spirit to reveal to us what we do not understand.

Our Father never intended for us to understand His ways through human understanding. We also are told in the New Testament that we cannot figure everything out with the limitations of our human logic and reasoning. "...The Lord knows the thoughts and reasonings of the [humanly] wise and recognizes how futile they are" (I Corinthians 3:20).

Unbelievers have to live entirely within the limitation of their minds. We are told that this reasoning can be absolutely *futile*. The Bible is filled with numerous examples of events that actually occurred that make *no sense whatsoever* to the limitations of our human understanding.

Genesis 6:5 through Genesis 8:22 tells us the story of Noah and the ark. God was so displeased at that time with the wickedness on the earth that He decided to destroy mankind by flooding the entire earth. God told Noah to build a large ark for himself and his family and two of each species of animals and seven pairs of some animals.

These instructions from God could not have made any sense whatsoever to the limitations of Noah's logic and understanding. The Bible tells us that it had *never rained* on the earth up to that time. *How* could Noah possibly comprehend the entire earth being flooded and the necessity of building a large ark for himself, his family and these animals if he had never even seen rain?

Aren't you glad that Noah did not lean upon the limitations of his human logic and understanding? The Bible tells us that Noah spent one hundred and twenty years building this ark. He was constantly ridiculed by other people during this period of time. Noah obeyed God because he did not put the limitations of his human understanding ahead of his absolute trust in the Lord.

Luke 1:34-35 tells us that a virgin named Mary gave birth to baby Jesus. Anyone who has ever asked Jesus to be his or her Savior had to turn away from the limitations of human logic that says that a virgin cannot have a baby. We must trust the Word of God when it says that this virgin woman *did* have a baby whose name was Jesus Christ.

John 2:3-10 tells about the first miracle that Jesus Christ performed. While Jesus was attending a wedding, He was informed that the supply of wine had run out. Jesus ordered six large water containers to be filled with water and brought to Him. Jesus then changed the water in these containers to wine. Human understanding cannot comprehend how all of those gallons of water could have been changed into wine, but we must believe what the Bible tells us.

John 11:1-45 tells us about a man named Lazarus who died. Jesus did not do anything when He first heard about the death of Lazarus. He waited for several days before He raised Lazarus from the dead. Most people cannot comprehend with the limitations of their human understanding why Jesus would wait or how people can be raised from the dead.

Matthew 14:21-31 tells us that Jesus walked on the water as He approached His disciples who were in a boat. We then are told that Peter, who was a normal human being with obvious weaknesses and shortcomings just like each of us, *actually was able to walk on the water*. Human understanding cannot comprehend how human beings can walk on water, but there is no question that Peter joined Jesus in walking on the water.

Matthew 14:15-20 tells about a large crowd of five thousand men, women and children who had very little food. There were only five loaves of bread and two fishes to feed all of these people. The Bible tells us that, after Jesus Christ prayed, there was enough food to feed every one of these people with sixteen baskets full of food remaining after everyone was fed.

Matthew 15:32-38 tells about a similar occurrence with four thousand hungry men, women and children. This group of people had only seven loaves of bread and a few small fish. Human logic and reasoning tell us that all of these people could not have been fed with such a small amount of food. Nevertheless, we are told that Jesus prayed and that there was enough food for all of these people with seven baskets full of food remaining.

Matthew 17:27 explains how Jesus received money to pay taxes for the apostle Peter and Himself. Jesus told Peter to go down to the sea and throw in a hook. Jesus told Peter that the first fish that came up on that hook would have enough money in its mouth to pay their taxes. How can human logic possibly comprehend receiving money for taxes from the mouth of a fish?

Luke 5:5-7 tells about a group of professional fishermen who had fished all night and caught nothing. These fishermen were tired and discouraged. Jesus Christ Who was not a professional fisherman appeared at that time. He told them to lower their nets again.

How could these weary professional fishermen who had made their living for so many years catching fish lower the nets again after going all night and catching nothing? Nevertheless, they did what Jesus said. In the face of all human logic and understanding, these men caught so many fish that they had to call for another boat to handle the excess. They caught so many fish that both boats almost sank.

When Jesus was preparing for the Last Supper just before He was betrayed and crucified, He told Peter and John to go into the city. In Luke 22:8-13 we see that these men were instructed to keep going until they saw a man carrying a jug of water. They were instructed to follow this man into his house. Jesus told them that the man then would show them the room where they would have the Passover supper.

Peter and John trusted Jesus Christ far beyond the limitations of their human understanding. They obeyed His instructions. They found this man and he led them to the room where the Last Supper was held.

The Bible tells us that Jesus was crucified on a cross at Calvary. John 20:1-18 tells us that Jesus was raised from the dead. If we trust Jesus Christ for our eternal salvation, we know that He was raised from the dead after He paid the full price for all of the sins of every person in the world. Human logic and understanding may tell us that Jesus could not have been raised from death. When we grow in our understanding of the nature of God, believing what God has done, is doing and will do is natural.

You just have read eleven examples of specific facts from the holy Scriptures that do not line up with the limitations of human understanding. The Bible is filled with many additional facts pertaining to events that actually took place that make no sense whatsoever to our limited human understanding. Many times things seem to be a certain way, but they are not as they seem to be. "There is a way which seems right to a man and appears straight before him, but at the end of it is the way of death" (Proverbs 14:12).

We have seen that the Bible uses repetition for purposes of emphasis. Our Father repeated this statement in the Book of Proverbs when He said, "There is a way that seems right to a man and appears straight before him, but at the end of it is the way of death" (Proverbs 16:25).

Doing what seems right to us can lead to spiritual death and, ultimately, to premature physical death. We cannot possibly understand God's ways without the guidance of the Holy Spirit. "...the mind of the flesh [which is sense and reason without the Holy Spirit] is death..." (Romans 8:6).

We should place all of our trust in the Lord, knowing that we cannot figure out His ways which are far different from and far superior to the limitations of our human understanding. Our Father has given us a comprehensive Book of Instructions. He wants us to follow these instructions exactly. "…be doers of the Word [obey the message], and not merely listeners to it, betraying yourselves [into deception by reasoning contrary to the Truth]" (James 1:22).

Some Christians *know* what the Word of God says to do, but they *do not do* what the Word of God tells them to do. Their human reasoning which is contrary to God's Word often stops them from doing what the Word of God tells them to do. Satan is a deceiver. Christians who make this mistake allow Satan to deceive them. We always give Satan and his demons the opportunity to deceive us when we fail to obey our Father's specific instructions.

Instead of giving Satan and his demons a foothold by trying to figure everything out intellectually, we are instructed to bring every one of our thoughts into obedience to Jesus Christ. "[Inasmuch as we] refute arguments and theories and reasonings and every proud and lofty thing that sets itself up against the [true] knowledge of God; and we lead every thought and purpose away captive into the obedience of Christ (the Messiah, the Anointed One)…" (II Corinthians 10:5).

This passage of Scripture tells us that we should "refute" the limitations of human reasoning. When we refute something, we prove that it is wrong. We must learn to identify the erroneous thoughts that Satan and his evil spirits try to put into our minds that are contrary to the teaching of the Word of God. When this passage of Scripture speaks about "every proud and lofty thing that sets itself up against the true knowledge of God," I believe it refers to Satan and his demons.

Many scholars have come to faith in Christ Jesus as a result of trying to prove that the Bible is false. In our lifetime, archaeological studies have revealed more and more evidence of the truth of the Bible. What people who lived centuries before us had to accept by faith, we now see with scientific proof. Although the Bible is truth and stands up under the most stringent scholarly scrutiny, every one of us must first take that one step of faith to trust in God our Father Who loves us so very much.

In this chapter we have seen how the human logic and intellectual beliefs that the world lives by can cause people to draw erroneous conclusions. In the next chapter we will look into the Word of God for additional information on the limitations of human logic and understanding.

Chapter 19

We Can Miss God through the Limitations of Human Logic

The same human logic that helps us to understand things in the world can be a spiritual veil that blocks us from clearly understanding God's truths that exist in the spiritual realm. The only way we can live the way our Father wants us to live is to learn how to get out of the natural realm so that we can get into the spiritual realm (the kingdom of God) and stay there.

We only can accomplish this goal if we obey our Father's instructions to continually fill our eyes, our ears, our minds, our hearts and our mouths with the supernatural power of His living Word. If we obey God's instructions in this area, we will constantly increase our sensitivity to the Holy Spirit.

Unbelievers have no alternative. They must attempt to solve difficult problems with their limited human logic and intellectual understanding without the wisdom of God. Christians should be very careful not to live the way that unbelievers live. The apostle Paul said, "…you must no longer live as the heathen (the Gentiles) do in their perverseness [in the folly, vanity, and emptiness of their souls and the futility] of their minds" (Ephesians 4:17).

Unbelievers have to live in the emptiness and futility of their human understanding. All things become gloriously new when we are born spiritually as a result of trusting Jesus Christ for our eternal salvation. "...if any person is [ingrafted] in Christ (the Messiah) he is a new creation (a new creature altogether); the old [previous moral and spiritual condition] has passed away. Behold, the fresh and new has come!" (II Corinthians 5:17).

When Jesus Christ becomes our personal Savior, our human logic and understanding are superceded by the wisdom of God. We are "new creatures altogether." We do not have to live the way we lived before. We are able to enter into a wonderful new realm and live in it.

We no longer have to view life from only the human perspective. We are able to see life from God's divine perspective because He lives inside of us. All that we have experienced and all that we have becomes touched by the power of God. Even our most painful experiences can work for good as we receive and understand God's forgiveness and His provision for us (see Romans 8:28).

The Word of God will cleanse us and make us whole and brand new daily if we obey our Father's instructions to renew our minds in His Word each day, to meditate continually on the holy Scriptures throughout the day and night and to constantly yield control of our lives to the Holy Spirit. The indwelling presence of God brings healing and wholeness.

We see a good example of this principle by observing how airplane pilots fly with absolute faith in the reliability of the instruments in their planes. These pilots must trust completely in their instruments when they are flying thousands of feet above the earth and they cannot see anything because of darkness or atmospheric conditions. All of their security comes from their faith in the reliability of these instruments. They cannot even think of following their senses because they know that their senses will deceive them.

Can you imagine what it must be like to fly an airplane thousands of feet above the earth without being able to see anything outside of the cockpit of the plane? Pilots who face these conditions have absolutely no alternative - they must have absolute faith in their instruments. *We also have no alternative* when we are faced with difficult challenges in our lives. We must learn to trust completely in God just as pilots learn to trust completely in the instruments in their planes when their visual comprehension is ineffective.

Sometimes we cannot trust our senses. We cannot always trust our emotions. Our Father wants our senses and our emotions to be controlled by our recreated spirits which should be filled with His Word and yielded to the Holy Spirit.

We have to turn away from the limitations of human logic when we ask Jesus Christ to be our Savior. Jesus becomes our Savior through faith. This faith in God will grow if we continually fill our minds and our hearts with the Word of God. "Let the word [spoken by] Christ (the Messiah) have its home [in your hearts and minds] and dwell in you in [all its] richness..." (Colossians 3:16).

Over the years I have found that continual meditation on the Word of God causes the Word of God to take up residence in our hearts to progressively give us the firm, solid and unwavering spiritual foundation we must have to trust God with simple child-like faith. We must understand that our hearts are the key to our lives. The "real us" is what we truly are deep down inside of our *hearts.* "...as he thinks in his heart, so is he..." (Proverbs 23:7).

True

Whenever we face a severe crisis, we always will react based upon whatever we truly believe in our hearts. Our Father wants us to react to the crises in our lives with deep and unwavering faith in Him because our hearts are solidly anchored upon His Word. We know that we are weak in our human abilities, but through hearts that are filled with God's Word and through the continual guidance of the Holy Spirit, we will grow more and more into the character and strength of God.

Every child of God should obey the instructions that King Solomon gave to his son when he said, "My son, attend to my words; consent and submit to my sayings. Let them not depart from your sight; keep them in the center of your heart. For they are life to those who find them, healing and health to all their flesh. Keep and guard your heart with all vigilance and above all that you guard, for out of it flow the springs of life" (Proverbs 4:20-23).

These instructions that King Solomon gave to his son also are our Father's instructions to each of us. Our Father wants us to pay close attention to His Word. He wants us to learn and obey all of the instructions He has given to us in His marvelous Book of Instructions. He does not want us to allow His Word to "depart from our sight." He wants our eyes to be filled as often as possible with His Word as we faithfully obey His instructions to meditate on His Word throughout the day and night.

Lamplight Ministries has published ten sets of Scripture Meditation Cards to help Christians to keep the Word of God in front of their eyes throughout the day and night. These Scripture cards can help you to obey your Father's instructions to keep His Word constantly in front of your eyes. We will be able to live exactly the way our Father has instructed to live if we will just mix a little imagination with absolute dedication to obey our Father's instructions pertaining to Scripture meditation.

Our hearts will be filled with the Word of God if we obey God's instructions to not allow His Word to depart from our sight and to meditate constantly on the holy Scriptures. The Word of God is alive and full of the power of God. Proverbs 4:23 tells us that we will be spiritually alive when our hearts are filled with the Word of God. We also are told that we will enjoy good health if we obey these instructions from God.

This passage of Scripture goes on to tell us that we should "keep our hearts with all vigilance." When we do something vigilantly, we pay very close attention to what we are doing. We do not vary in the slightest from the instructions we have been given.

Our Father wants us to place the spiritual condition of our hearts "above all that we guard." We should not allow anything to come ahead of filling our hearts continually with the supernatural power of the living Word of God.

We have seen that our hearts are the key to our lives. If we constantly fill our hearts with the Word of God, we will continually draw closer to Jesus Christ Who lives in our hearts. Jesus said, "If you live in Me [abide vitally united to Me] and My words remain in you and continue to live in your hearts, ask whatever you will, and it shall be done for you" (John 15:7).

There are two conditions to this wonderful promise from Jesus Christ. First, we must "live in Christ" if we sincerely desire to receive whatever we ask for in prayer. We should "abide vitally united to Him." When we are united to other people, we stay close to them. Nothing can separate us when we understand that a close relationship with someone is vital. We will be very determined to stay close to that person. Jesus told us that *it is absolutely vital for us to abide in Him* – to center every aspect of our lives around His indwelling presence.

The second condition that Jesus gave us in this passage of Scripture is for His Word to *live in our hearts continually*. We will meet this condition if we constantly fill our hearts with the Word of God by obeying our Father's instructions to meditate on His Word throughout the day and night.

In the last two chapters we have seen that the Word of God repeatedly tells us that we are not limited to human logic and understanding. We have the mind of Christ which surpasses all human wisdom and knowledge (see I Corinthians 2:16). I believe that we are able to "tune in" to the mind of Christ to the degree that we obey our Father's instructions to continually fill our minds and our hearts with His Word.

Chapter 20

Beware of the Bondage
of Religious Tradition

Some people are worried and afraid because they are under the bondage of religious tradition. Their traditional religious beliefs stop them from being able to draw close enough to the Lord to trust Him in the face of extremely difficult circumstances.

Christianity was alive during the first few hundred years after the earthly ministry of Jesus Christ. However, over a period of time, Christianity became more and more "watered down." Christianity became more religious, traditional and ceremonial.

Human beings created new doctrines. They began to teach principles that were not in accordance with the teaching of the Bible. More and more people were negatively influenced by this religious tradition as the centuries went by.

Religion is centered upon what human beings do. Christianity is based upon what Jesus Christ already has done for us. Religion is man reaching up to God. Christianity is God reaching down to man.

Many religious people say and do things that sound good, but they have no true relationship with the living God. "…this people draw near Me with their mouth and honor Me with their lips but remove their hearts and minds far from Me, and their fear and reverence for Me are a commandment of men that is learned by repetition [without any thought as to the meaning]…"(Isaiah 29:13).

The Bible says that God looks at our hearts instead of looking at us externally (see I Samuel 16:7). Isaiah 29:13 speaks of seemingly religious people whose hearts and minds are far from the Lord even though they say the right words. These people do not truly fear the Lord and hold Him in reverent awe.

This passage of Scripture tells us that these religious people obey commandments that come from men. People who are under the bondage of religious tradition carry out man-made doctrines instead of doing what God tells them to do. They live their lives based upon the religious tradition that has been taught to them by human beings even though this religious tradition is not solidly anchored upon the Bible.

I believe that our generation lives in the last days before Jesus Christ returns. The Bible teaches us that many people in these last days will seem to be religious even though they actually have no personal knowledge of the power of God. "…[although] they hold a form of piety (true religion), they deny and reject and are strangers to the power of it [their conduct belies the genuineness of their profession]. Avoid [all] such people [turn away from them]" (II Timothy 3:5).

When this passage of Scripture speaks of "profession," it refers to what some of these religious people profess to be. This passage of Scripture refers to the words these people speak with their mouths. These people seem to be religious,

o then unto your way

but they actually "deny and reject and are strangers to" the power of God.

Their religion is a surface religion without the true depth that only can be experienced by Christians whose lives are solidly anchored upon the Word of God and the Holy Spirit living in their hearts. Our Father wants us to avoid these people. He does not want us to be influenced by their unscriptural teaching.

The Pharisees were the epitome of religious tradition during the earthly ministry of Jesus Christ. They were extremely self-righteous. They added hundreds of additional rules to the basic Ten Commandments. They carefully obeyed all of these man-made rules and regulations. They thought that everyone who did not do what they did was wrong.

Religious tradition is very similar today. We must not make the mistake of attempting to live our lives based upon man-made concepts. Our Father wants us to live our lives in obedience to the specific instructions He has given us in the Bible.

Throughout His earthly ministry, Jesus Christ was supportive of many people who were looked down upon by other people. However, the one group of people that Jesus often criticized was the Pharisees. Jesus consistently condemned religious tradition.

During the earthly ministry of Jesus Christ, religious people constantly attempted to put their tradition upon others. They attempted to persuade people to adhere to the things they told them to do. Religious tradition has not changed over the years. Religious tradition still attempts to persuade people to adhere to many different doctrines that have nothing to do with the instructions from God that are contained in the Bible.

Many seemingly religious people faithfully attend church once and sometimes twice a week. They pray for a few minutes each day. They do their best to live a good life. However, their lives have very little spiritual depth. Their minds and their hearts are not filled with the holy Scriptures. They have little or no knowledge of how the Holy Spirit can live in our hearts. They fail to continually yield control of their lives to the Holy Spirit.

When we ask Jesus Christ to be our Savior, we are given the power and authority to break loose from the bondage of religious tradition. Unfortunately, some Christians fail to take advantage of this opportunity.

These Christians do not comprehend the tremendous spiritual power that has been made available to them because of the victory Jesus Christ won for them. Jesus said, "…having the power of seeing, they do not see; and having the power of hearing, they do not hear, nor do they grasp and understand. In them indeed is the process of fulfillment of the prophecy of Isaiah, which says: You shall indeed hear and hear but never grasp and understand; and you shall indeed look and look but never see and perceive. For this nation's heart has grown gross (fat and dull), and their ears heavy and difficult of hearing, and their eyes they have tightly closed, lest they see and perceive with their eyes, and hear and comprehend the sense with their ears, and grasp and understand with their heart, and turn and I should heal them" (Matthew 13:13-15).

These words that Jesus spoke many years ago apply to us today. Some Christians fail to see truths in the spiritual realm they have been given the power to see. They fail to hear truths they have been given the power to hear. They do not understand the great spiritual truths that are available to them if they would just study and meditate on the holy Scriptures every day and learn about, trust in and yield control of their lives to the Holy Spirit Who lives in their hearts.

Some believers merely go through the motions of being Christians. They have little or no concept of being guided by the Holy Spirit or of living lives that have been completely set free from religious tradition. These people will give in to fear and worry about the circumstances in their lives because their lives are anchored upon religious tradition. They do not have the solid scriptural foundation that we must have to live our lives the way our Father wants us to live.

Many people who are under the bondage of religious tradition are essentially good people. They have good intentions. They want to do the right thing. They have absolutely no concept of the degree that they have been bound by religious tradition.

These religious people go to churches where they hear little or nothing of substance from the Bible. They might hear an occasional passage of Scripture at the services they attend, but most of the theology they are taught is a social doctrine that is not solidly anchored upon the holy Scriptures. The services in the churches they attend usually place a great deal of emphasis on ceremony and ritual and very little emphasis on the supernatural power of the living Word of God.

The Bible teaches us that our faith in God increases by continually hearing the Word of God (see Romans 10:17). Religious people who seldom or never hear the Word of God cannot experience continually increasing faith in God. They are especially vulnerable to worry and fear because their faith in God is not strong enough to override the difficult challenges they face.

These people do not understand that we should live in a permanent state of clinging to God for our very lives. God is our shelter and our strength. We can find the nature of God in the Bible that is filled with instructions and promises that will help us in every circumstance.

Jesus strongly criticized the Pharisees for their man-made traditions. He said, "In vain (fruitlessly and without profit) do they worship Me, ordering and teaching [to be obeyed] as doctrines the commandments and precepts of men. You disregard and give up and ask to depart from you the commandment of God and cling to the tradition of men [keeping it carefully and faithfully]" (Mark 7:7-8).

We must understand that we will live our lives in vain if we live according to a doctrine created by human beings instead of devoting our lives continually to obedience to the instructions in the Bible and to the guidance of the Holy Spirit. Jesus then told the Pharisees, "…You have a fine way of rejecting [thus thwarting and nullifying and doing away with] the commandment of God in order to keep your tradition (your own human regulations)!" (Mark 7:9).

The Bible is filled with the supernatural power of Almighty God. Nevertheless, Jesus Christ taught us that *religious tradition actually is able to make the Word of God ineffective.* He said, "…you are nullifying and making void and of no effect [the authority of] the Word of God through your tradition…" (Mark 7:13).

We must not allow ourselves to be caught in the trap of religious tradition. I believe that some of Satan's demons are religious spirits who attempt to influence people to live under the bondage of religious tradition. — Interesting

So True!

Satan does not want us to learn from the Word of God and to live our lives according to the instructions in God's Word. He does not want us to fill our minds and our hearts with the holy Scriptures. He knows what will happen to him if we do these things. "...the Word of God is [always] abiding in you (in your hearts), and you have been victorious over the wicked one" (I John 2:14).

Satan's demons know that they constantly will be defeated by Christians whose eyes, ears, minds, hearts and mouths are filled with the Word of God. They attempt to influence us to be "religious." They try to put a veil over our eyes.

Satan and his demons are not concerned if we attend churches that are not solidly anchored upon the Word of God. They are not concerned if we spend time in religious activities that seem to be beneficial. However, they absolutely do not want the supernatural power of the living Word of God to fill our minds and our hearts.

Religious people who have little or no knowledge of the living Word of God or of the personal living God Who lives in their hearts have weak faith. They are unable to place deep and unwavering trust in God because they do not have a close relationship with Him. Religious tradition teaches that God is far away and virtually unapproachable. The Bible tells us that just the opposite is true. The Word of God says that God is so close to us that He lives in our hearts as soon as we choose to believe in Jesus Christ as our Redeemer and our Messiah. Our Father wants to have a close personal relationship with each of His beloved children throughout every day of our lives (see James 4:8).

Jesus Christ died on a cross at Calvary to set us free from the bondage of religious tradition. "You must know (recognize) that you were redeemed (ransomed) from the useless (fruit-less) way of living inherited by tradition from [your] forefathers…" (I Peter 1:18).

We have a difficult issue if our parents and/or grandparents grew up in religious tradition. We must pray about keeping peace in the family as we seek to be set free in the Spirit of God.

Jesus Christ wants us to enjoy the abundant life He has provided for us (see John 10:10). He wants every aspect of our lives to be centered around His indwelling presence. He wants us to constantly fill our minds and our hearts with the supernatural power of the Word of God.

We must not make the mistake of obeying traditional religious teaching that disregards the teaching of Jesus Christ. "See to it that no one carries you off as spoil or makes you yourselves captive by his so-called philosophy and intellectualism and vain deceit (idle fancies and plain nonsense), following human tradition (men's ideas of the material rather than the spiritual world), just crude notions following the rudimentary and elemental teachings of the universe and disregarding [the teachings of] Christ (the Messiah)" (Colossians 2:8).

During these last days before Jesus Christ returns, many people are teaching religious doctrine that sounds good. Careful examination of what they teach will clearly show that their teaching is solidly anchored upon human tradition. These people completely disregard the power of God through Jesus Christ.

Many good and well-intentioned people who do their best to live good lives are trapped by the bondage of religious tradition. They do not even begin to comprehend that they have been trapped by the bondage by religious tradition. Their lifestyle has been taught to them throughout their lives. Their religious tradition seems to be good, worthwhile and meaningful.

We cannot separate Christianity from our daily living. Christianity is not something we do for an hour or two on Sunday mornings. *Every* aspect of the lives of committed Christians should be centered around the Lord Jesus Christ.

Religion and Christianity are very different. Religion is segmented into certain times of the day in certain days of the week. Christianity is a living relationship with Jesus Christ twenty-four hours a day, seven days a week and fifty-two weeks each year throughout every year of our lives.

Religious people are similar to someone who is on a treadmill. They are walking continually, but they aren't going anywhere. They always are busy doing things that seem to be worthwhile, but they seldom or never do anything of eternal significance because their lives are not surrendered to the Word of God and the Spirit of God living in their hearts.

Many people go to a church simply because their parents went to a church of that particular denomination. Worshipping together as a family is beautiful. Unfortunately, the Spirit of God is not present in many churches. He has been closed out because of ceremonies and tradition.

Today many families attend the same church because they always have attended that church. The church may have become bogged down in tradition apart from the living Lord. This issue is very sensitive. Our prayer is that the whole family will worship together in a church that is alive with the Spirit of God.

This book is filled with scriptural concepts that are exactly the opposite of religious tradition. Anyone who has been blinded by religious tradition should constantly learn and obey the instructions our Father has given us in the Bible. Fill your mind and your heart continually with the Word of God. Meditate constantly on the promises of God so that worry and fear cannot obtain a foothold in your life. Know that God's promises are true.

Chapter 21

Trust the Lord with Your Future

Most people who worry are concerned about things they think might happen in the future. Jesus Christ told us exactly what to do in regard to worrying about the future. He said, "...do not worry or be anxious about tomorrow, for tomorrow will have worries and anxieties of its own. Sufficient for each day is its own trouble" (Matthew 6:34).

This passage of Scripture will be our theme for the next three chapters. In these chapters we will study the Word of God to learn what it says about the future, the past and the present. Anyone who carefully reads these chapters and meditates on God's specific instructions in these three areas will learn some very practical and helpful scriptural truths.

We have just seen that Jesus definitely does not want us to worry about the future. Satan always is the opposite of Jesus. Satan *does* want us to worry about the future. Satan and his demons continually try to put worried thoughts about the future into our minds. They hope that we will accept these thoughts and worry about them continually.

I don't remember where I originally read the following facts about worrying. I know that I copied this "worry table" from something I read more than thirty years ago. I cannot tell you that the following percentages have been proven statistically. I can say that, after many years of personal experience, I believe the following percentages are accurate:

Things We Worry About

Things that never happen	40%
Things that can't be changed by all the worry in the world	35%
Things that turn out better than expected	15%
Petty, useless worries	8%
Legitimate worries	2%
Total	100%

This "worry table" shows us that the odds are 50 to 1 that all of us worry about things that should not concern us. Many people are tormented with worried thoughts about the future that are absolutely useless. Whenever we worry about the future, we open our minds to continued torment from Satan's demons. True believers will understand that the two percent of so-called "legitimate worries" actually are marvelous opportunities for us to trust God completely. Christians should not worry about *anything*.

We complicate our lives unnecessarily if we make the mistake of worrying about anticipated problems that we think might occur. We have just seen in Matthew 6:34 that Jesus instructs us to live our lives one day at a time. Jesus does not want us to complicate our lives. He wants us to keep our lives simple by obeying His instructions to live our lives one day at a time and trusting Him completely to bring us safely through each day.

We put our minds on "overload" if we are concerned about everything we think might happen in the future in addition to whatever issues we face today. God did not create our minds to handle the multiplicity of worried thoughts that many of us put into our minds. We must not make the serious mistake of violating the specific instructions that Jesus gave us by spending considerable time and energy worrying about the future.

Many people are worried about what they think might happen in the future because they know that what they are worrying about is beyond their ability to control. Our Father wants us to trust Him completely whenever we face circumstances that may cause worry or fear to rise up inside of us. "Fear nothing that you are about to suffer. [Dismiss your dread and your fears!]..." (Revelation 2:10).

Please highlight or underline the word "nothing," the word "you" and the two times the word "your" is used in this passage of Scripture. Know that God is speaking to *you* when He uses the words "you" and "your" three times in this short passage of Scripture.

There is no question that our Father does not want us to be worried or afraid about *anything* that might happen in the future. He tells us to "dismiss" these thoughts. When we dismiss a thought, we send it away. We put that thought out of our minds. We refuse to think about it any more.

Unfortunately, many of God's children disobey the specific instructions that the Word of God gives us in regard to worrying about the future. Instead of worrying about the future, we should rest upon our absolute certainty of God's indwelling presence. We should have absolute faith in the reliability of the thousands of promises our Father has given us in His Word.

Why would we ever worry about the future if we are absolutely certain that Almighty God is with us at all times? *Why* would we ever worry about the future if we know a large number of our Father's promises to us and we have absolute faith in Him?

We have seen that our Father wants us to trust Him completely just as little children here on earth place complete trust in their parents. Little children do not provide anything for themselves. All of their needs are provided by their parents. Little children live their lives one day at a time. They do not worry about the future.

Our Father wants us to have this same childlike trust in Him. He can and will help us with every problem we face now and every problem we will face in the future if we have total, absolute and unwavering faith in Him.

We do not know what the future holds. Unless we are able to hear the voice of the Holy Spirit, we do not know anyone who truly knows what the future holds. "He does not know what is to be, or who can tell him how or when it will be…" (Ecclesiastes 8:7).

We should seek the Lord's will for our lives one day at a time instead of worrying about the future. "…you do not know [the least thing] about what may happen tomorrow. What is the nature of your life? You are [really] but a wisp of vapor (a puff of smoke, a mist) that is visible for a little while and then disappears [into thin air]. You ought instead to say, If the Lord is willing, we shall live and we shall do this or that [thing]" (James 4:14-15).

We should always seek the Lord's will instead of making overly detailed and elaborate plans for the future without seeking God. Our Father is omniscient, omnipotent and omnipresent. He knows everything that is happening throughout the world and everything that will happen in the future. He has all power. He can be in an infinite number of places at the same time. Our Father wants us to trust Him completely with the future.

In these last days before Jesus Christ returns, we have to deal with a proliferation of news media that has increased substantially in recent years. In addition to reading newspapers and magazines that are filled with concerns about the future, some Christians listen frequently to the twenty-four hour radio and television news stations. They are bombarded constantly with concerns about the uncertainty of the future.

Some people are overly concerned about the future. Other people drown any concerns about the future by drinking alcoholic beverages to excess. "Come, say they, We will fetch wine, and we will fill ourselves with strong drink! And tomorrow shall be as this day, a day great beyond measure" (Isaiah 56:12).

People who drink alcoholic beverages to drown out any concerns they have about the future are correct in not worrying about the future, but they are wrong in the way they attempt to achieve this goal. Instead of drinking to forget the future or spending emotional energy worrying about the future, we are instructed by God to meditate continually on His Word (see Joshua 1:8 and Psalm 1:2-3).

I believe that our meditation on the Word of God should be constant when everything is going well in our lives. I know from many years of experience that one of the best things we can do when we face the temptation to be concerned about the future is to spend *even more time* meditating on God's promises.

The Word of God is filled with thousands of promises from God. These promises are absolute. They are not changed in any way by the circumstances we face today or by any circumstances we might face in the future. Instead of focusing on the changing, temporal and uncertain world we live in, our Father wants us to focus continually on His unchanging, supernatural and eternal promises. We also must obey any conditions that our Father places with any promise.

We can be assured that our Father will tell us whenever He wants us to know anything about the future. He has promised to reveal through the Holy Spirit whatever we need to know about the future. Jesus Christ, speaking of the Holy Spirit, said, "...He will announce and declare to you the things that are to come [that will happen in the future]" (John 16:13).

I am *not* saying that we shouldn't plan for the future. We are wise to prayerfully make short-term and long-term goals, but we must not worry about the future. Planning for the future and worrying about the future are vastly different.

All of our future plans should be based upon God's plans. We should continually seek God's will for our lives. We should never make plans for the future without seeking direction from God. Our plans for the future should be flexible. We should be able to adapt to the changes that inevitably will occur while we trust the Bible as our compass and the Holy Spirit as our guide.

When we plan ahead, we are doing something that is constructive. When we worry about the future, we are doing something that is destructive. Our Father wants us to do the very best we can to carry out His will for our lives by focusing on Him at all times and trusting completely in Him as we seek His will for our lives one day at a time.

Chapter 22

Our Father Does Not Wants Us to be Concerned About the Past

In the last chapter we saw that our Father does not want us to worry about the future. In this chapter we will see that He does not want us to be concerned about events that took place in the past. We cannot do what our Father has called us to do with our lives if we have our attention focused too much on the future or too much on the past. Jesus Christ said, "…No one who puts his hand to the plow and looks back [to the things behind] is fit for the kingdom of God" (Luke 9:62).

Jesus spoke these words to His disciples who wanted to take care of seemingly important details before accompanying Him. Jesus told them to forget about the past and to concern themselves solely with following Him. This same spiritual principle applies to each of us today.

If we insist on focusing on the past, we are very likely to miss out on doing what God has called us to do with our lives. Our Father has specific plans for each of His beloved children. He wants each of us to "put our hands to the plow" as we move steadily forward to carry out the assignment He has given us.

We each should have a deep and sincere desire to do what God has called us to do with our lives. We should be like the apostle Paul who said, "…one thing I do [it is my one aspiration]: forgetting what lies behind and straining forward to what lies ahead, I press on toward the goal to win the [supreme and heavenly] prize to which God in Christ Jesus is calling us upward" (Philippians 3:13-14).

If Paul wanted to dwell on the past, he could have focused on many events in his past when he was Saul of Tarsus that could have stopped him from doing what God called him to do with his life. Saul of Tarsus was violently opposed to Christians. He persecuted Christians unmercifully.

Paul refused to allow anything from his past to influence him. We can see how single-minded he was to carry out the goal that God gave him when we read the words "…this *one* thing I do [it is my *one* aspiration]…" In this passage of Scripture we can see that Paul refused to allow his thoughts to wander. He focused completely on Jesus Christ.

Many of us would be able to do much more for God with the remainder of our lives if we were set free from all concerns about the future or the past. Our Father wants each of us to constantly move toward the goals He has for us. If you would like to learn more about God's plan for your life, you might want to meditate consistently on the scriptural instructions in our Scripture Meditation Cards, *Find God's Will for Your Life,* and listen to our detailed eighty-five minute cassette tape on this subject.

Yesterday is over and done with. Yesterday has no more value. We should learn what we can from the experiences of the past and then step expectantly into the newness of today. Many Christians are hindered from becoming what God wants them to become because they are held back by things that happened to them in the past. God can and will use our worst experiences for our good (see Romans 8:28).

Our Father wants to do fresh, new things in us and through us regardless of what happened to us in the past. "…you shall forget your misery; you shall remember it as waters that pass away. And [your] life shall be clearer than the noonday and rise above it; though there be darkness, it shall be as the morning. And you shall be secure and feel confident because there is hope…" (Job 11:16-18).

These words that were spoken to Job many years ago apply to Christians today. One of the biggest mistakes any of us can make is to carry the burdens of the past into the present. Our Father wants us to trust Him to give us a fresh new start. He wants us to look forward to the future with hope and optimism because we place all of our trust in Him.

Any issues we have faced in the past will decrease in intensity if we devote our lives to doing what our Father has called us to do. Like Job, we can "rise above" past problems. We should be secure in our confidence in the Lord as we focus on what He is doing in our lives today. At dawn each day the darkness gives way to the morning light. God uses this daily occurrence to show us that He is willing to give each of us a fresh new start if we will refuse to focus on what happened in the past.

Some of us are so caught up with the problems of yesterday that we miss out completely on the new things the Lord has for us today. "Do not [earnestly] remember the former things; neither consider the things of old. Behold, I am doing a new thing! Now it springs forth; do you not perceive and know it and will you not give heed to it? I will even make a way in the wilderness and rivers in the desert" (Isaiah 43:18-19).

These words that the Lord spoke through the prophet Isaiah many years ago apply to us today. Each of the three passages of Scripture we have just studied tells us to forget the past and to move forward to the wonderful new things that God can and will do in our lives. God is the God of the past, the present and the future. He has great plans for each of His children.

Our Father can and will bring us through every trial as we rest in Him. He even says that He will "make a way in the wilderness" for us. He said that He will create "rivers in the desert" if we refuse to focus on the past and focus instead on the "new things" He wants to do in our lives.

We have seen that many people are held back by problems that took place in the past. Some people go to the opposite extreme. They focus too much on "the good old days." They live in the past because they believe their past was better than the present or the future. "Do not say, Why were the old days better than these? For it is not wise or because of wisdom that you ask this" (Ecclesiastes 7:10).

We must not focus too much on good things or bad things that happened in the past. We are told that "it is not wise" to dwell on the "good old days." Some people are so caught up with the good things (or the bad things) that happened in the past that they miss out completely on the good things God has for them now.

Some people have no purpose in life. They have nothing to anticipate. Time hangs heavily on their hands. Some of these people devote their lives to a constant pursuit of pleasure. We must understand that we are not here on earth to pursue selfish goals. We are here to carry out God's will for our lives.

Our Father wants us to serve Him throughout our lives. He wants us to look ahead instead of looking back. Today is the first day of the rest of your life. If we want to remain young at heart as we grow older, we must keep our thoughts focused on God's present and future goals for us instead of dwelling on the past.

I believe there are two exceptions to forgetting about the past. The first exception is to learn from the past. We should not allow the past to influence our lives today except for what we have learned as a result of what we have been through. George Washington, the first president of the United States, said, "We ought not to look back unless it is to derive useful lessons from past errors."

Past failures have no relevancy to whatever we face today except for what we have learned that will help us to be more effective today. Our lives are ahead of us, not behind us. We need to learn the lessons we should learn from the past and be done with the past. These lessons have served the purpose of preparing us for the present and for the future.

Some people are overly preoccupied with sins they have committed in the past. They cannot imagine how God possibly could bless them or use them. Some of these people do not even bother to ask God to help them or to use them. They believe they are totally unworthy.

This type of thinking comes from the influence of Satan. Satan wants us to identify with past failures. He wants us to focus continually on the mistakes we have made in the past. Satan's demons constantly try to put thoughts into our minds that will cause us to relive the problems of yesterday.

We could not make a bigger mistake. If we have sinned against God, our Father wants us to admit our sins to Him. He wants us to know that He will forgive us when we truly repent of our sins and ask Him for forgiveness.

God is the God of a "fresh new start." The shed blood of Jesus Christ has cleansed us from all sin. We must not allow Satan to influence us by tempting us to dwell on any past mistakes we have made.

Our Father will forgive our sins and give us a fresh new start if we will humbly receive His grace because of the price that Jesus Christ paid for us at Calvary. "If we [freely] admit that we have sinned and confess our sins, He is faithful and just (true to His own nature and promises) and will forgive our sins [dismiss our lawlessness] and [continuously] cleanse us from all unrighteousness [everything not in conformity to His will in purpose, thought, and action]" (I John 1:9).

If we repent of our sins and ask our Father to forgive us for past errors, we can be certain that He will give us a clean slate. In addition to forgiving our sins, God *does not even remember them any more.* "I, even I, am He Who blots out and cancels your transgressions, for My own sake, and I will not remember your sins "(Isaiah 43:25).

If Satan's demons try to bring a picture of our past mistakes into our minds, we should laugh at their attempts. Our past mistakes *do not exist any more* if we have repented of them and asked God to forgive us. These sins have been cancelled, wiped clean, forgiven and forgotten.

Some Christians make the mistake of continuing to feel guilty about things they have done in the past even though God has forgiven them. Our Father wants us to *forget* these mistakes just as He has forgotten them. "...I will be merciful and gracious toward their sins and I will remember their deeds of unrighteousness no more" (Hebrews 8:12).

When we confess our sins to our Father and ask Him to forgive us, we can be absolutely certain that He has forgiven us and that He has forgotten our sins. We should not be burdened with past sins if we know that our Father has forgiven them. Too many of us are punishing ourselves constantly for mistakes we made in the past. When our Father forgives us, we also must forgive ourselves and go on with our goal of carrying out His plan for our lives.

There is one other thing our Father wants us to remember about the past. In addition to learning from our past mistakes, He wants us to remember the many times in the past when He has brought us through difficult circumstances. "...you shall [earnestly] remember all the way which the Lord your God led you..." (Deuteronomy 8:2).

These words that God spoke to the Israelites about bringing them through forty years in the wilderness apply to each of us today. Some of us who have been Christians for a long time have exercised our faith in God many times. We have many testimonies pertaining to God's faithfulness. Some of us became Christians in the first place because God delivered us out of very difficult problems.

We can and we should look to the past to receive encouragement. Newer Christians who do not have personal testimonies of what God did for them in the past can be encouraged by the numerous stories in the Bible that tell us how God brought many people safely through difficult circumstances. They can be encouraged by numerous Christian books and articles in Christian magazines that are filled with additional testimonies of God's faithfulness.

In this chapter we have learned what our Father wants us to receive from the past. Our Father does *not* want us to dwell on the past with the exception of these positive things. He wants us to focus our attention entirely on what He is doing in our lives now.

In the next chapter we will look carefully into the Word of God for specific instructions about living our lives one day at a time. We will learn many valuable scriptural truths that will help us to live our lives one day at a time without being concerned about the future or the past.

Chapter 23

Our Father Wants Us to Live One Day at a Time

In Chapter 21 we studied Matthew 6:34 and other passages of Scripture that tell us that we should not worry about the *future*. In the last chapter we studied several passages of Scripture that tell us that we should not allow things that happened in the *past* to pull us down. Now that we have seen that our Father does not want us to worry about the future or to be concerned about the past, we have come down to the only thing that remains – *today*. We have seen in the last part of Matthew 6:34 that Jesus said, "…Sufficient for each day is its own trouble."

Our Father wants each of us to live our lives *one day at a time*. Several years ago I read about Dr. William Osler, a Canadian physician, who instructed his patients to live in "day-tight compartments." I have never forgotten these words. If we live in day-tight compartments, the past cannot affect our lives and we will not worry about the future. We will focus entirely upon today.

Dr. Osler told his patients to pull down a mental curtain each night to shut out the past. He told them to pull down another mental curtain each night to shut out the future. He told them to go to sleep at night without being concerned about burdens from the past or being concerned with any anxiety about the future. He told them to awaken the next morning to concentrate only on that day as they continued to shut out the past and the future.

Dr. Osler's teaching was scripturally correct according to the instructions Jesus gave us in Matthew 6:34. Our Father does not want the past or the future to drain any of the mental, physical and emotional energy we need to live our lives effectively today.

We see a scriptural example of this principle in the manna the Lord provided for food for the Israelites when they were in the wilderness on the way to the Promised Land. The Israelites awakened each morning to find that the Lord had made supernatural provision for the food they needed for that day. "In the evening quails came up and covered the camp; and in the morning the dew lay round about the camp. And when the dew had gone, behold, upon the face of the wilderness there lay a fine, round and flakelike thing, as fine as hoarfrost on the ground. When the Israelites saw it, they said one to another, Manna [What is it?]. For they did not know what it was. And Moses said to them, This is the bread which the Lord has given you to eat" (Exodus 16:13-15).

God provided this food for the Israelites when their food ran out. The Israelites named the food God had provided for them when they asked "Manna?" which means "What is it?".

Moses instructed the Israelites to take as much manna as they would need for themselves and the other people in their tents. "This is what the Lord has commanded: Let every man gather of it as much as he will need, an omer for each person, according to the number of your persons; take it, every man for those in his tent. The [people] did so, and gathered, some more, some less. When they measured it with an omer, he who gathered much had nothing over, and he who gathered little had no lack; each gathered according to his need" (Exodus 16:16-18).

Moses told the Israelites to take only as much food as they could use for the remainder of that day and night. He told them that they should not have any food left over for the next day, but they did not do what he said. "Moses said, Let none of it be left until morning. But they did not listen to Moses; some of them left of it until morning, and it bred worms, became foul, and stank; and Moses was angry with them. They gathered it every morning, each as much as he needed, for when the sun became hot it melted" (Exodus 16:19-21).

We can see from this example that God provided for the needs of the Israelites one day at a time. The Israelites who refused to obey Moses tried to keep enough manna to last until the next day, but they found that this manna "stank" – it spoiled, smelled bad and was filled with worms. They learned to gather only as much manna as they needed each morning for the upcoming day because any excess melted when the sun became hot.

This biblical principle is consistent with the instructions that Jesus gave us in Matthew 6:34 to live one day at a time. Jesus reiterated this principle when He prayed asking God to provide food. Jesus said, "Give us daily our bread [food for the morrow]" (Luke 11:3).

I believe the word "daily" in this passage of Scripture is very significant. Jesus did not pray for food for a month. He did not pray for food for a week. He prayed for food for one day. Our Father wants us to trust Him to meet our needs one day at a time without worrying about the future.

Our days come to us one at a time. When each day is over, it will never come again. Our Father wants us to make the most that we can out of each day. Our Father wants us to treat each new day as the precious gem that it is. He does not want us to be careless about even one day of our lives.

Many people do not understand how important each day is. They squander days, weeks, months and years in the pursuit of selfish goals that have no eternal value. As some of us grow older, we begin to see the importance of seeking and fulfilling the assignment God has given to us. We understand how precious each day is.

I believe we should ask ourselves each night, "What did I do today that had eternal significance?" This vitally important question gives us a standard of measurement to measure the effectiveness of each day from God's perspective. Our Father wants us to use each day He has given us for activities that will last into eternity instead of wasting these precious days on activities that have no eternal significance.

I believe we should live each day under the guidance of the Holy Spirit so that the results of our daily activity will be eternally significant. We should plant many eternal spiritual seeds each day through prayer, through sharing Jesus Christ with other people, through Bible study and meditation, through obeying God's instructions, through believing God's promises and through successfully completing God's plan for our lives for that day. As we turn away from the temptations of the world to seek God's will throughout each day of our lives, we will find that we spend more and more of our time on activities that have eternal significance.

Each new day in our lives is a gift from the Lord. He gives us each day to be used for what He wants us to do with that day. He wants us to be grateful for each day of our lives. He wants us to be glad because of the opportunity we have been given to serve Him during the upcoming day. "This is the day which the Lord has brought about; we will rejoice and be glad in it" (Psalm 118:24).

Our Father wants us to look forward to each new day of our lives. He wants us to be optimistic and excited about each new day He gives us. He wants us to rejoice because we know that each day is a fresh new opportunity to serve Him and to trust Him.

We all have learned from experience that the problems we face seem to be much more severe when we are tired. A problem at the end of the day when we are tired and ready for bed often will not seem as difficult when we look at this same problem after a good night's sleep.

When our Father gives us a fresh new day, He gives us a new opportunity to cleanse our minds of the past and the future. He gives us an opportunity to enter into and remain in His rest throughout the upcoming day. "…He sets a definite day, [a new] Today, [and gives another opportunity of securing that rest]…" (Hebrews 4:7).

The Word of God capitalizes the word "Today" in this passage of Scripture. I believe this word is capitalized to place emphasis on the vital importance of resting in God as we seek His plan for each day of our lives. This passage of Scripture is part of the instructions God gives us in the third and fourth chapters of the Book of Hebrews to enter into His rest by trusting Him completely. We only can enter into God's rest when we comprehend the finished work of the cross.

We are given a fresh new opportunity to enter into God's rest every morning of our lives. Each day we receive God's precious gift of twenty-four fresh, new hours. We should prayerfully ask our Father what He wants us to do with these hours.

Our Father loves us so much that He gives each of us a fresh new supply of His love every morning. We should awaken each morning to an awareness of the magnificence of our Father's love, grace, mercy and compassion for us during the upcoming day.

We do not need enough of our Father's love, grace, mercy and compassion for tomorrow, next week, next month or next year. Our Father promises to give us these blessings every day. "It is because of the Lord's mercy and loving-kindness that we are not consumed, because His [tender] compassions fail not. They are new every morning; great and abundant is Your stability and faithfulness" (Lamentations 3:22-23).

I believe that we should meditate often on this wonderful promise from God as we begin a new day. We should begin the day by thanking God for the love, grace, mercy and compassion He has provided for us. We should rejoice because we know that our Father has given each of us a fresh new start every morning. We can be assured that our Father has given us an abundant supply of stability to trust Him throughout the upcoming day.

I believe that our first thoughts and our first words each morning should be focused upon the Lord. When I wake up I usually begin my day by saying something like the following: "Dear Father, thank You for this wonderful day You have made. I rejoice and I am glad in it. Thank You for Your love, Your grace, Your mercy and Your compassion. I yield control of my life to You this day. Guide me throughout this day to do what You want me to do. Live Your life in me and through me this day. Thank You in the precious name of Jesus Christ for answering this prayer. Amen."

My prayer at the beginning of each day is not always exactly the same. However, the preceding prayer is typical of what I pray most mornings. I believe that we should always thank our Father for the fresh new opportunity He gives us each morning. We should dedicate each day to Him. We should yield our God-given ability to control our own lives by voluntarily giving each day of our lives back to God.

Our Father has a specific plan for each of His children for each day. He had this definite plan for every day of our lives before He created us. "Your eyes saw my unformed substance, and in Your book all the days [of my life] were written before ever they took shape, when as yet there was none of them" (Psalm 139:16).

I believe that these words from the psalmist David apply to each of us today. Our Father wants us to dedicate each day to seeking, finding and carrying out His plan for our lives. He wants us to allow Him to do in us and through us whatever He wants to do throughout the upcoming day. He wants us to allow each day of our lives to unfold at His pace. He wants us to trust Him to bring us safely through our lives one day at a time.

I believe we should start each day with a time of prayer, a time of praise and thanksgiving and precious quiet time before the Lord. I believe we should begin each day with Bible study and meditation. We then should continue throughout the day and night to meditate on the Word of God as Joshua 1:8 and Psalm 1:2-3 instruct us to do.

Our Father does not want negative thoughts and emotions that are caused by the circumstances we face to obtain a foothold in our minds and in our hearts. We should constantly fill our minds and our hearts with God's Word so that negative thoughts and emotions cannot control our lives. The worried, anxious and fearful thoughts that Satan's demons try to put into our minds will not be able to get a foothold if our minds and our hearts are constantly being filled with the supernatural power of the living Word of God.

Our primary goal each day should be to enter into and remain in the Lord's presence. We should be like the psalmist who said, "One thing have I asked of the Lord, that will I seek, inquire for, and [insistently] require: that I may dwell in the house of the Lord [in His presence] all the days of my life, to behold and gaze upon the beauty [the sweet attractiveness and the delightful loveliness] of the Lord and to meditate, consider, and inquire in His temple" (Psalm 27:4).

We should pray consistently to dwell in the presence of the Lord throughout every day of our lives. We will see how beautiful God is when we are in His presence. We will think about God constantly. We will trust Him completely.

Our Father promises to carry our burdens one day at a time if we will place all of our faith in Him when we face difficult problems each day. "Blessed be the Lord, Who bears our burdens and carries us day by day..." (Psalm 68:19).

This passage of Scripture does not tell us that the Lord will bear our burdens tomorrow or next week, next month or next year. We are told that He will bear our burdens and carry us through the difficult times in our lives "day by day."

Our Father wants us to have absolute faith that He will bear our burdens for us. We can be assured that He will carry all of our burdens one day at a time if we live in day-tight compartments because we trust Him completely. Our Father wants us to trust Him to provide the strength we need for each day of our lives. "...as your day, so shall your strength, your rest and security, be" (Deuteronomy 33:25).

We can meditate on this promise to be certain that our Father will give us the strength we need one day at a time. Our Father wants us to rest in Him each day. He wants us to turn to Him for security instead of looking to external sources for security.

I am very goal-oriented. Each day I seek God's will for my life. I do my very best to do what I believe He wants me to do. I have worked from a daily list of things to do for almost fifty years. I have never come close to being caught up. I know that I never will be caught up. I like to always have much more to do than I can accomplish in any given day. I believe that those of us who want to "bite off more than we can chew" should be determined to make every day of our lives count for the Lord as much as we possibly can.

Our Father wants us to spend our time so carefully each day that we will receive wisdom from Him to do what is important to Him. Our Father wants us to effectively utilize the precious time He has allotted to us during that day. "...teach us to number our days, that we may get us a heart of wisdom" (Psalm 90:12).

Our Father does not want us to waste any of the precious days He has given us. He does not want us to allow ourselves to be overwhelmed by the many things we have to do. He wants us to learn to do one thing at a time just as He wants us to learn to live one day at a time. We can break each day down into small segments once we learn how to live one day at a time. We should live each segment of each day as efficiently as possible because we continually are able to receive God's wisdom by faith (see James 1:5-8).

We should be realistic. We should know that we will face several challenges each day. We must not make the mistake of trying to look at all of the challenges of the day at the same time. The same principle that we have learned about not looking into the future applies to the various challenges we face daily. We can be certain that our Father is with us as we go through each day. We sin if we rush ahead of God. "...to be overhasty is to sin and miss the mark" (Proverbs 19:2).

In the past three chapters we have studied scriptural instructions that tell us what to do about the future, what to do about the past and how to live our lives one day at a time. I hope that these instructions from heaven have been a blessing to you. I pray that you will learn to live your life in day-tight compartments and that each day of your life will be completely dedicated to our precious Lord.

Chapter 24

Know the Importance of a
Close Relationship with the Lord

Adam and Eve enjoyed a close and intimate relationship with God. Their sin caused them to lose this wonderful relationship. All of us are descendants of Adam and Eve. We all are born separated from God.

The sacrifice that Jesus Christ made at Calvary has restored the ability for each person who receives Him as Savior to enjoy a close relationship with God. All Christians should take full advantage of the precious privilege we have been given to constantly draw closer to God. If we learn how to stay close to God, we will *not* worry about *anything*.

We do not deserve the opportunity to enjoy a close relationship with God. All of the money in the world cannot buy the priceless privilege of a personal relationship with God. We are able to enjoy this wonderful relationship only because of the price that Jesus Christ paid for us at Calvary. We make a major mistake if we fail to enjoy this wonderful gift we have been given.

Some people are unable to comprehend that the same awesome God Who created the earth, the stars, the sun, the moon and all of the planets and galaxies in the universe and every person on earth wants to enjoy a close personal relationship with each of us. "When I view and consider Your heavens, the work of Your fingers, the moon and the stars, which You have ordained and established, what is man that You are mindful of him, and the son of [earthborn] man that You care for him?" (Psalm 8:3-4).

Our Father desires a much closer relationship with us than we can possibly comprehend. I do not believe that anything is more important to God than to enjoy a close relationship with each of His beloved children. Nothing should be more important to us. "Behold, I stand at the door and knock; if anyone hears and listens to and heeds My voice and opens the door, I will come in to him..." (Revelation 3:20).

These words were spoken by Jesus Christ. Jesus constantly knocks on the door of our hearts asking us to let Him in. "Come close to God and He will come close to you..." (James 4:8).

If we read the last part of this passage of Scripture first, we can see that God wants to come close to us. Our Father has done His part. He has provided a bridge to Himself through Jesus Christ. God has prepared the way to receive each of us whenever we choose to come close to Him.

If we truly desire to know God, we will obey the following wise advice that King David gave to his son, Solomon, when he said, "And you, Solomon my son, know the God of your father [have personal knowledge of Him, be acquainted with, and understand Him; appreciate, heed, and cherish Him] and serve Him with a blameless heart and a willing mind. For the Lord searches all hearts and minds and understands all the wanderings of the thoughts. If you seek Him [inquiring for and of Him and requiring Him as your first and vital necessity] you will find Him..." (I Chronicles 28:9).

These words King David spoke to his son apply to each of us today. Our Father has instructed each of us to "have personal knowledge of Him, be acquainted with, and understand Him." Isn't it wonderful to know that *you* actually can know God personally and enjoy a close personal relationship with Him? We actually can begin to understand many things about God while we are here on earth, although full understanding of God cannot be obtained until we are in heaven (see I Corinthians 13:12).

Our Father wants us to fully appreciate the opportunity we have been given to know Him intimately. We are instructed to "cherish Him." When we cherish a relationship with someone, we fully appreciate the opportunity to enjoy this relationship. We should have a deep and sincere desire to serve God "with a blameless heart and willing mind."

This passage of Scripture goes on to tell us that the Lord is able to search the hearts and the minds of every person on earth. Before the time of computers, understanding how God could know every thought of every person on earth was difficult for some people to comprehend. Now, because of the Internet and all of the detailed facts available through computers, we can see how the God of the Universe actually can know and keep track of each precious person.

The implementation of the computer solved some faith questions. More discoveries will solve more faith questions. Nevertheless, until we see God face to face, we will have to live by faith. Entering into and staying in God's presence should be the deepest yearning of our hearts. We should step out in faith each day with a deep and sincere desire to constantly draw closer to God.

I Chronicles 28:9 goes on to tell us that we can only find God and enjoy a close relationship with Him if this desire is our "first and vital necessity." A close relationship with God is not a "nice to have" – a close personal relationship with Almighty God should be *vitally important* to each of us. We never will do anything that is more important than to continually draw closer to God. We are told that we *will find God* if we seek Him continually.

Please stop and think about what we have just learned. What else do you do in your life that could possibly be more important than to pursue a close and intimate relationship with Almighty God? Are you determined to enjoy the wonderful privilege you have been given to fellowship continually with the Lord?

We each should have a deep yearning to know our precious Lord much more intimately than the closest relationship we have with any member of our families or any other person on earth. This close relationship with the Lord will make our relationship with other people much better than it could be otherwise.

Every aspect of our lives should spring from our deep and constant desire to enjoy a close personal relationship with the Lord. We can be assured that every other aspect of our lives will improve if we put this close relationship with our precious Lord in first place where it belongs.

Our Father wants our relationship with Him to deepen and widen because we continually seek a closer relationship with Him. Once we experience the blessings of this closer relationship, we will be absolutely determined to stay close to

Him. We will be like the psalmist who said, "My whole being follows hard after You and clings closely to You; Your right hand upholds me" (Psalm 63:8).

The Lord will hold us up when we are so close to Him that we actually cling to Him. Can you truly say that you yearn for a close relationship with the Lord? "...let us know (recognize, be acquainted with, and understand) Him; let us be zealous to know the Lord [to appreciate, give heed to, and cherish Him]..." (Hosea 6:3).

We are instructed to "be zealous" in our desire to know the Lord intimately. When we are zealous about something, we pursue this goal wholeheartedly. We are consumed constantly by this goal. Once again, the amplification repeats the instructions from I Chronicles 28:9, telling us to "appreciate, give heed to and cherish" a close relationship with the Lord.

The apostle Paul was totally committed to knowing Jesus Christ more intimately. Paul said, "...I count everything as loss compared to the possession of the priceless privilege (the overwhelming preciousness, the surpassing worth, and supreme advantage) of knowing Christ Jesus my Lord and of progressively becoming more deeply and intimately acquainted with Him [of perceiving and recognizing and understanding Him more fully and clearly]. For His sake I have lost everything and consider it all to be mere rubbish (refuse, dregs), in order that I may win (gain) Christ (the Anointed One)" (Philippians 3:8).

The apostle Paul emphasized that we should never allow anything to come ahead of the "priceless privilege" we have been given to know the Lord more intimately. The amplification of this passage of Scripture tells us that the privilege of knowing the Lord intimately is "overwhelming precious." This privilege surpasses in value anything else we ever will experience.

Paul refers to the closeness of our relationship with the Lord as a "supreme advantage." We must not miss out on this wonderful advantage that has been made available to us. Knowing Jesus intimately is the highest and most treasured experience in our lives on earth. We each should have a deep and consuming desire to "progressively become more deeply and intimately acquainted with Him."

Knowing Jesus Christ intimately is a progressive process. We will find that the intimacy of our relationship with Jesus will increase constantly as we draw closer to Him over a period of time. The amplification says that we will be able to "perceive Him clearly." We are told that we will "recognize Him." We will be able to "understand Him more as we continually draw closer to Him."

Would *you* like to see Jesus clearly, to recognize Him while you are here on earth and to continually understand Him more and more? Paul said that anything we allow to come ahead of a fervent desire to draw closer to Jesus Christ is "*mere rubbish.*"

Shortly after making this statement, Paul expounded even more on his fervent desire to draw closer to Jesus Christ. He said, "[For my determined purpose is] that I may know Him [that I may progressively become more deeply and intimately acquainted with Him, perceiving and recognizing and understanding the wonders of His Person more strongly and more clearly], and that I may in that same way come to know the power outflowing from His resurrection [which it exerts over believers], and that I may so share His sufferings as to be continually transformed [in spirit into His likeness even] to His death, [in the hope] that if possible I may attain to the [spiritual and moral] resurrection [that lifts me] out from among the dead [even while in the body]" (Philippians 3:10-11).

Paul's absolute and total commitment to a closer relationship with Jesus Christ is a wonderful example for each of us. The amplification tells us that Paul was determined to progressively know Jesus more deeply and more intimately. We are told that Paul had a constant desire to "perceive, recognize, and understand the wonders of His Person more strongly and more clearly."

We each should have this same deep, sincere and intense desire to know Jesus more intimately. As we know Jesus more intimately, we personally will experience "the power outflowing from His resurrection."

Paul went on to say that he also desired to share in the suffering of Jesus Christ so that he continually would be transformed to "attain a spiritual and moral resurrection." Paul knew that being tortured for Jesus would result in partaking of His nature. He said that he would be honored to suffer for Jesus because he knew that he would become more like Jesus. This same spiritual principle applies to each of us when we actually draw closer to Jesus because of adversity in our lives.

Jesus loves us so much that He reaches out to us when we face adversity. "The Lord is close to those who are of a broken heart and saves such as are crushed with sorrow for sin and are humbly and thoroughly penitent" (Psalm 34:18).

If our hearts are broken, we are in a perfect position to draw closer to Jesus. Jesus will be very close to us if we seek Him wholeheartedly. He has provided salvation for anyone who is sorry for his or her wrongdoing and decides to change his or her ways.

If we have a deep and sincere desire to draw closer to God, we should praise Him and worship Him constantly as we pour out our heartfelt gratitude to Him. We should study and meditate on His Word continually. We should speak His Word with faith throughout every day and night of our lives. We should pray continually. We should constantly intercede for others. We should listen continually to hear what He is saying to us.

Now that we have seen how important it is for each of us to draw closer to our precious Lord, we are ready to look into the Word of God for specific instructions that tell us how to draw closer to the Lord. We also will learn more about the wonderful blessings we will receive as we draw closer to the Lord.

Chapter 25

Stay Close to the Lord and Refuse to Worry

One of the best ways to draw closer to the Lord is to continually feed on the spiritually nutritious food of His Word. We have seen previously that God and His Word are the same. "In the beginning [before all time] was the Word (Christ), and the Word was with God, and the Word was God Himself" (John 1:1).

We will draw closer and closer to God if we continually fill our minds and our hearts with the Word of God. Once again, I want to emphasize that we must not make the mistake of ignoring our Father's instructions to renew our minds in His Word on a daily basis (see Romans 12:2, II Corinthians 4:16 and Ephesians 4:23). This book will repeatedly emphasize that we must not make the mistake of ignoring our Father's instructions to meditate on His Word continually throughout the day and night (see Joshua 1:8 and Psalm 1:2-3).

Unfortunately, only a very small percentage of Christians faithfully obey these specific instructions from God. They do not realize the severe long-term implications of their failure to continually study and meditate on the Word of God. We cannot draw closer to God without obeying His instructions to constantly fill our minds and our hearts with the supernatural power of His living Word. We fill our minds and our hearts with God Himself when we continually fill our minds and our hearts with His Word.

We cannot know God intimately unless we learn how He wants us to live our lives and then obey the specific instructions He has given to us. "…this is how we may discern [daily, by experience] that we are coming to know Him [to perceive, recognize, understand, and become better acquainted with Him]: if we keep (bear in mind, observe, practice) His teachings (precepts, commandments)" (I John 2:3).

Would you like to know God more intimately on a daily basis? Do you truly have a deep and sincere desire to "perceive, recognize, understand and become better acquainted with Him?" This passage of Scripture tells us exactly what we should do if we sincerely desire to draw close to God.

Our Father tells us that we can achieve these very desirable goals by continually being aware of His instructions and by doing what He has instructed us to do. The amplification of this passage of Scripture clearly shows us the specific relationship that exists between knowing God more intimately, learning how He wants us to live and faithfully obeying the specific instructions He has given to us.

We are proud, ignorant or lazy if we ignore our Father's instructions to constantly fill our minds and our hearts with His Word. We are cheating ourselves if we pursue selfish desires instead of studying and meditating on the Word of God as God has instructed us to do. Actually, the more we know our Father, the more we will desire His holy Word, the Bible.

If we are humble and teachable, we will be able to continually draw closer to God. If we are proud, we will keep Him at a distance. "...though the Lord is high, yet has He respect to the lowly [bringing them into fellowship with Him]; but the proud and haughty He knows and recognizes [only] at a distance" (Psalm 138:6).

Pride always will keep us away from God. Proud people attempt to elevate themselves into God's position. They are their own little gods. Proud people disregard what God has instructed them to do. Proud people do what they want to do.

This passage of Scripture tells us that *we must be "lowly"* if we sincerely want to enjoy close fellowship with the Lord. We should humble ourselves before the Lord and before one another. We should not have an exaggerated opinion of our own importance.

Proud people are influenced by Satan's demons who fell from heaven because of their pride. Satan's demons do their very best to get into our minds to influence us to make the same mistake they made. They want us to be proud because they know that proud people cannot know God intimately.

Humble Christians absolutely refuse to give in to this attempt to influence them by appealing to pride. Humble and teachable Christians faithfully obey their Father's instructions to fill their minds and hearts with His Word. As we continually draw closer and closer to God, we will trust Him more and more with a simple, childlike trust that proud people cannot even begin to comprehend.

If we continually draw closer to God, we will turn away from an earthly perspective. We will be able see our lives more and more from our Father's heavenly perspective. As we continually draw closer and closer to God, we will begin to comprehend how awesome, great and magnificent He is. The problems that seemed so impossible to us will not seem to be so difficult if we learn how to enter into and remain in God's presence.

The same God Who created heaven and earth can do anything. *Nothing is too difficult for Almighty God.* "Alas, Lord God! Behold, You have made the heavens and the earth by Your great power and by Your outstretched arm! There is nothing too hard or too wonderful for You…" (Jeremiah 32:17).

Jeremiah knew how powerful God is. The apostle Paul also knew how powerful God is. Paul prayed that the Ephesians would know and understand the mighty power of God. This same mighty power is available to each of us today *if* we will draw close to God "…[so that you can know and understand] what is the immeasurable and unlimited and surpassing greatness of His power in and for us who believe, as demonstrated in the working of His mighty strength, which He exerted in Christ when He raised Him from the dead and seated Him at His [own] right hand in the heavenly [places]…" (Ephesians 1:19-20).

The amplification in this passage of Scripture tells us that we have been given the ability to know and understand the mighty power of God. The "immeasurable, and unlimited and surpassing greatness" of the power that raised Jesus Christ from the dead is available to each of God's children who know their Father intimately and trust Him completely. God's unlimited power surpasses anything we can even begin to comprehend with the limitations of our human understanding.

Awareness of God's mighty power is only available to us by faith. The continually increasing awareness of the power of Almighty God is available to "us who believe." If we do not know and understand how great and powerful God is, we will be very apprehensive when we face severe problems. If we know and believe that God's mighty power truly is available to us, we will see our problems as the opportunities they actually are for the mighty power of God to be released.

We must not limit God. Our Father lives in the hearts of every one of His children. We must know that God's mighty power is at work deep down inside of us. If we place all of our trust and confidence in God, He can and will do much more than we can comprehend. The Bible speaks of "...Him Who, by (in consequence of) the [action of His] power that is at work within us, is able to [carry out His purpose and] do superabundantly, far over and above all that we [dare] ask or think [infinitely beyond our highest prayers, desires, thoughts, hopes, or dreams] – To Him be glory in the church and in Christ Jesus throughout all generations forever and ever. Amen (so be it)" (Ephesians 3:20-21).

Please go back and *meditate carefully and thoroughly* on this wonderful promise that your loving Father has given to *you*. I don't know of any passage of Scripture in the Bible that describes the immense power of God more clearly. We must know and believe without reservation that Almighty God Who lives in our hearts is able to carry out His purpose for our lives by doing "superabundantly, far over and above all that we dare ask or think."

This passage of Scripture does not just tell us that God is able to do more than we ask Him to do or more than we think He can do. The word "superabundantly" tells us that there are absolutely *no limits* to what God can and will do on our behalf *if* we are close enough to Him and if we truly desire to carry out His purpose for our lives. If we have a close and intimate relationship with God, we will be able to trust Him completely at all times and in the face of every circumstance.

The amplification of this marvelous promise from heaven tells us that God is able to respond to each of us in a way that is "infinitely beyond our highest prayers, desires, thoughts, hopes or dreams." We must not limit the One Who knows no limits.

When we continually draw closer to God, we will know deep down inside of ourselves that He really *does* have the answer to *every* problem we will face. We must know that the seemingly complex problems we face are not at all difficult for God to solve. Jesus Christ said, "…With men [it is] impossible, but not with God; for all things are possible with God" (Mark 10:27).

Many of God's children are overwhelmed by the seeming impossibility of solving the severe problems they face. We must know and believe deep down in our hearts that "*all* things are possible with God." Know that the word "all" includes whatever problems *you* face at this time, no matter how impossible these problems may seem to be from your limited human comprehension.

We must not focus on the problems we face. Our so-called problems actually are marvelous opportunities for God. When we face difficult problems, we should turn away from these problems to draw closer and closer to God. "Let us all come forward and draw near with true (honest and sincere) hearts in unqualified assurance and absolute conviction engendered by faith (by that leaning of the entire human personality on God in absolute trust and confidence in His power, wisdom, and goodness)…" (Hebrews 10:22).

Once again, you can be certain that the word "all" in this passage of Scripture includes *you*. Our Father wants *all* of His children to draw close to Him. If we have a close relationship with God, we will have "unqualified assurance and absolute conviction" in the power of Almighty God. If we faithfully obey God's instructions to draw near to Him, our faith in God *will not waver* regardless of the seeming severity of any problems we face.

This passage of Scripture goes on to tell us that God's power is "engendered by faith." The word "engendered" means "to bring into being." The amplification of this passage of Scripture says that, as we draw closer to God, we will lean on Him with "absolute trust and confidence in His power, wisdom and goodness." We will be absolutely certain that He can and will do exactly what He says He will do.

Our relationship with God should be at the absolute center of every aspect of our lives. Our lives should be centered around our constant awareness of God's indwelling presence. "For in Him we live and move and have our being..." (Acts 17:28).

Our lives must not be centered around ourselves. We "live and move and have our being" in God when every aspect of our lives revolves around our absolute certainty that the God of the universe actually lives in our hearts. We should have a deep and consuming desire to live by the Spirit instead of being controlled by the dictates and impulses of the flesh.

Putting our total confidence in God does not come naturally to us. We are naturally inclined to place our trust in people and things because we are descendants of a fallen Adam. People who are worldly-oriented place their trust in things they can contact with their senses. They place their trust in things they can see with their eyes, hear with their ears and touch with their hands. They trust other people more than they trust God.

We may not see God with our physical eyesight. We may not hear God with our physical ears. We cannot touch God physically with our hands. We can know and feel the presence of the Holy Spirit. We must learn how to trust God by obeying the specific instructions He has given us that tell us how to continually draw closer to Him so that we *will* be able to trust Him completely.

If we sincerely desire to draw closer to God, we need to turn away from the influence of the world throughout every day of our lives. We must understand that "…the whole world [around us] is under the power of the evil one" (I John 5:19).

Anyone who sincerely desires to trust God completely cannot trust in the things of the world. This passage of Scripture tells us that the world we live in is greatly influenced by the power of Satan. All that we have to do to understand this spiritual truth is to look around us to see how much more evil the world has become in recent years.

I believe that we live in the last days before Jesus Christ will return to earth. The influence of Satan on the world has ascended to a degree that never has been experienced in the past. We absolutely must not make the mistake of placing our trust in the things of this world.

Unfortunately, some Christians look at God as a distant God. God seems to be far away from them. They have a difficult time trusting God Who seems to be so far away. The Holy Spirit confirms that God lives in our hearts.

Christians who make an absolute commitment to draw closer to God will find that God actually will become their closest friend and their constant companion. When we develop an intimate relationship with God, we will be able to trust Him in a way that was absolutely impossible when He seemed to be far away. We will understand that He could not be closer to us because He lives in our hearts. We will *know* that our Father loves us with a love that is beyond the limitations of our human comprehension.

Please stop for a moment to think about the one or two people here on earth whom you trust above everyone else. Please do not resume reading this book until you have identified these people. Have you identified these names? Now we are ready to move on.

Why do you trust this person or these people so much? Don't you trust each of these people *because you have developed a close and intimate relationship* with them over a period of time? Don't you tend to be skeptical when people you don't know intimately make promises when you have no history of their faithfulness to their word? On the other hand, if someone you know and trust completely makes a promise to you, do you doubt this person?

The Word of God is filled with thousands of awesome and magnificent promises from Almighty God. These promises from heaven may seem to be too good to be true to some of us. However, as we draw closer and closer to God, we will be able to trust His Word completely just as we are able to trust the word of the people on earth who are closest to us.

In reality, even these people may occasionally disappoint us, but God never will disappoint us. "…they who know Your name [who have experience and acquaintance with Your mercy] will lean on and confidently put their trust in You, for You, Lord, have not forsaken those who seek (inquire of and for) You [on the authority of God's Word and the right of their necessity]" (Psalm 9:10).

The amplification of this passage of Scripture tells us that we will trust God *if* we know Him well enough to have had "experience and acquaintance with His mercy." We will be able to "lean on" God as our faith in Him progressively increases. We will be able to "confidently put our trust in Him." We will be absolutely certain that God will never forsake us when we continually seek Him based upon the authority and the power of His Word.

If we have a close relationship with God that has been developed over a period of time, we will not have to struggle, strain and work at having faith in God. Trusting God is natural and normal for all of His children who are close to Him. Our trust in God should be spontaneous. This trust should not be something that we have to labor over or think about.

We now are ready to learn more about actually coming into the presence of God. In the next chapter we will look into the Word of God to learn what it says about coming into God's presence and staying there so that we will be able to trust Him totally, completely and absolutely at all times.

Chapter 26

Be Secure in the Presence of the Lord

We will begin this chapter by looking into the Word of God to see what it says about the relationship between the fear of the Lord and a close personal relationship with the Lord. When we fear the Lord, we hold Him in *reverent awe* at all times. We have a deep and sincere desire to humble ourselves before Him and to serve Him because He is so wonderful.

Satan and his demons will do everything they can do to stop us from fearing God. They attempt to influence us to be externally oriented. They want our lives to be focused on people, places, things and events in the world. Our Father wants us to turn away from the world. He wants us to see the world from His perspective. He wants us to have such a reverent fear and awe of Him that we always will stay close to Him. "…I will put My [reverential] fear in their hearts, so that they will not depart from Me" (Jeremiah 32:40).

Would you like to enjoy continual companionship with the Lord? We will enjoy this companionship if we always have a reverent fear and awe of the Lord. "The secret [of the sweet, satisfying companionship] of the Lord have they who fear (revere and worship) Him…" (Psalm 25:14)

This passage of Scripture *tells us the secret of a wonderful, close relationship with the Lord.* We will enjoy this relationship when we fear and revere the Lord so much that we worship Him continually. We should be in such awe of the Lord and our hearts should be so full of gratitude to Him that words of heartfelt praise and worship will pour out of our mouths spontaneously throughout every day of our lives.

The Bible also tells us that God's children who truly fear Him and revere Him will trust Him completely. Our Father is very close to His children who fear Him and revere Him. We will trust God completely if we have a continual consciousness of His presence. "In the reverent and worshipful fear of the Lord there is strong confidence, and His children shall always have a place of refuge" (Proverbs 14:26).

We have just studied three passages of Scripture pertaining to the fear of the Lord. We have learned that we will *walk closely* with the Lord if we truly fear Him. We have seen that we will *trust the Lord completely* if we truly fear Him. We always will be able to enter into the "place of refuge" our Father has provided for us if we truly fear Him and revere Him.

Our Father wants us to *abide* in the place of refuge He has provided for us. He wants us to come into this refuge and stay there. *How* do we abide in the Lord? "All who keep His commandments [who obey His orders and follow His plan, live and continue to live, to stay and] abide in Him, and He in them. [They let Christ be a home to them and they are the home of Christ.] And by this we know and understand and have the proof that He [really] lives and makes His home in us: by the [Holy] Spirit Whom He has given us" (I John 3:24).

Our Father has made it possible for each of us to have *proof* that Jesus Christ really does make His home in our hearts. He has given us the Holy Spirit Who will give assurance of the indwelling presence of Jesus Christ to all of God's children who continually learn and obey the instructions our Father has given us in His Word. We will *abide* constantly in Jesus Christ if we faithfully study and meditate on the Word of God and if we live our lives in absolute obedience to its instructions.

Worry and fear *cannot* get a foothold in our hearts when we are absolutely certain that Jesus Christ lives in our hearts and when we abide in Him by staying in His presence. *How* can worry and fear ever have a continuing influence on us if we truly have a close personal relationship with our Lord Jesus Christ?

Many Christians would like to be in the presence of the Lord. We should do more than just wish we had a close relationship with the Lord. We should have a deep, fervent and constant desire to be in His presence. "Seek the Lord and His strength, yearn for and seek His face and to be in His presence continually!" (I Chronicles 16:11).

We are instructed to continually seek the Lord and His strength. We should yearn to be in the Lord's presence at all times. We are not given any greater privilege during our lives here on earth than to come into and remain in the presence of the Lord. "…I know the thoughts and plans that I have for you, says the Lord, thoughts and plans for welfare and peace and not for evil, to give you hope in your final outcome. Then you will call upon Me, and you will come and pray to Me, and I will hear and heed you. Then you will seek Me, inquire for, and require Me [as a vital necessity] and find Me when you search for Me with all your heart. I will be found by you, says the Lord, and I will release you from captivity…" (Jeremiah 29:11-14).

This promise that God made to the Israelites applies to each of us today. God had specific plans for the Israelites when

He made this promise. He has a definite plan for each of our lives today. Our Father wants us to seek His will for our lives wholeheartedly.

We are told that God's plans for us include our welfare and our peace. God's plans for us do *not* include evil. We will not give in to the evil temptations of Satan and his demons if we turn away from our selfish desires to continually seek God's will for our lives.

Our Father promises eternal life to us that begins the moment we believe and receive Jesus Christ as our Messiah. Our Father tells us that He wants us to "call upon Him." He wants us to pray continually. He promises that He *will* hear our prayers and that He will answer our requests.

Our Father then goes on to tell us that *we will find Him* if we seek Him and "require Him as a vital necessity." A close personal relationship with the Lord is not a "nice to have." A close personal relationship with the Lord is absolutely necessary. No personal desire should come ahead of our desire to continually draw closer to our precious Lord.

We will search for the Lord with all of our hearts *if* we understand the vital importance of walking closely with Him and being in His presence. He promises that we *will* find Him if we search for Him wholeheartedly. He will "release us from captivity" just as He released the Israelites from captivity at the appointed time.

Please do not pass over this passage of Scripture quickly. Please take the time to meditate carefully on the many specific instructions and promises that are contained in this passage of Scripture. Any Christian who consistently meditates on this wonderful truth from God and obeys these specific instructions will find that his or her life will be *absolutely transformed.*

We have seen that we should have a deep, fervent and continual desire to enter into and remain in the presence of the Lord. How do we enter into God's presence? We have seen that our Father wants us to study and meditate on His Word and to obey His instructions. We have seen that our Father wants us to fear Him and hold Him in reverent awe. We have seen that our Father wants us to pray continually.

Our Father wants us to praise Him and thank Him continually because we have a constant attitude of gratitude that wells up from our hearts. Our hearts will sing with joy if we can even begin to comprehend the magnificence of our Father's love for us and His marvelous grace, mercy and compassion.

We must understand that we deserve to live eternally in the horror of the lake of fire (see Revelation 20:10-15 and 21:8). However, we can be absolutely certain that everyone who has asked Jesus Christ to be his or her Savior will live eternally with Him in the paradise of heaven (see Revelation 21:4, 21:10-27 and 22:1-7).

Our hearts will sing with joy if we are absolutely certain that everything we need here on earth has been provided for us (see Chapters Two and Three). We will know that we did not earn and do not deserve the blessings our Father has provided for us. These blessings are given to us by the grace of God.

If we understand these great spiritual truths, we will be very humble. We will be in constant awe of everything our loving Father has provided for us. We will have a deep inner desire to praise Him and thank Him constantly. Words of praise and thanksgiving will spontaneously flow out of our mouths throughout every day. Our constant words of thanksgiving will bring us into the presence of the Lord. "Let us come before His presence with thanksgiving…" (Psalm 95:2).

Humble Christians will have a constant attitude of gratitude because they know that everything they are and everything they have has come to them because of the grace of God. If we truly are grateful to God, we will rejoice constantly. The songs in our hearts will pour out of our mouths (see Matthew 12:34). Our lives will be joyful. God instructs us to come to Him singing. "Serve the Lord with gladness! Come before His presence with singing!" (Psalm 100:2).

We are instructed to come into the presence of the Lord with songs and words of praise and thanksgiving constantly pouring out of our mouths. "Enter into His gates with thanksgiving and a thank offering and into His courts with praise! Be thankful and say so to Him, bless and affectionately praise His name!" (Psalm 100:4).

God instructs us to come to Him with gratitude. Before Jesus Christ came to earth, God required a blood sacrifice of a perfect animal. Jesus Christ was the sacrifice Who made us righteous before God. We should be very grateful for our salvation. Our praise to God should be natural and spontaneous.

Coming into the Lord's presence is not complicated. We should revere the Lord, obey the Lord, be grateful to the Lord, thank the Lord and praise the Lord continually. We should study the Word of God each day and meditate on the Word of God continually. Some of us are so self-oriented that being quiet before God is difficult. We must learn to listen to God and enjoy being still before Him.

Focusing continually on God does not come naturally to us. We must learn through practice and experience to still our minds and quiet our hearts. Only then will our spirits soar because we are in God's presence.

We will be completely humbled as we continually come into the presence of the Lord. We will see how great and mighty and powerful He is. We will know how insignificant we are. "Humble yourselves [feeling very insignificant] in the presence of the Lord, and He will exalt you [He will lift you up and make your lives significant]" (James 4:10).

The Lord will lift us up and make our lives significant when we are completely humbled because we are in His presence. The Lord will honor our humility and our faith in Him by blessing us and lifting us up and making our lives full, meaningful and significant.

Our hearts will sing with joy when we are in the presence of the Lord. "You have made known to me the ways of life; You will enrapture me [diffusing my soul with joy] with and in Your presence" (Acts 2:28).

Our Father has told us in His Word and by the guidance of the Holy Spirit exactly how He wants us to live our lives. We will come into His presence if we faithfully obey these instructions.

If we remain in the presence of the Lord, we will walk constantly in the victory that our Lord Jesus Christ has won for us. If we live godly lives and remain in God's presence, Satan and his demons will not be able to influence us. God says, "...Sit at My right hand [associated with Me in My royal dignity] till I make your enemies a stool for your feet..." (Hebrews 1:13).

Satan and his demons cannot remain in the presence of God. They know what will happen to them when they are near God. They also know what will happen to them when God's children come into His presence and remain there. If we remain in God's presence, Satan and his demons always will be under our feet.

We open the door for Satan and his demons and the circumstances in our lives to pull us down whenever we come out of

God's presence. We will be safe and secure at all times if we learn how to remain in God's presence and obey these instructions.

In the first twenty-six chapters of this book we have studied more than two hundred Scripture references that teach us exactly what we should do to overcome worry, anxiety and fear. In the twenty-two chapters that remain we will learn how to be quiet and calm in the face of problems. We will learn how to receive the perfect peace of God that is so great that it surpasses the limitations of our human understanding. As we prepare to learn these wonderful scriptural truths, we can be certain that the key to a calm, quiet and peaceful heart is to remain in the presence of the Lord.

Chapter 27

Trust the Lord When You Face Adversity

We can face severe problems with calm and quiet confidence in the Lord if we have learned how to come close to the Lord and how to remain in His presence. In the next two chapters we will learn exactly what our Father instructs us to do so that we will be able to remain calm when we face a crisis. "...thus says the Lord God, Behold, I am laying in Zion for a foundation a Stone, a tested Stone, a precious Cornerstone of sure foundation; he who believes (trusts in, relies on, and adheres to that Stone) will not be ashamed or give way or hasten away [in sudden panic" (Isaiah 28:16).

The Book of Isaiah is a prophetic book. The prophet Isaiah refers to the coming Messiah, Jesus Christ, when he refers to "that Stone." The New Testament also refers to Jesus Christ as a "Living Stone." "Come to Him [then, to that] Living Stone which men tried and threw away, but which is chosen [and] precious in God's sight" (I Peter 2:4).

This passage of Scripture tells us to come to Jesus Christ. Jesus was chosen by God. He is precious to God, yet men crucified Him and threw Him away.

Jesus Christ should be our rock-solid foundation throughout every day of our lives. If we trust Him completely, we *will not panic* when we face a crisis. People who react negatively when they face a crisis situation react in this way because they do not have a close personal relationship with Jesus Christ. Jesus always was and is calm.

When everything that can go wrong seems to go wrong, we show by our reaction whether we will panic or whether we trust completely in Jesus Christ Who lives in our hearts. If we have a close relationship with Jesus, we will not panic because we will be absolutely certain that He can and will bring us safely through every problem we face if we focus continually on Him instead of focusing continually on the circumstances in our lives. "Be not afraid of sudden terror and panic, nor of the stormy blast or the storm and ruin of the wicked when it comes [for you will be guiltless], for the Lord shall be your confidence, firm and strong, and shall keep your foot from being caught [in a trap or some hidden danger]" (Proverbs 3:25-26).

We should not panic when we face storms in our lives. We can have absolute confidence in our Lord Jesus Christ. He has all power in heaven and on earth (see Matthew 28:18). Jesus does not want us to react with worry, anxiety and fear when we face difficult problems. He said, "...Do not be seized with alarm and struck with fear; only keep on believing" (Mark 5:36).

Jesus spoke these words when He told a man that he should not be afraid even though he had just been told that his daughter had died. Jesus is a miracle-working God. He told this man to "keep on believing." This advice applies to each of us today.

We cannot control many of the events that take place in our lives, but we *can* control our reaction to the circumstances we face. We should obey the instructions the apostle Paul gave to the Thessalonians when he said, "…we beg you, brethren, not to allow your minds to be quickly unsettled or disturbed or kept excited or alarmed…" (II Thessalonians 2:1-2).

Please highlight or underline the word "allow" in this passage of Scripture. We each decide whether we will allow ourselves to be upset when we face adversity. Some people immediately panic when they face a difficult situation. They fall apart emotionally. Satan's demons scream into their minds, "Do something. Do anything. Don't just sit there and do nothing."

If we react to the problems we face with anxiety, fear and tension, our reaction shows that we really do not trust the Lord. Why would we ever react in this way if we truly trust the Lord? Consistent awareness of the presence and power of God will enable us to be quiet and calm whenever we face a crisis. We must understand that we actually are able to block ourselves from receiving the mighty power of God through doubt and unbelief (see Mark 6:1-6).

When we face any problem we should pause and say something like the following — "Dear Lord, You are in complete control. I know that You will work everything out in this situation. I trust You completely. I ask for Your wisdom, Your knowledge, Your understanding, Your counsel and Your might. Thank You, dear Lord."

I pray that many people reading this book will be able to learn how to react to crises with absolute faith in God. As we grow and mature, we each should come to the realization that we will face many challenges in our lives. We should rest in the Lord whenever we face difficult problems. We should rest in the Lord instead of struggling and straining. "Better is a handful with quietness than both hands full with painful effort, a vain striving after the wind and feeding on it." (Ecclesiastes 4:6).

We strive in vain if we try to do everything ourselves. We have learned that our Father has provided everything we need. He wants us to be quiet and calm. Over the years I have found that the one passage of Scripture that helps me more than anything else in a crisis situation instructs us to "…be still, and know (recognize and understand) that I am God…" (Psalm 46:10).

We must understand the context in which these words were written. Psalm 46 speaks of earthquakes and tidal waves. We always should react with quiet and calm confidence in God no matter how severe the circumstances in our lives might seem to be. Time after time when I have faced a crisis situation, I have spoken the first two words of this passage of Scripture. Again and again I have said, "Be still." "Be still." "Be still." "Be still." "Be still." "Be still." I say these words because I know that God is in complete control of every circumstance in my life.

I have found that repeatedly speaking these words brings me into the presence of God and the power of God. Being still in the face of a crisis may be the last thing we feel like doing, but we will be able to react calmly if we have drawn close to the Lord on a daily basis over a period of time.

When we face a crisis, we should focus continually on God Who is omnipotent, omniscient and omnipresent. God has all power. He knows everything. He is with each of His children at all times. Psalm 46:10 instructs us to *be still* because we *know that He is God.* Our Father wants us to be quiet and calm because we identify with His mighty power instead of worrying about the seeming severity of the problems we face.

Tension is not still. Tension races. Tension hurries. Tension worries. Tension comes from the influence of Satan and from preoccupation with self. Stillness comes from focusing constantly upon God. Tremendous spiritual power is released when we are calm and quiet because we trust God. We are receptive to God when we are relaxed.

Hurry, worry and tension often block us from receiving the help our Father has provided for us. Doubt and unbelief block us from being able to hear our Father speaking to us and guiding us. We must learn to be still. "Be still, all flesh, before the Lord..." (Zechariah 2:13).

Know that the words "all flesh" in this passage of Scripture include *you*. Know that the Lord wants you to learn how to be still, quiet and calm whenever you face a crisis situation. "[Hush!] Be silent before the Lord God..." (Zephaniah 1:7).

Zephaniah is referring to the coming of the Lord in this passage of Scripture. I believe that this spiritual principle applies to every circumstance in our lives. "...Fear not; stand still (firm, confident, undismayed) and see the salvation of the Lord which He will work for you today. For the Egyptians you have seen today you shall never see again. The Lord will fight for you, and you shall hold your peace and remain at rest" (Exodus 14:13-14).

The Word of God repeatedly tells us to *be still* whenever we face difficult problems. We will rest in the Lord when we are still. We will wait patiently for Him. We will lean on Him while we wait. "...stand still and consider the wondrous works of God" (Job 37:14).

Our Father wants us to be still and quiet because we focus continually on His indwelling presence. He wants us to reflect upon the times in our lives when He has brought us safely through difficult circumstances. He wants us to learn from the many stories in the Bible that tell us how He brought many people through seemingly impossible situations.

He wants us to be still, calm and quiet because we have absolute and unwavering faith in Him. We should be the like psalmist who said, "...He leads me beside the still and restful waters. He refreshes and restores my life (my self)..." (Psalm 23:2-3).

The Twenty-third Psalm has comforted many people who have faced difficult circumstances. Our wonderful Lord will lead us into quietness and calmness when we willingly yield control of our lives to Him because we trust Him completely. He will "lead us beside the still and restful waters." He will refresh us and restore us.

In this chapter we have seen that the holy Scriptures consistently instruct us to react to the circumstances we face with calm and quiet trust in the Lord. In the next chapter we will carefully study what the Word of God tells us about God's strength being released to help us whenever we are quiet and calm because we trust Him completely.

Chapter 28

Quiet Confidence
Releases the Lord's Strength

Why would we ever worry about anything if we *are absolutely certain* that the Lord's strength is available to us at all times? The Word of God repeatedly tells us that the strength of the Lord is available to us whenever we need it.

We need to learn the promises in the Bible pertaining to the Lord's strength. We then need to meditate continually on these great spiritual truths until we *know* with deep inner certainty that, by faith, we can and will receive the strength of the Lord whenever we need it. We will be quiet, calm and confident whenever we face any crisis. "…in quietness and in [trusting] confidence shall be your strength…" (Isaiah 30:15).

A tranquil spirit strengthens us. An agitated spirit weakens us and brings trouble. Christians who allow themselves to become agitated, worried, fearful and upset clearly indicate that they do not trust the Lord. This negative reaction to a crisis situation blocks us from receiving the Lord's mighty strength to work in us and through us.

We often bring the very things we fear into manifestation in our lives because we are not calm, quiet and confident in the Lord. Our worry and fear are like a magnet that reaches out into the spiritual realm to attract whatever we fear. Job said, "...the thing which I greatly fear comes upon me, and that of which I am afraid befalls me. I was not or am not at ease, nor had I or have I rest, nor was I or am I quiet, yet trouble came and still comes [upon me]" (Job 3:25-26).

This passage of Scripture is filled with scriptural truth that applies to each of us whenever we face a crisis. Job said that the very thing he was most afraid of *came upon him*. *Why* did Job receive manifestation of his fears? Job received manifestation of his fears because he *was not at ease*, because he *did not rest* in the Lord, because he *was not quiet and calm* in the face of adversity and because he placed his focus on that which he feared.

We must understand that a definite relationship exists between our quiet confidence and trust in the Lord and receiving His strength to help us. We may find that the things we are most afraid of actually will happen in our lives if we are not calm, quiet and confident in the Lord. "...be quiet, fear not..." (Isaiah 7:4).

The holy Scriptures repeatedly emphasize the relationship between being quiet and not being afraid. The ability to react calmly to a crisis situation does not develop suddenly. We cannot force ourselves to relax. Force and relaxation do not go together. We only can be still before the Lord *if* we really know Him and trust Him.

Calm and quiet faith in the Lord only can be developed from daily quiet time with the Lord over a sustained period of time. Each day of our lives we should turn completely away from the things of this world to draw closer to our precious Lord. We should prepare ourselves for the future by spending quiet time alone with the Lord each day in quiet fellowship, prayer, praise, thanksgiving, Bible study and Scripture meditation.

Our Father wants us to be consistent in our time with Him. He doesn't want our precious quiet time with Him to be an "on again, off again" situation. He wants our quiet time with Him to be in absolute first place in our lives. We should not allow anything to come ahead of our daily quiet time with the Lord.

If we are serving God and being led by Him daily, His virtue often will be tapped and emptied from us. Just as Jesus felt the virtue leave Him when a lady touched the hem of His robe, we also can be drained by being God's vessels of salvation and hope daily. We must spend time in His presence to be *filled again* with His power and strength so that we will not burn out or feel tired or weary.

The cumulative effect of this quiet time with the Lord will be a constantly increasing calmness and quietness inside of us. We will find that we normally and naturally turn quietly and calmly to the Lord whenever we face difficult problems. We will not allow ourselves to become upset because of the circumstances we face. The problems in our lives actually are opportunities for believers who are victorious in Jesus Christ.

Christians who are able to remain calm, quiet and confident when they face a crisis situation have prepared themselves by constantly filling their minds and their hearts with the supernatural power of the living Word of God. We *will* be able to remain calm, quiet and confident in a crisis *if* we repeatedly have breathed the life of God into our hearts by meditating constantly on His Word.

Our Father is calm, quiet and confident at all times. Whenever we face seemingly difficult problems, He wants us to rest completely in Him. Sometimes God calms the storms in our lives.

Other times He calms us in the midst of the storms. Our Father will only be able to calm us during the storms in our lives *if* we willingly surrender control of our lives to Him and *if* we trust Him completely.

I believe that our Father is very pleased when we are calm, quiet and confident in the face of adversity. He does not want us to allow the circumstances in our lives to cause us to be anxious, fearful and tense. The Bible speaks of "…the hidden person of the heart, with the incorruptible and unfading charm of a gentle and peaceful spirit, which [is not anxious or wrought up, but] is very precious in the sight of God" (I Peter 3:4).

The "hidden person of the heart" is the "real us." The hidden person of the heart is who we really are deep down inside of ourselves. Many times people in the world judge us by external standards. They judge us by what we look like and by what we seem to be. Our Father judges us by what we *really are*. "…the Lord sees not as man sees; for man looks on the outward appearance, but the Lord looks on the heart" (I Samuel 16:7).

The hidden person of the heart is the part of us that has changed and developed as a result of consistent daily time alone with the Lord. We will become much calmer and much more peaceful if we obey our Father's instructions to draw close to Him. We will have "a gentle and peaceful spirit which is not anxious or wrought up."

This peaceful spirit "is very precious in the sight of the Lord." I believe that our Father is delighted when His children are calm and peaceful in a crisis because we trust completely in Him. "Our inner selves wait [earnestly] for the Lord; He is our Help and our Shield" (Psalm 33:20).

Please note the reference in this passage of Scripture to "our inner selves." There is no question that the key to receiving help from the Lord is what we really are deep down inside of ourselves. The Lord will be "our Help and our Shield" *if* we wait quietly on Him because we trust Him completely.

We will prepare ourselves to learn from the Lord how to stay calm if we have paid the price of filling our minds and our hearts continually with His Word over a period of time. "Blessed (happy, fortunate, to be envied) is the man whom You discipline and instruct, O Lord, and teach out of Your law, that You may give him power to keep himself calm in the days of adversity…" (Psalm 94:12-13).

Let's look first at this wonderful promise from God by seeing what He promises to do for us. *He promises to give us power to remain calm when we face adversity.* He will discipline and instruct us. He will teach us from His Word. What does He instruct us to do to receive these blessings?

Our Father wants our minds and our hearts to be filled with His Word so that we will have within us what He wants us to have so that He can teach us how to be calm in the face of adversity. We will be calm, cool and collected in a crisis if we learned what our Father wants us to learn. "…a man of understanding has a cool spirit" (Proverbs 17:27).

This passage of Scripture tells us that "a man of understanding" is cool, quiet and calm. We will be calm and quiet when we understand what our Father wants us to understand because our minds and our hearts are filled with His Word and every aspect of our lives is yielded to the Holy Spirit. Our Father wants each of us to be "…be calm and cool and steady, accept and suffer unflinchingly every hardship…" (II Timothy 4:5).

Our Father does not want us to flinch when we face adversity. People who flinch draw back from whatever threatens them. Our Father wants us to "be calm and cool and steady" whenever we face adversity. The Word of God compares this calm quietness with little babies after they have been weaned from their mothers. "Surely I have calmed and quieted my soul; like a weaned child with his mother, like a weaned child is my soul within me [ceased from fretting]" (Psalm 131:2).

Little babies fret when they first are weaned from their mother's milk. They eventually become calm and quiet as they become accustomed to food other than their mother's milk. The Word of God is God's spiritual "milk" that enables us to be calm in the face of a crisis. "Like newborn babies you should crave (thirst for, earnestly desire) the pure (unadulterated) spiritual milk, that by it you may be nurtured and grow unto [completed] salvation..." (I Peter 2:2).

Our Father wants us to be like "newborn babies" who crave their mother's milk. He wants us to be constantly thirsty because we have a deep and constant desire to partake of "the pure, unadulterated spiritual milk" of His Word. We only can grow into the completeness of our salvation if we constantly fill our minds and our hearts with the Word of God.

We now are ready to learn from the specific advice the apostle Paul gave to the Philippians when he told them how he learned to be content regardless of the circumstances he faced. Paul said, "...I have learned how to be content (satisfied to the point where I am not disturbed or disquieted) in whatever state I am. I know how to be abased and live humbly in straitened circumstances, and I know also how to enjoy plenty and live in abundance. I have learned in any and all circumstances the secret of facing every situation, whether well-fed or going hungry, having a sufficiency and enough to spare or going without and being in want" (Philippians 4:11-12).

Paul says that he has *learned* how to be content at all times. *We can learn* as Paul learned to be quiet, calm and content in good times and in bad times. Paul refers to *"the secret* of facing every situation." *Do you know what this secret is?*

The next verse of Scripture gives us the secret to always being calm, quiet and content, regardless of circumstances. "I have strength for all things in Christ Who empowers me [I am ready for anything and equal to anything through Him who infuses inner strength into me; I am self-sufficient in Christ's sufficiency]" (Philippians 4:13).

We *can and will* be content, regardless of the circumstances we face *if* we refuse to focus on these circumstances because we always are focused upon the indwelling presence of Jesus Christ. This passage of Scripture assures us that we *can* receive the strength we need for *all things* from Jesus Christ.

The amplification of this wonderful promise tells us that we can and will be "ready for anything and equal to anything" because of the inner strength Jesus has provided for us. We must focus on His indwelling presence instead of focusing on the circumstances in our lives. *Know* that you have the strength for whatever you will face because Jesus Christ will "infuse inner strength" into you.

Philippians 4:13 is my favorite passage of Scripture. On many different occasions I have meditated over and over on this magnificent promise from heaven. I urge you to meditate constantly on this promise when you face difficult circumstances. Speak it out loud. Repeat it. Say it again…and again…and again…

Personalize this wonderful promise from God. Apply this promise to whatever circumstance you face. Refuse to allow any circumstance to pull you down. Instead of focusing on the problems you face, focus continually on Jesus Christ Who lives in your heart.

The fourth chapter of Philippians is a beautiful chapter. Paul wrote all of this spiritual truth under the anointing of the Holy Spirit *when he was in a prison cell.* Paul was able to share many great truths with us because he learned these truths when he faced adversity. When we think about these wonderful truths that God has given to us through the apostle Paul we should understand some of the things Paul went through while he was learning to be content at all times. We must prepare ourselves for whatever we may face in these last days before Jesus returns..

The following verses of Scripture tell us about just a few of the many ordeals Paul faced. "Five times I received from [the hands of] the Jews forty [lashes all] but one; three times I have been beaten with rods; once I was stoned. Three times I have been aboard a ship wrecked at sea; a [whole] night and a day I have spent [adrift] on the deep; many times on journeys, [exposed to] perils from rivers, perils from bandits, perils from [my own] nation, perils from the Gentiles, perils in the city, perils in the desert places, perils in the sea, perils from those posing as believers [but destitute of Christian knowledge and piety]; in toil and hardship, watching often [through sleepless nights], in hunger and thirst, frequently driven to fasting by want, in cold and exposure and lack of clothing" (II Corinthians 11:24-27).

Please go back and carefully meditate on the ordeals Paul faced while he learned the great truths he shared with us. Compare Paul's ordeals with the circumstances in your life. If Paul could learn to be content with all he went through, you can be assured that *you can learn* how to be content. *The secret to perfect contentment* through-out our lives is to focus continually on the indwelling Person of Jesus Christ and His mighty strength that is always available to us.

Paul learned to be content because of his close relationship with Jesus Christ and his absolute trust in Him. This relationship never changed, regardless of the severity of the circumstances Paul faced. We also can and will learn the secret of being content regardless of the circumstances we face if we will draw close to Jesus Christ throughout every day of our lives.

We now are ready to study in detail what the Bible teaches us about peace with God and the peace of God. In the next two chapters we will study what the Word of God teaches about *peace with God*. The remainder of the book will be devoted to an intensive study of *the peace of God*.

Chapter 29

One Man's Trespass Separated All of Us from God

As we begin to study the subject of peace, we need to learn the difference between *peace with God* and *the peace of God.* No one can be at peace with God without asking Jesus Christ to be his or her Savior. We must be at peace with God if we want to receive the wonderful blessings of the peace of God.

Because of the sin of Adam, no one is born with the ability to immediately be at peace with God. We all are descendants of Adam. His sin is passed to us when we are born. Babies are separated from God when they are born just as Adam and Eve were separated from God when they sinned in the Garden of Eden. We all are born in a spiritual position where we actually are opposed to God. We each are born as "…children of [God's] wrath and heirs of [His] indignation, like the rest of mankind" (Ephesians 2:3).

How can anyone be further from peace with God than to be "children of God's wrath and heirs of His indignation?" The Bible says that the sin of Adam caused all of his descendants (each and every one of us) to be separated from God. "…one man's trespass [one man's false step and falling away led] to condemnation for all men…" (Romans 5:18).

Please highlight or underline the words "all men" in this passage of Scripture. Please understand that, because of the sin of Adam, *you* were born under condemnation from God. No person who was born condemned from God can live a good enough life on earth to live eternally in heaven.

Many people all over the world are trying to "earn" their way to heaven. They do their best to live a godly life. They do not understand that a "good life" is not a "ticket to heaven." No matter how hard we try to live a good life, we still are sinners before God unless we ask Jesus Christ to be our Savior. "…None is righteous, just and truthful and upright and conscientious, no, not one" (Romans 3:10).

Please think of the finest person you have ever known. This person probably is (or was) kind, loving, caring and compassionate. Know that *no* person, "no, not one," no matter how good that person may seem to be, is "righteous, just, truthful and upright" before God without Jesus Christ. No person can live eternally in heaven with God based solely upon how good his or her life seems to be.

God does not have degrees of sin. He does not allow people to come to heaven because they have lived a "pretty good life" that is superior to the lives of many other people. We *all* are sinners from God's perspective.

Many unbelievers search for peace. They have no conception of how to obtain peace with God or the peace of God. We cannot experience peace with God or the peace of God through human efforts. Unbelievers do not understand that they have been separated from God since birth. "….being ignorant of the righteousness that God ascribes [which makes one acceptable to Him in word, thought, and deed] and seeking to establish a righteousness (a means of salvation) of their own, they did not obey or submit themselves to God's righteousness" (Romans 10:3).

Although this passage of Scripture refers to Israel, I believe that this same principle applies to each of us today. Unbelievers are ignorant regarding what God wants them to do so that their thoughts, words and actions will be acceptable to Him. Many people strive and strain in a vain attempt to establish their own righteousness. They do not understand that they cannot receive peace with God through their own efforts.

Unbelievers cannot understand the ways of God because they have been blinded by Satan. "Their moral understanding is darkened and their reasoning is beclouded. [They are] alienated (estranged, self-banished) from the life of God [with no share in it; this is] because of the ignorance (the want of knowledge and perception, the willful blindness) that is deep-seated in them, due to their hardness of heart [to the insensitiveness of their moral nature]" (Ephesians 4:18).

Satan darkens the moral understanding of all unbelievers. Their thinking is cloudy. They are unable to clearly see and understand spiritual truths. Satan's deception influences them to continue the estrangement from God that existed when they were born. These people have no comprehension of the ways of God.

This passage of Scripture says that these people actually are "willfully blind" to the ways of God. They do not want to understand the truth from God's perspective. Their hard hearts were inherited from their ancestor, Adam. Their hearts are made harder by the influence of Satan and by the influence of the lost and dying world we live in.

This short chapter lays a foundation that clearly indicates our undeniable need for peace with God. This dark and gloomy chapter does not paint a pretty picture. This brief chapter is absolutely necessary so that anyone who reads it can understand that *we all are born separated from God.*

This seeming intolerable situation does have a solution. God has made provision for *every* person to be at peace with Him. In the next chapter we will see exactly what God has done to enable each person who cannot be at peace with Him through his or her own efforts to come into peace with Him because of the magnificent sacrifice Jesus Christ made for us.

Chapter 30

We Only Can Experience Peace with God through Jesus Christ

In the last chapter we saw that no one can experience peace with God through human effort. God has made a wonderful provision to offset this deplorable situation. "While we were yet in weakness [powerless to help ourselves], at the fitting time Christ died for (in behalf of) the ungodly" (Romans 5:6).

God paid the greatest price that could be paid. His beloved Son, Jesus Christ, willingly left the glory of heaven to come to earth to take upon Himself all of the sins of mankind. "Now it is an extraordinary thing for one to give his life even for an upright man, though perhaps for a noble and lovable and generous benefactor someone might even dare to die. But God shows and clearly proves His [own] love for us by the fact that while we were still sinners, Christ (the Messiah, the Anointed One) died for us" (Romans 5:7-8).

God loves *every* person on earth *so much* that He gave His beloved Son to die for our sins. God has provided a spiritual bridge that enables us to be set free from the penalty of our sins and to be at peace with Him. "...let it be clearly known and understood by you, brethren, that through this Man forgiveness and removal of sins is now proclaimed to you; and that through Him everyone who believes [who acknowledges Jesus as his Savior and devotes himself to Him] is absolved (cleared and freed) from every charge from which he could not be justified and freed by the Law of Moses and given right standing with God" (Acts 13:38-39).

Please note the words "everyone" and "every charge" in this passage of Scripture. There is no question that *God has made provision for every person on earth* to be set free from his or her sins. "In Him we have redemption (deliverance and salvation) through His blood, the remission (forgiveness) of our offenses (shortcomings and trespasses), in accordance with the riches and the generosity of His gracious favor..." (Ephesians 1:7).

Jesus Christ shed His precious blood on the cross at Calvary so that each of us could be forgiven for all of our "offenses, shortcomings and trespasses." We did not earn this redemption. We do not deserve redemption for our sins. We are able to receive this magnificent redemption from our sins because of the generous grace and favor of Jesus Christ.

Every person who has not asked Jesus Christ to be his or her Savior will live throughout eternity in the horrible lake of fire. "...if anyone's [name] was not found recorded in the Book of Life, he was hurled into the lake of fire" (Revelation 20:15).

We are not talking about "nice to haves" here. *We are talking about the biggest, most important decision any person will ever make.* We are talking about the decision to ask Jesus Christ to be our Savior. We will be at peace with God if we make this decision. The Book of Life contains the name of every person who has asked Jesus Christ to be his or her Savior.

Anyone who fails to make this decision is doomed to a life on earth without the peace of God. Anyone who fails to make this decision also is doomed to an endless eternity of suffering in the lake of fire. "...the smoke of their torment ascends forever and ever; and they have no respite (no pause, no intermission, no rest, no peace) day or night..." (Revelation 14:11).

I pray that you will understand and that you will share with your friends and loved ones the horrible eternal price that every person who does not ask Jesus Christ to be his or her Savior will pay. The difference between believers and unbelievers is staggering.

Believers can learn how to enjoy the peace of God throughout their lives on earth. They will live eternally with God in the paradise of heaven. Unbelievers cannot enjoy the peace of God while they are on earth. They will live eternally in anguish in the lake of fire (hell) where Jesus said, "...there will be weeping and wailing and grinding of teeth" (Matthew 13:42).

God has done everything He can do. We can live at peace with God throughout eternity because of His magnificent sacrifice of His Son and the willingness of Jesus Christ to leave the glory of heaven to come to earth to pay the full price for every one of our sins. "...God purposed that through (by the service, the intervention of) Him [the Son] all things should be completely reconciled back to Himself, whether on earth or in heaven, as through Him, [the Father] made peace by means of the blood of His cross" (Colossians 1:20).

We have seen that every person on earth was estranged from God at birth. This passage of Scripture tells us that Jesus Christ stood in our place and took our sins upon Himself so that we could be reconciled back to God. "And although you at one time were estranged and alienated from Him and were of hostile attitude of mind in your wicked activities, yet now has [Christ, the Messiah] reconciled [you to God] in the body of His flesh through death, in order to present you holy and faultless and irreproachable in His [the Father's] presence" (Colossians 1:21-22).

This passage of Scripture is absolutely mind-boggling. There is no question that all of us were "at one time estranged and alienated" from God. Jesus Christ has provided the means for us to be reconciled and at peace with God. Every person is able to be "presented holy and faultless and irreproachable" before God because Jesus Christ took our sins upon Himself through death.

No greater gift ever has been given than the sacrifice of Jesus Christ. We must understand that we will make a tremendous mistake with dire eternal consequences if we fail to receive this marvelous gift from God that we have not earned and do not deserve.

Any person who has carefully read the Scripture references in the last two chapters can clearly see that the *only way* we can experience peace with God, righteousness before God and forgiveness of our sins, is by asking Jesus Christ to be our Savior. If Jesus Christ is not your Savior, you can make the decision at this very moment to experience peace with God.

If you now are ready to make the decision to receive Jesus Christ as your Savior, you can be absolutely certain that Almighty God is drawing you to Him. Jesus said, "No one is able to come to Me unless the Father Who sent Me attracts and draws him and gives him the desire to come to Me..." (John 6:44).

Do you understand that you are not at peace with God and that you were born with a sin nature that will cause you to live eternally in the lake of fire? Are you ready to ask Jesus Christ to be your Savior? If you answer these questions affirmatively, you can be absolutely certain that Almighty God has drawn you to Himself.

The time has come for you to repent of every one of your sins. Jesus said, "…unless you repent (change your mind for the better and heartily amend your ways, with abhorrence of your past sins), you will all likewise perish and be lost eternally" (Luke 13:5).

This statement that Jesus Christ made to a group of people many years ago was recorded in the Bible to provide a message to *you* today. We cannot receive salvation through Jesus Christ unless we admit that we are sinners and unless we repent of our sins. Many people who are trying to get to heaven through living what they believe is a good life will live eternally in the lake of fire *unless they freely admit that they actually are sinners* and unless they *repent* of these sins and change their sin nature to God's nature through faith in Jesus Christ.

We are told that we must "abhor our past sins or we will all perish and be lost eternally." Do you admit that you are a sinner? Do you abhor your sins? Do you repent of these sins? Are you willing to change your life to walk closely with God? The Word of God tells us exactly what we should do if we have come to this decision. "…if you acknowledge and confess with your lips that Jesus is Lord and in your heart believe (adhere to, trust in, and rely on the truth) that God raised Him from the dead, you will be saved" (Romans 10:9).

This passage of Scripture explains how to receive eternal salvation through Jesus Christ. We must believe that Jesus came from heaven to earth to die on the cross at Calvary to pay the price for our sins. *We will be saved* if we believe these great spiritual truths in our hearts and if we confess with our mouths that Jesus Christ has died for our sins and that God has raised Him from the dead.

We now can experience wonderful peace with God because of the magnificent sacrifice Jesus Christ has made for us. People who once were far away from God can be at peace with God because of the sacrifice of Jesus Christ. "...now in Christ Jesus, you who once were [so] far away, through (by, in) the blood of Christ have been brought near. For He is [Himself] our peace (our bond of unity and harmony). He has made us both [Jew and Gentile] one [body], and has broken down (destroyed, abolished) the hostile dividing wall between us..." (Ephesians 2:13-14).

This passage of Scripture explains that Jesus Christ is our peace. We must understand that we can experience wonderful peace with God and that we can come into unity with God and harmony with God because of the price that Jesus Christ has paid for us.

God has made provision for His people, the Jews, and for all Gentiles (to become His adopted children) to be united together at peace with one another and at peace with Him. "By abolishing in His [own crucified] flesh the enmity [caused by] the Law with its decrees and ordinances [which He annulled]; that He from the two might create in Himself one new man [one new quality of humanity out of the two], so making peace" (Ephesians 2:15).

The Hebrew Law was very difficult to adhere to. We are told that Jesus Christ abolished the bitterness that existed because of the provisions of the Law. Jesus annulled this Law by combining Jews and Gentiles to be at peace with God and with one another. "And [He designed] to reconcile to God both [Jew and Gentile, united] in a single body by means of His cross, thereby killing the mutual enmity and bringing the feud to an end" (Ephesians 2:16).

We can be at peace with God because we are justified before God as a result of the sacrifice of Jesus Christ. "...since we are justified (acquitted, declared righteous, and given a right standing with God) through faith, let us [grasp the fact that we] have [the peace of reconciliation to hold and to enjoy] peace with God through our Lord Jesus Christ (the Messiah, the Anointed One)" (Romans 5:1).

A spiritual miracle occurs when we ask Jesus Christ to be our Savior. This miracle enables us to turn away from our previous separation from God *to actually become God's children* when we ask Jesus Christ to be our Savior. "…to as many as did receive and welcome Him, He gave the authority (power, privilege, right) to become the children of God, that is, to those who believe in (adhere to, trust in and rely on) His name – who owe their birth neither to bloods nor to the will of the flesh [that of physical impulse] nor to the will of man [that of a natural father], but to God. [They are born of God!]" (John 1:12).

Every person who has asked Jesus Christ to be his or her Savior has been given the privilege of becoming a child of God. We are born spiritually into God's family if we have complete faith in our Lord Jesus Christ. We have achieved through Jesus Christ what we could not achieve through our "natural father" as a result of the sins of Adam. Our new spiritual birth actually means that "we are born of God!"

People all over the world are frantically searching for peace. They do not realize how hopeless their quest is. True peace only can come to us through the sacrifice of Jesus Christ. We cannot experience the peace of God without first experiencing peace with God. If we are not at peace with God, we cannot experience God's peace deep down inside of ourselves and we cannot truly live in peace with other people.

Now that we have clearly seen what is required to be at peace with God, we are ready to explore throughout the remainder of this book exactly what the Word of God tells us to do to receive the peace of God. You will learn how to turn away from all worry, fear and anxiety to experience the peace of God at all times regardless of the circumstances you face.

Please contact us if you have made the decision to join the family of God, if you have made a renewed commitment to God or if you are not certain and now are certain of your salvation. Our address, telephone number, fax number and email address are listed at the beginning of this book. We would be so pleased to hear from you. We love you and we would be honored to hear from you. We want to rejoice with you and to welcome you as our brother or sister in Christ.

Chapter 31

Experience the Incredible Blessing of the Peace of God

All of the money that has ever existed on earth cannot purchase the peace of God. The peace of God is a wonderful *gift* from our loving Father to each of His children. The incredible magnitude of the blessing of God's peace is beyond the limitations of our human comprehension.

In the last two chapters we saw why we need to be righteous before God so that we can be at peace with God. We only can become righteous before God as a result of choosing to receive the sacrifice that Jesus Christ made for us when He paid the price for all of our sins. The peace of God is available to each of us once we have received Jesus Christ as our Savior. "...the effect of righteousness will be peace [internal and external], and the result of righteousness will be quietness and confident trust forever" (Isaiah 32:17).

Would you like to enjoy internal and external peace forever? Would you like to experience quiet and confident trust in God forever? These incredible blessings are available to us when we are righteous before God through Jesus Christ.

The peace of God will be normal and natural when we are in heaven. None of the events that rob us of peace on earth will occur in heaven. "God will wipe away every tear from their eyes; and death shall be no more, neither shall there be anguish (sorrow and mourning) nor grief nor pain any more, for the old conditions and the former order of things have passed away" (Revelation 21:4).

No one in heaven suffers from anguish, sorrow, grief or pain. The peace of God that everyone in heaven enjoys is available to us while we are here on earth, but we *must learn* how to live in God's peace. Christians who have not learned how to receive God's peace forfeit a tremendous blessing that our Father already has provided for us. We will learn from the Word of God *how* to receive the peace of God throughout the remainder of this book. We will study many specific instructions from the holy Scriptures that tell us *exactly* what we should do to receive God's peace.

We will begin this study with a definition of the peace of God. I like the definition of peace in the following amplification from *The Amplified Bible* which speaks of "…those who work for and make peace [in themselves and in others, that peace which means concord, agreement, and harmony between individuals, with undisturbedness, in a peaceful mind free from fears and agitating passions and moral conflicts]" (James 3:18).

Our Father has offered peace to us in three different areas. First, we have seen that He offers us peace with Himself when Jesus Christ becomes our Savior. Second, He has made His peace available to us so that we can react to difficult circumstances in our lives with "a peaceful mind free from fears." Third, our Father has given us specific instructions that tell us how to remain peaceful within ourselves regardless of how other people treat us. We can respond in love because God Who is love lives inside of us.

When we study the gospels of Matthew, Mark, Luke and John, we see many examples of the peace of God that Jesus Christ exhibited throughout His earthly ministry. This same wonderful peace is available to each of us today by faith. The Bible tells us that Jesus Christ was sent to earth "…to direct and guide our feet in a straight line into the way of peace" (Luke 1:79).

This Scripture reference refers to peace with God. I believe that it also applies to the peace of God. Christians must understand the tremendous difference between the peace of the world and the peace of God. The peace of God always comes from the *inside out* while the peace of the world comes from the *outside in.*

The world's peace is dependent upon the absence of problems. The peace of God does not change no matter how severe our problems might be. Dr. Billy Graham once explained the difference between the world's version of peace and God's peace by giving an example of two artists who were asked to paint a picture that depicted their understanding of peace.

One artist painted a picture of a beautiful lake that was surrounded by mountains. The lake was calm and tranquil. Its blue waters reflected the rays of the sun. This artist portrayed the world's version of peace. The other artist painted a picture of a violent, raging storm. In the midst of the storm, on a branch of a tree, was a bird's nest. In that nest was a small bird sleeping peacefully, absolutely unconcerned by the turmoil caused by the storm. This artist captured the conception of God's peace. I used a painting of a bird sleeping peacefully in a storm on the cover of *Deep Inner Peace,* a book that I wrote almost twenty years ago.

Peace that is based upon external conditions is very fragile. The world's peace constantly goes up and down depending on external circumstances. This peace is conditional. The world's peace depends upon favorable circumstances. God's peace transcends any crisis.

Believers can be at peace in the face of every trial because of their absolute and unshakable trust that the Lord will bring them safely through *all* of the trials they face. "Many evils confront the [consistently] righteous, but the Lord delivers him out of them all" (Psalm 34:19).

Christians who are committed to God will face much evil in the world. We can trust the Lord to deliver us from this evil. We can be certain that the Lord is always with us and that His peace is always upon us.

Some Christians lose their peace because of minor irritations such as the rudeness of other people, unexpected interruptions and frustrating delays. We all will face many irritating circumstances throughout our lives. We cannot escape from these frustrating circumstances, but we can be certain that our Father has given us the ability to receive His peace rather than give in to irritation.

Our Father wants us to react to the circumstances we face with absolute faith in His indwelling presence and in the promises in His Word. He wants us to learn how to remain calm in the face of frustrating circumstances. Instead of complaining, we should praise God and thank Him continually because we trust Him to lead us through every crisis. We will grow and mature as Christians if we dwell in the Lord instead of focusing on the irritations and frustrations in our lives.

Unbelievers continually attempt to create the circumstances they believe will give them peace. Some people attempt to find peace in expensive automobiles, luxurious homes, vacation trips and other external possessions that can be purchased with money.

These possessions only can give them temporary worldly peace for a short period of time.

Some people find that their peace fluctuates constantly. They start their day with peace in the morning only to become completely frustrated later in the day. Some people experience more peace on the weekends than when they are working during the week. Some people experience more peace when the weather is good than they do during unpleasant weather.

Too many people are looking outside of themselves for the peace that only can be found within because of the indwelling presence of the Holy Spirit. Our generation spends more money on entertainment than any generation in history, but the level of frustration in the world today is very high.

God did not create us in such a way that we can receive lasting peace from any external source. People who lust after expensive new possessions or vacations in beautiful places will find that their desire for peace from external sources cannot possibly produce lasting satisfaction. "...[the lust of] the eyes of man is never satisfied" (Proverbs 27:20).

God's peace is priceless. Some Christians who constantly face undesirable circumstances in their lives experience much more peace than many other Christians and unbelievers who enjoy much more favorable circumstances in their lives.

Our Father wants us to face severe problems calmly because our peace comes from Him instead of the circumstances in our lives. We can learn how to live in the peace of God when we are in the valleys of life and when we are on the mountaintops.

Our peace should *not* be determined by the circumstances in our lives. Our peace should *not* be determined by what other people do or do not do to us. Our peace should *not* be determined by what Satan and his demons attempt to do to us.

The circumstances in our lives have no authority over us. These circumstances *cannot* rob us of the peace of God if we do our very best to learn and obey the instructions our Father has given us pertaining to His peace. These circumstances cannot rob us of God's peace if we know, believe and step out in faith upon several of God's promises pertaining to His peace.

In this chapter we have laid a foundation that will enable us to learn about the peace of God. In the next chapter we will study several Scripture references that show us how to receive the peace of God that is available to *all* of God's children at *all* times.

Chapter 32

Receive the Peace That Jesus Christ Has Provided for You

The Bible is filled with many promises pertaining to peace from God. Our Father wants us to be certain that He has made full provision for each of His beloved children to experience His wonderful peace. "...the Lord will bless His people with peace" (Psalm 29:11).

We can expect to receive peace from God because the Word of God tells us that our Father will bless us with His peace. God always does exactly what He says He will do. The Bible refers to Him as "...[our] peace-giving God..." (Romans 15:33).

Satan wants us to experience constant frustration because of the circumstances we face and the influence of his evil spirits. We must not allow Satan and his demons to steal our peace. Satan and his demons are peace-stealers. Jesus Christ is our peace-giver.

Jesus paid the full price for every problem we have faced, every problem we face now and every problem we will face. Jesus wants each of us to walk in the peace He has provided for us. He does not want us to give up this precious peace because of the circumstances in our lives or because of the influence of Satan and his demons. Our Father has called each of His children to live in peace with Him, in peace deep down inside of ourselves and in peace with one another. "...God has called us to peace" (I Corinthians 7:15).

We will have a great big hole in our lives if we do not walk constantly in the peace God has provided for us. We cannot experience the peace of God if we seek this wonderful gift passively. Our Father wants each of us to have a deep and constant desire to walk in the wonderful peace He has made available to us. The peace of God is not a "nice to have." The peace of God is a "have to have." "...seek, inquire for, and crave peace and pursue (go after) it!" (Psalm 34:14).

This passage of Scripture contains two active words – "crave" and "pursue." Our Father wants us to crave His peace. When we crave something, we want it very badly. We have a deep, strong and constant desire for anything we crave. Unfortunately, some of God's children crave things that our loving Father does not want us to crave. Some of us fail to crave the peace our Father has told us to crave.

Our Father instructs us to "pursue" His peace. The amplification in this passage of Scripture tells us to "go after" God's peace. Our Father wants us to be very determined to receive the peace He has provided for us. He wants us to abide in His wonderful peace throughout every day of our lives.

There is no comparison between the quality of our lives without the peace of God and the quality of our lives with the peace of God. We would place our desire for God's peace near the top of our priority list if we could even begin to comprehend how marvelous our lives would be if we were able to live in God's peace at all times. We would not make the mistake that some Christians make of spending a great deal of time and energy pursuing selfish goals instead of utilizing the same amount of energy to pursue the peace of God.

Our Father gives us additional instructions to actively pursue His wonderful peace. "…search for peace (harmony; undisturbedness from fears, agitating passions, and moral conflicts) and seek it eagerly. [Do not merely desire peaceful relations with God, with your fellowmen, and with yourself, but pursue, go after them!]" (I Peter 3:11).

Please stop for a moment to think about how emphatic our Father is in these instructions to seek His wonderful peace. He tells us that we should "search" for this peace. Searching is not passive. Searching always is active. Whenever we search for something, we explore carefully and examine thoroughly.

Our Father wants our lives to be in absolute harmony with Him. We have seen that He does not want worry, anxiety, fear or any other negative emotions to influence us. Instead, He instructs us to seek His peace "eagerly." Our Father does not want us to merely desire His peace. We are instructed to "pursue" and to "go after" peace with Him, peace with other human beings and peace deep down inside of ourselves.

Some people wish that their life was free from problems. A problem-free life does not exist (see Job 5:6-7, Psalm 34:19 and John 16:33). The problems we face will not be able to overcome us if we know that we will experience many problems in our lives and if we have a deep and sincere desire to walk in God's peace that never is affected by circumstances. The problems we face will not be able to overcome us if we trust completely in the victory Jesus Christ won for us when He rose from the dead (see Matthew 28:18).

I hope you will meditate continually on all of God's promises that show us that our loving Father has provided His peace for us.

Our Father has given us specific instructions telling us exactly what He wants us to do to receive this peace in our lives. He wants us to believe these promises with unwavering faith in Him. He wants us to obey the specific instructions He has given to us. Take a deep breath and close your eyes. Enjoy God's presence right now.

The peace of God is the peace that our beloved Savior, Jesus Christ, offers. Jesus said, "Peace I leave with you; My [own] peace I now give and bequeath to you. Not as the world gives do I give to you. Do not let your hearts be troubled, neither let them be afraid. [Stop allowing yourselves to be agitated and disturbed; and do not permit yourselves to be fearful and intimidated and cowardly and unsettled.]" (John 14:27).

This passage of Scripture is the foundation for everything else that is contained in this book. Please stop for a moment to consider the impact these words from Jesus must have had upon His disciples. Shortly before He made this promise to them, Jesus had told them that He would be leaving them. Every aspect of the lives of these men revolved around Jesus Christ. They suddenly were faced with the knowledge that He no longer would be with them.

Jesus knew exactly how His disciples would feel, so He gave them the instructions pertaining to His peace that we just read in John 14:27. We must understand that this wonderful promise and these same instructions apply to each of us today.

Please personalize this promise from Jesus Christ. Stop for a moment to underline or highlight the *six* times in this passage of Scripture that the words "you," "your" and "yourselves" are used. Speak this passage of Scripture boldly, substituting *your name* in each of these six places. Speak it again. Speak it again. Know that Jesus is speaking directly to *you*.

The peace of Jesus Christ is vastly different from the peace of the world. Jesus emphasized that He did *not* give us the same peace the world searches for. The peace of Jesus Christ is so real, so great, so strong and so powerful that it is independent of circumstances. The peace of Jesus Christ cannot be swayed by any problems we face.

Jesus tells us that we should not allow our hearts to be troubled. He does not want us to allow worry, anxiety and fear to obtain a foothold in our lives. Please highlight or underline the words "allowing" and "permit" in the amplification of this passage of Scripture. We each make continual decisions whether or not we will *allow* the circumstances in our lives to cause us to "be agitated and disturbed."

Jesus went on to tell us that we should not *permit* ourselves to be "fearful, intimidated, cowardly and unsettled." The word "permit" implies that we decide whether or not we will allow the circumstances in our lives to cause us to be afraid. We choose whether we will allow these circumstances to affect us or whether we constantly will walk in the peace that our Lord Jesus Christ has provided for us.

Jesus tells us that *He has given us His very own peace.* The *same* peace that Jesus Christ maintained through all of the challenges He faced during His earthly ministry is available to *you* today. Know and understand the magnificence of this promise that Jesus has given to you. We can be assured that this peace lives inside of us because we know that Jesus Christ lives inside of every Christian (see Galatians 2:20).

We must understand what a precious gift we have been given when Jesus Christ says that He has given us His very own peace. We should not take this magnificent gift lightly. We each should have a deep and sincere desire to learn how to receive the marvelous peace Jesus has provided for us.

The glorious and magnificent peace of Jesus Christ is so great that nothing in the world can begin to compare with it. His peace is so great and so deep that we can face great crises and remain in His perfect peace. If we learn how to rest in the peace that Jesus has given us, we will be able to face every challenge with the supernatural peace of Jesus Christ instead of reacting to these challenges emotionally with human worry, anxiety and fear.

This chapter is filled with specific facts from the Word of God pertaining to the peace of God that has been provided for every child of God. Carefully review the passages of Scripture in this chapter. Meditate on them continually. Know that each of these promises applies to *you* personally.

In the next chapter we will learn more truths from the Word of God pertaining to the peace our Father has made available to every one of His children. This practical gift can change your everyday life. Your life will be absolutely transformed if you learn how to live continually in the peace of God that has been made available to you.

Chapter 33

Refuse to Give Up Your Peace

In the last chapter we studied John 14:27 that tells us about the peace Jesus Christ gave to His disciples. This peace is available to each of us today. Shortly after that, Jesus explained to His disciples that His peace would see them through every crisis they would face. Jesus said, "I have told you these things, so that in Me you may have [perfect] peace and confidence. In the world you have tribulation and trials and distress and frustration; but be of good cheer [take courage; be confident, certain, undaunted]! For I have overcome the world. [I have deprived it of power to harm you and have conquered it for you]" (John 16:33).

Please highlight or underline the five times the word "you" is used in this passage of Scripture. Personalize this promise. *Know* that it applies to you. Speak this promise boldly. Speak it again. Speak it again.

Jesus tells us that we *will* experience "tribulations, trials, distress and frustration." We should not be surprised by the trials and tribulations we face. We will face circumstances that could cause us to be distressed *if* we react negatively to these circumstances.

Jesus went on to tell us that we should "be of good cheer" when we face trials and tribulations. Our hearts should sing with joy regardless of the circumstances in our lives. Jesus wants us to face these trials and tribulations with courage and with unwavering confidence in Him.

We can learn more about the peace of Jesus Christ by carefully examining the biblical account of what took place when Jesus and His disciples faced a severe storm in the middle of a lake. "...He and His disciples got into a boat, and He said to them, Let us go across to the other side of the lake. So they put out to sea. But as they were sailing, He fell off to sleep. And a whirlwind revolving from below upwards swept down on the lake, and the boat was filling with water, and they were in great danger" (Luke 8:22-23).

A whirlwind is similar to a hurricane except that a whirlwind is a current of air that swirls upward violently and spirals around a forward-moving axis. The disciples were professional fishermen. They knew they were in deep trouble when they observed this whirlwind sweeping down after swirling upward to begin to fill their boat with water.

The disciples were afraid. They immediately awakened Jesus. "And the disciples came and woke Him, saying, Master, Master, we are perishing! And He, being thoroughly awakened, censured and blamed and rebuked the wind and the raging waves; and they ceased, and there came a calm" (Luke 8:24).

The disciples knew they would be in great trouble if their boat sank in the midst of the swirling wind and violent waves. Jesus spoke boldly to the storm. He rebuked the wind and the waves that were sweeping over the boat. The wind stopped. The water became calm.

Jesus then spoke words to His disciples that apply to each of us whenever we face storms in our lives today. "And He said to them, [Why are you so fearful?] Where is your faith (your trust, your confidence in Me – in My veracity and My integrity)? And they were seized with alarm and profound and reverent dread, and they marveled, saying to one another, Who then is this, that He commands even wind and sea, and they obey Him?" (Luke 8:25).

Apply these words from Jesus Christ to the storms that you face in *your* life. Jesus told us that we should not be afraid, regardless of the seeming severity of the storms in our lives. He told us that we should have absolute faith, trust and confidence in Him.

The disciples were amazed at what Jesus did. They had seen Him perform many miracles, but they "marveled" when they saw His deep peace in the midst of this storm. You can be certain that Jesus Christ Who lives in *your heart* is much more powerful than any storm you will face. Jesus wants us to *keep our eyes on Him.*

Jesus has not changed. He is exactly the same today as He was during that severe whirlwind in the middle of the lake. "Jesus Christ (the Messiah) is [always] the same, yesterday, today, [yes] and forever (to the ages)" (Hebrews 13:8).

The same Jesus Christ Who calmed this torrential storm many years ago lives inside of every Christian believer today. Jesus wants us to be certain that He can and will calm the storms in our lives *if* we will walk in His peace and allow His peace to be manifested in us and, through us, to others.

The winds and the sea obeyed Jesus Christ in the midst of that storm. The storms in our lives will yield before the mighty power of His indwelling presence *if* we will yield control of our lives to Him and trust Him completely.

Jesus wants us to be absolutely certain that He is much greater and much more powerful than any problem we will face. Just before Jesus ascended into heaven He said, "…All authority (all power of rule) in heaven and on earth has been given to Me" (Matthew 28:18).

Some Christians block themselves from receiving the mighty power of Jesus Christ because of their doubt and unbelief. There is no question that our doubt and unbelief can block the enormous power of Jesus Christ. When Jesus went to His home town of Nazareth, He must have wanted to perform the healing miracles He had been performing in many other places. However, the people in His home town did not believe He was the Messiah. They looked at Him as the carpenter who had lived among them for many years.

The former neighbors of Jesus Christ did not exhibit deep and unwavering faith in Him. Their doubt and unbelief blocked them from receiving the mighty healing miracles that Jesus had been performing throughout the land. "…He was not able to do even one work of power there, except that He laid His hands on a few sickly people [and] cured them." (Mark 6:5).

Please highlight or underline the words "was not able." These words show us that doubt and unbelief *can* block the mighty power of Jesus Christ from working in our lives. We must not give up the peace Jesus has given to us. We must not allow our faith in Jesus to waver. Jesus can and will do wonderful things in our lives today if we rest in Him and allow His peace to calm our storms.

This chapter is filled with facts from the Word of God about the peace that Jesus Christ wants us to have at all times and especially when we face storms in our lives. In the next chapter we will learn that Jesus Christ actually is the Prince of Peace. We will learn more scriptural truth that tells us how to receive His peace in our lives today.

Chapter 34

Trust the Prince of Peace
to Control Your Life

The prophet Isaiah prophesied several times about the forthcoming Messiah, Jesus Christ. On one occasion Isaiah referred to Him as the Prince of Peace. He said, "For to us a Child is born, to us a Son is given; and the government shall be upon His shoulder, and His name shall be called Wonderful Counselor, Mighty God, Everlasting Father [of Eternity], Prince of Peace" (Isaiah 9:6).

There is no question that Isaiah was referring to Jesus Christ because there is no other Son of God (see John 3:16). This passage of Scripture tells us about the mighty power of Jesus Christ. We can trust Jesus to give us wonderful counsel when we need it. He is our everlasting Father throughout eternity. Jesus Christ is the Prince of Peace.

If you have asked Jesus Christ to be your Lord, you can be certain that the same mighty and powerful Jesus Christ Who is described in this passage of Scripture lives in *your* heart. Why would any of us ever allow the circumstances in our lives to steal our peace if we are absolutely certain that the Prince of

Peace lives inside of us? Some Christians place far too much emphasis on the problems they face and far too little emphasis on the Prince of Peace Who lives in their hearts.

We must not allow ourselves to be distracted by the circumstances we face. We should turn away from all distractions to focus constantly on Jesus Christ. "Looking away [from all that will distract] to Jesus, Who is the Leader and the Source of our faith [giving the first incentive for our belief] and is also its Finisher [bringing it to maturity and perfection]..." (Hebrews 12:2).

Some unbelievers focus continually on the problems in their lives. They have no other alternative. They know they cannot overcome extremely difficult problems with their limited human abilities. They are filled with worry, fear, doubt and apprehension when they face problems they know they cannot possibly solve.

Christians should *not* react the way unbelievers react. We should never focus on the problems in our lives. We are instructed to "look away" from the problems we face. We must not allow the circumstances in our lives to distract us from focusing continually on Jesus Christ Who is our "Leader and the Source of our faith."

We also are told that Jesus Christ is the "Finisher" of our faith. We can be assured that Jesus can and will bring whatever we are trusting Him for "to maturity and perfection." The Prince of Peace always will bring us safely through the problems we face if we refuse to give up our peace because we trust Him completely.

We have seen that Isaiah referred to Jesus Christ as the Prince of Peace. The next verse of Scripture gives us more facts about our marvelous Leader. Isaiah said, "Of the increase of His government and of peace there shall be no end..." (Isaiah 9:7).

You can be certain that the peace of God will *increase* constantly throughout the remainder of your life *if* you will focus constantly on the Prince of Peace instead of allowing yourself to be distracted by the problems you face. The peace of Jesus Christ is infinite. Jesus wants to give each of us more and more of His peace throughout our lives on earth.

We will experience the peace of Jesus Christ in direct proportion to our relationship with Him. We make a tremendous mistake if we fail to draw closer to Jesus on an ongoing basis throughout every day of our lives.

The Word of God tells us that the peace of Jesus Christ should be like an "umpire" in our lives. An umpire in a baseball game is an official who is in charge of everything that happens in that game. "...let the peace (soul harmony which comes) from Christ rule (act as umpire continually) in your hearts [deciding and settling with finality all questions that arise in your minds, in that peaceful state] to which as [members of Christ's] one body you were also called [to live]. And be thankful (appreciative), [giving praise to God always]" (Colossians 3:15).

The amplification of this passage of Scripture refers to peace as "soul harmony." Our souls consist of our minds, our emotions and our will. Our souls consist of what we think, what we feel and what we decide. Our thoughts, our feelings and our decisions should be immersed in Jesus Christ. We should reflect Him in all that we say and all that we do.

Our thoughts, our emotions and our decisions always will be in harmony and at peace if we allow the peace of Jesus

Christ to rule our lives and to "act as umpire continually." Jesus will "decide and settle with finality all questions that arise in our minds" if we yield to Him because we trust Him completely.

Whenever we face difficult problems, we can be certain that Jesus knows exactly what we are going through. "For we do not have a High Priest Who is unable to understand and sympathize and have a shared feeling with our weaknesses and infirmities and liability to the assaults of temptation, but One Who has been tempted in every respect as we are, yet without sinning" (Hebrews 4:15).

Jesus is not a distant God who does not know what we are experiencing. Jesus came from heaven to live on earth as a man. He knows from His personal experience exactly what kind of trials and temptations we face. Jesus never once sinned by allowing any trial or temptation to overcome Him.

The next verse of Scripture tells us that we should confidently approach the throne of God whenever we need help. "Let us then fearlessly and confidently and boldly draw near to the throne of grace (the throne of God's unmerited favor to us sinners), that we may receive mercy [for our failures] and find grace to help in good time for every need [appropriate help and well-timed help, coming just when we need it]" (Hebrews 4:16).

The throne of God is referred to as "the throne of grace" because we did not earn and we do not deserve the right to approach this throne. We only can approach the throne of God because of the grace of God that is available to us because of the sacrifice that Jesus Christ made on our behalf.

This passage of Scripture tells us that God will give us "help in good time for every need." Please highlight or underline the words "good time" and the words "every need." Know that your loving Father will help *you* in His perfect timing with *every* need that you have. The amplification in this passage of Scripture assures us that we will receive "appropriate help and well-timed help, coming just when we need it."

God's timing often is very different from our timing. Our Father wants us to trust His timing completely just as we trust Him in every other area of our lives. "The Lord does not delay and is not tardy or slow about what He promises, according to some people's conception of slowness…" (II Peter 3:9).

Our Father does not want us to give up. He wants us to persevere in our faith in Him. "…let us not lose heart and grow weary and faint in acting nobly and doing right, for in due time and at the appointed season we shall reap, if we do not loosen and relax our courage and faint" (Galatians 6:9).

We will reap a harvest from our faith in God *if* we do not give up. If we live the way our Father wants us to live and if we refuse to give up, God will honor our faith in Him "in due time and at the appointed season."

Our Father wants us to follow the example of farmers who calmly and patiently waited for the harvest from the seeds they planted. "…See how the farmer waits expectantly for the precious harvest from the land. [See how] he keeps up his patient [vigil] over it until it receives the early and late rains. So you also must be patient…" (James 5:7-8).

When this passage of Scripture refers to early rain, it refers to the fact that farmers tried to plant seeds at a time when rain would fall shortly after the seeds had been put into the ground. This early rain helped the seeds to germinate. The farmers then continued to wait until rain at a later time caused their crops to ripen. Farmers learn very quickly that they must be extremely patient. Our Father wants us to learn this same lesson.

The last four chapters have been filled with wonderful scriptural truths pertaining to the peace that is available to us through our Lord Jesus Christ. In the next chapter we will study the Word of God to see exactly what it says about *perfect peace*. We then will learn how to receive manifestation of this perfect peace that Almighty God has provided for us throughout every day of our lives.

Chapter 35

God's Perfect Peace Is Available to You

We will see that our Father promises to guard and protect each of us. He also promises that He will keep each of us in perfect peace. This promise is a conditional promise. The Word of God says that we should do *two things* consistently if we sincerely desire to receive these blessings from God. *Do you know* what your loving Father has instructed you to do so that He will guard you and keep you in perfect peace?

The following passage of Scripture tells us exactly what our Father wants us to do to receive these blessings. "You will guard him and keep him in perfect and constant peace whose mind [both its inclination and its character] is stayed on You, because he commits himself to You, leans on You, and hopes confidently in You. So trust in the Lord (commit yourself to Him, lean on Him, hope confidently in Him) forever…" (Isaiah 26:3-4).

Everyone in heaven enjoys God's perfect peace at all times. Christians who are able to appropriate this wonderful blessing from God will experience a preview of heaven during their lives on earth.

When our Father speaks of perfect peace, He speaks of His peace that has no qualifications, defects or shortcomings. He speaks of His peace that never changes for even one moment, regardless of the circumstances we face. Perfect peace is available to every child of God. Our loving Father has done His part to give us His perfect peace. Will we do what He instructs us to do to receive this blessing?

What exactly does our Father want us to do so that He will guard us at all times and keep us in perfect and constant peace? First, our Father tells us to keep our minds "stayed" on Him. If we truly want to experience God's perfect peace, we should give every burden to Him and focus continually on Him. *How* do we keep our minds focused on God? The remainder of this passage of Scripture tells us that our Father wants us to trust Him – to commit ourselves to Him, to lean on Him and to place all of our hope and confidence in Him.

In this chapter we will focus entirely on the first part of God's requirement – to keep our minds *stayed* on God. In the next two chapters we will focus on the second requirement our Father has given to us to receive His perfect peace.

What does it mean to keep our minds "stayed" on God? I believe that the word "stay" in this context is similar to glue. I believe this passage of Scripture could be translated to say that we should keep our minds "glued" to God. Our inclination and our character should be God-centered rather than self-centered.

Unfortunately, some of us do *exactly the opposite* of what our loving Father instructs us to do. Many people, when they face a difficult problem, *keep their minds stayed upon the problem.* They think about the problem constantly.

When God created us, He gave each of us the ability to direct our thoughts just as He gave us the ability to direct our arms, our hands, our legs and our feet. We direct our appendages instinctively, but we need to *learn* how to direct our thoughts.

Our Father has given us the opportunity to "program" our thinking throughout every day of our lives. Our thoughts and our character should increasingly be conformed to God's thoughts and character. Our Father has instructed us to constantly renew our minds in His Word. Christians who disregard these instructions from God ultimately will pay a severe price for their disobedience.

We each make a decision throughout every day of our lives whether we will allow our thoughts and our emotions to control us or whether we will utilize our God-given ability to control our thoughts and our emotions. We do *not* have to react mentally, emotionally or physically to the challenges we face. We do not have to accept the thoughts of worry, fear and anxiety that Satan's demons try to put into our minds. We cannot stop these thoughts from coming at us, but we can choose to immediately replace these thoughts with godly thoughts.

None of us can control the circumstances in our lives, but *we are able to control our reaction to these circumstances.* Our *reaction* to the circumstances in our lives is much more important than the actual challenges we face. When God created us, He gave each of us the ability to react to the challenges in our lives by obeying the specific instructions He has given us in His Word and by reacting to every challenge with deep and unwavering faith in Him.

Whenever we face difficult challenges, we each will make the decision whether we will think the way our Father wants us to think or whether we will think the way Satan wants us to think. Satan wants us to dwell on the problems we face. Our Father wants us to look at these problems as opportunities for Him to bless us according to our faith in Him (see Matthew 9:29).

The presence and power of God enable us to be part of the solution instead of being part of the problem. Our Father has given each of us the ability to develop a peaceful mind that is absolutely free from the effect of all worried, anxious and fearful thoughts.

We should not ignore the problems we face. I believe that a problem that is well defined is half solved. However, once we have identified a potential problem, we then must *stop thinking about the problem.* We make a tremendous mistake if we dwell upon the challenges we face. Instead, we should follow our Father's instructions to focus on Him continually.

Keeping our minds stayed on God is not a mental exercise. We actually live in God when our minds are stayed upon Him. Every aspect of our lives should be expressive of our relationship with God. We should not even think of dwelling upon the problems we face because we are safe and secure in our relationship with our Father.

Some people are so consumed with the problems in their lives that they think about these problems and talk about these problems constantly. Some people allow these problems to overwhelm them because they do not have a close personal relationship with the Lord. They cannot trust Him completely because they do not know Him intimately. Several chapters of this book contain specific scriptural instructions that explain how to develop a close personal relationship with the Lord.

We cannot think about two different things at the same time. Every time that Satan's demons try to get into our minds with worried and anxious thoughts, we should come right back at them with specific facts from the Word of God. The promises of God are *much more powerful* than any thoughts that Satan's demons attempt to put into our minds.

Christians who worry have a divided mind. Their minds go back and forth from a desire to trust God to thoughts of worry and fear. Our Father does not want us to be double-minded. Jesus said, "…no city or house divided against itself will last or continue to stand" (Matthew 12:25).

Christians with a double-minded thought life are engaged in a continual "tug of war" between God and the devil. When we face difficult problems, Satan's demons often hammer away at our minds. They want us to think continually about the problems we face.

Our Father wants us to do just the opposite. He wants our minds to be filled with a steady infusion of His Word as we obey His instructions to study and meditate on the holy Scriptures throughout the day and night. Our Father wants us to be single-minded. He wants us to keep our minds focused on Him at all times.

Our eyes, our ears, our minds, our hearts and our mouths should be constantly filled with the Word of God. We should have glorious praise and worship music playing continually. We should always be conscious of God's presence.

Hopefully we will grow and mature to the point where we do not allow our minds to constantly go back and forth between faith in God and worrying about the challenges we face. We should obey God's instructions to "…set your mind and heart to seek (inquire of and require as your vital necessity) the Lord your God…" (I Chronicles 22:19).

Our Father wants us to "set" our minds and our hearts on Him so that we do not waver in our faith in Him. He wants us to know that focusing on Him at all times is a "vital necessity." When something is a necessity, we do not have a choice. We cannot afford to disobey God's instructions in this area.

Our Father wants us to hunger for Him as if we were starved. He wants us to thirst for His glorious presence. He wants us to seek Him continually with every ounce of strength we have.

This process is not an idea or a thought. This process is a spiritual, emotional and physical quest to reach God. Our Father wants us to seek Him with our whole being. When we are in His presence, we will experience joy that cannot be described.

We must not allow the circumstances we face to pull us down. Our Father has instructed us repeatedly to keep our minds focused on Him instead of focusing on anything that is taking place in the world. "…set your minds and keep them set on what is above (the higher things), not on the things that are on the earth" (Colossians 3:2).

We cannot afford to allow our minds to dwell upon worldly concerns. We shut out the peace of God when we allow fear, worry and frustration to enter our minds. Now that we have carefully studied the first part of God's requirement for perfect peace, we are ready to go on to His remaining instructions and examine them in detail.

Our Father told us that He wants us to commit ourselves to Him, to lean on Him constantly and to place all of our hope and confidence in Him. In the next two chapters we will thoroughly study God's instructions in this area.

Chapter 36

Experience God's Perfect Peace in Your Heart

In addition to keeping our minds stayed upon God, we need to learn how to fill our *hearts* with the Word of God. Our Father wants us to see life from His perspective. He wants us to live in His peace and by His power because we have learned how to come into His presence.

I believe that our *minds* are filled with the Word of God by *studying* facts from the holy Scriptures each day. I believe that we fill our *hearts* with the Word of God by *meditating* constantly on the holy Scriptures. In the next two chapters I will explain what I believe is the difference between studying the Word of God and meditating on the Word of God.

Instead of dwelling upon any worldly concerns, our Father wants us to meditate on His promises continually. Meditation on worldly concerns always blocks us from receiving God's perfect peace. Our faith in God will increase constantly if we enjoy God's presence and meditate continually on the magnificent promises our Father has given to us.

Joshua was concerned when he learned that he would succeed Moses as the leader of Israel. God gave Joshua specific instructions. God said, "This Book of the Law shall not depart out of your mouth, but you shall meditate on it day and night, that you may observe and do according to all that is written in it. For then you shall make your way prosperous, and then you shall deal wisely and have good success" (Joshua 1:8).

The instructions that God gave to Joshua apply to each of us today. This passage of Scripture tells us how to succeed from God's perspective. Worldly success and success from God's perspective are vastly different. We should faithfully obey these specific instructions from God if we want to be successful in receiving God's perfect peace or any other blessings our Father has provided for us.

Our Father has given us three specific instructions in this passage of Scripture. We should meditate on His Word throughout the day and night. We should speak God's Word continually. We should learn exactly how our Father wants us to live and we then should carefully obey His instructions.

All Christians will say that they want to be successful from God's perspective, but I believe that *only a very small percentage* of God's children faithfully obey these instructions from God that tell us how to succeed. Our Father has provided magnificent blessings for each of His children who faithfully obey these instructions. He promises that we will be prosperous, that we will make wise decisions and that we will be successful.

In addition to these instructions from Joshua 1:8, our Father has given us additional instructions about meditating on the holy Scriptures throughout the day and night. "...his delight and desire are in the law of the Lord, and on His law (the precepts, the instructions, the teachings of God) he habitually meditates (ponders and studies) by day and by night. And he shall be like a tree firmly planted [and tended] by the streams of water, ready to bring forth its fruit in its season; its leaf also shall not fade or wither; and everything he does shall prosper [and come to maturity]" (Psalm 1:2-3).

Our Father wants us to absolutely "delight" in His Word. He wants us to have a deep and constant desire to learn everything He wants us to learn. Our Father tells us exactly how He will bless us if we will obey His instructions to meditate throughout the day and night on His Word.

If we obey these instructions, we will be like a tree that is planted next to a stream of water. This tree will produce fruit in season even in the midst of a severe drought. Our Father promises that we will prosper in *everything* we do *if* we obey His instructions to meditate throughout the day and night on His Word.

Why would any child of God disobey these specific instructions and fail to receive the wonderful blessings our Father has provided for His children who faithfully obey these instructions? Trees that are planted next to a river or a stream are *not* dependent upon rainfall from the sky to produce fruit. The roots of these trees are able to reach down into the river or stream to bring up water so that they will be able to produce bountiful fruit regardless of external conditions.

This same principle applies to us. We can experience God's perfect peace regardless of the circumstances we face. If we want to live in God's perfect peace, we should faithfully obey our Father's instructions to meditate on His Word throughout the day and night. We should meditate constantly on the Word of God if we want to receive any of the other blessings that have been provided for us through the cross of Jesus Christ. These blessings will enable us to be a vessel of glory for God.

The circumstances in our lives will *not* be able to pull us down if we meditate continually on the Word of God. Because of our obedience to our Father's instructions for constant meditation, we will see these circumstances as opportunities for our character to be molded into the image of Christ. We will enjoy God's perfect peace because our minds and our hearts have been filled to overflowing with God's promises and instructions instead of being filled with worried and anxious thoughts about the future. I believe that Scripture meditation is *absolutely essential* for any of God's children to receive the fullness of the blessings our loving Father has provided for us.

When we meditate on a passage of Scripture we reflect quietly, deeply and thoroughly over a period of time on the specific instructions and/or promises from God in that passage of Scripture. We should look at each passage of Scripture as a personal message from our loving Father. We should turn these promises and instructions over and over in our minds. Throughout the day and night, we should speak with our mouths the Scripture references we are meditating upon.

Our faith in God will increase steadily as this process of Scripture meditation continues over a period of weeks, months and years. This continual meditation causes our faith in God to take root in our hearts where it will grow continually. Our deeply rooted and persevering faith in God will bring the blessings God has provided for us into manifestation.

Lamplight Ministries is so devoted to Scripture meditation that Judy and I spent five years to produce ten sets of Scripture Meditation Cards. We have spent thousands of hours in the Word of God to find, categorize and explain hundreds of passages of Scripture. Each set of fifty-two Scripture cards contains approximately eighty Scripture references.

These cards easily can be carried in a pocket or a purse so that any child of God can obey his or her Father's instructions to meditate on His Word throughout the day and night. The specific passage of Scripture being meditating upon can be placed on a table, a desk, the dashboard of an automobile and many other places.

This continual meditation causes us to focus constantly on God's promises and instructions. As we meditate, we should open our mouths throughout the day and night to continually speak the promises and instructions we have chosen. We are obeying God's instructions in Joshua 1:8 that tell us that His Word *should not depart from our mouths.*

We see an example of the importance of what we focus upon by an account from the Bible that tells how Jesus Christ approached a boat by walking on the water. His disciples who were in the boat emphatically expressed their fear when they saw Him. "…when the disciples saw Him walking on the sea, they were terrified and said, It is a ghost! And they screamed out with fright" (Matthew 14:26).

Jesus did not want His disciples to be afraid. He does not want us to be afraid. Jesus wants us to react with unwavering faith when we are in His presence. "…instantly He spoke to them, saying, Take courage! I AM! Stop being afraid!" (Matthew 14:27).

Peter responded to these instructions from Jesus. He stepped out on his faith in the Lord. "…Peter answered Him, Lord, if it is You, command me to come to You on the water. He said, Come! So Peter got out of the boat and walked on the water, and he came toward Jesus" (Matthew 14:28-29).

Peter actually was able to walk on the water *because he kept his eyes focused on Jesus.* Peter fell as soon as he took his eyes off Jesus and focused instead upon the wind and the waves. "…when he perceived and felt the strong wind, he was frightened, and as he began to sink, he cried out, Lord, save me [from death]! Instantly Jesus reached out His hand and caught and held him, saying to him, O you of little faith, why did you doubt?" (Matthew 14:30-31).

We see the same principle here that we saw in the first part of Isaiah 26:3. If we truly desire God's perfect peace, we must focus on God instead of focusing on the problems we face. We *will* focus on God constantly when we obey His instructions to continually meditate on passages of Scripture. We are not just studying facts. Continual meditation on the holy Scriptures will bring us more and more into God's presence.

We need Peter's boldness and readiness to step out on our faith in Jesus Christ. Peter walked in perfect peace as long as he kept his attention on Jesus. Peter was not frightened until he took his eyes off Jesus.

This same principle applies to us. We must keep our minds and our hearts focused continually on God if we want to experience His perfect peace. We cannot afford to focus on the circumstances in our lives.

All circumstances are temporary and subject to change. We should focus instead on our unchanging eternal God and on His unchanging eternal Word. "...consider and look not to the things that are seen but to the things that are unseen; for the things that are visible are temporal (brief and fleeting), but the things that are invisible are deathless and everlasting" (II Corinthians 4:18).

The natural mind cannot understand the way God wants us to live. All Christians are citizens of heaven who are able to receive divine power through Jesus Christ. We must turn away from the temporal problems of this world to focus continually on our eternal God. "…we walk by faith [we regulate our lives and conduct ourselves by our conviction or belief respecting man's relationship to God and divine things, with trust and holy fervor; thus we walk] not by sight or appearance" (II Corinthians 5:7).

Let's look at the last part of this passage of Scripture first. The Word of God tells us that we should *not* live our lives based upon what we see. We should not base our lives upon the circumstances we face. Instead of focusing on circumstances, we should step out on our faith in God.

This passage of Scripture says that our relationship with God should be a relationship of "holy fervor." Our Father wants us to have an intense passion for Him. He wants us to stay so close to Him and to trust Him so completely that we absolutely will not be swayed by any circumstances in our lives. "…he who believes in Him [who adheres to, trusts in, and relies on Him] shall not be put to shame nor be disappointed in his expectations" (Romans 9:33).

Our Father will never let us down. He is absolutely trustworthy. When we place all of our trust in Him, He will not disappoint us. "…whoever leans on, trusts in, and is confident in the Lord - happy, blessed and fortunate is he" (Proverbs 16:20).

The Word of God promises that we will be happy, that we will be blessed by God and that we will be fortunate when we joyfully place all of our trust in God. "[Most] blessed is the man who believes in, trusts in, and relies on the Lord, and whose hope and confidence the Lord is. For he shall be like a tree planted by the waters that spreads out its roots by the river; and it shall not see and fear when heat comes; but its leaf shall be green. It shall not be anxious and full of care in the year of drought, nor shall it cease yielding fruit" (Jeremiah 17:7-8).

Once again we see that our Father has made provision to bless us abundantly when we place all of our trust in Him. Our Father promises the same fruitfulness here that was described in Psalm 1:2 where we are told to meditate on the Word of God throughout the day and night.

Once again we are told that we will be like a tree that is planted next to a river. When a drought comes, this tree can reach its roots down into the river to find the water that is required to continue to produce fruit. The circumstances in our lives will *not* be able to overcome us if we turn away from these circumstances to place all of our deeply rooted faith in the Lord.

In this chapter we have established a scriptural foundation for obeying the second requirement of Isaiah 26:3 where we are told that we should commit ourselves to the Lord, lean on Him and place all of our hope and confidence in Him. In the next chapter we will study the Word of God to receive additional instructions that will tell us exactly what our Father wants us to do so that we will trust Him totally, completely and absolutely.

Chapter 37

Place All of Your Trust in the Lord

Christians who have not obeyed their Father's instructions to renew their minds in His Word every day and to meditate on His Word continually throughout the day and night *cannot comprehend the supernatural power of the Word of God.* We cannot appropriate the supernatural power of the Word of God unless our minds and our hearts have been filled to overflowing with this power.

Some Christians believe that the problems they face are more powerful than the Word of God. They cannot even begin to understand how words that are printed on paper can possibly be more powerful than problems that are very real and readily apparent. Our Father wants our faith in Him to grow continually so that we will be able to experience His perfect peace because we trust Him completely instead of being overwhelmed by the circumstances we face.

Whenever we face difficult circumstances, we need to *increase* our time alone with the Lord. We need to study and meditate on His Word throughout the day and night. We need to boldly speak His supernatural promises again and again and again. We need to personalize these promises. We need to communicate with the

Lord constantly by praying, by worshipping Him and by listening to Him.

As this process continues over a period of time, faith in God will rise up on the inside of us. As we continually draw closer to God, we will be able to see things more and more from God's perspective. Our faith in God will increase to the point at which we will be able to see the circumstances in our lives as God sees them. We will look down at these problems instead of looking up at them. "…whoever leans on, trusts in, and puts his confidence in the Lord is safe and set on high" (Proverbs 29:25).

All of us would like to be safe from the difficult problems in our lives. We would like to be lifted above these problems. This passage of Scripture says that *whoever* places all of his or her trust and confidence in the Lord *will* be "safe and set on high." The word "whoever" is an all-inclusive word. Know that this word refers to you. Lean completely on the Lord. Place all of your weight on Him.

As we continually draw closer to the Lord, we will be absolutely certain that He lives inside of us. We will be conscious of His presence throughout every day of our lives. We will be absolutely certain that He can and will keep us safe and lift us above the problems we face because our faith in Him is strong and unwavering.

Some of us have a tendency to exaggerate the severity of the problems we face. Our Father does not want us to make this mistake. He wants us to trust Him completely. "Those who trust in, lean on, and confidently hope in the Lord are like Mount Zion, which cannot be moved but abides and stands fast forever" (Psalm 125:1).

The word "Zion" in the Bible originally referred to a hill in Jerusalem that was captured by King David. Mount Zion also is a name that is used in the Bible to refer to heaven. Mount Zion is the heavenly city where God lives. "...you have come to Mount Zion, even to the city of the living God, the heavenly Jerusalem, and to countless multitudes of angels in festal gathering..." (Hebrews 12:22).

Nothing can destroy the holy city where God lives. There is no safer place than this heavenly city. If we place all of our hope, trust and confidence in the Lord, we will be like the immovable and impenetrable Mount Zion.

Whenever we face problems that seem to be overwhelming, we should focus constantly on our Father's magnificent love for us. If we obey our Father's instructions to meditate continually on the truth of His Word, we will not be afraid. Our consciousness of God's love will increase continually. We will be filled with God's peace, strength and power. "...O man greatly beloved, fear not! Peace be to you! Be strong, yes, be strong..." (Daniel 10:19).

Unfortunately, many of God's children do not have deeply rooted faith in their Father. They fail to obey His instructions to come close to Him on a daily basis. Deep spiritual roots only can be developed as a result of many hours spent alone with our precious Lord. "As you have therefore received Christ, [even] Jesus the Lord, [so] walk (regulate your lives and conduct yourselves) in union with and conformity to Him. Have the roots [of your being] firmly and deeply planted [in Him, fixed and founded in Him], being continually built up in Him, becoming increasingly more confirmed and established in the faith, just as you were taught, and abounding and overflowing in it with thanksgiving" (Colossians 2:6-7).

These words that the apostle Paul wrote in his letter to the Colossians tell us that we should do more than receive Jesus Christ as our Savior. We should gratefully make Jesus the Lord of every minute of every hour of every day of our lives. We should constantly draw closer to Him. Our greatest joy should be to live "in union with and conformity to Him."

When we live in union with another person, we are close to that person. Jesus Christ wants each of us to have an extremely close relationship with Him. He wants us to be so close to Him that our ways will conform completely to His ways.

This close relationship with Jesus will cause our faith in Him to be deeply rooted because this faith will be "firmly and deeply planted in Him." Jesus does not want us to have shallow faith in Him. He wants our deep and unwavering faith in Him to be established on a solid foundation that continually is built up as a result of constantly drawing closer to Him.

Jesus wants our faith in Him to become "increasingly more confirmed and established." When we confirm something, we establish it to be true and authentic. Jesus wants us to trust Him so much that our faith in Him will not waver in the face of any circumstance.

Jesus wants our faith in Him to be so strong that we will thank Him and praise Him continually even though we may face seemingly insurmountable problems. Our hearts will sing with joy as we constantly draw closer to Jesus. Spontaneous words of gratitude and thanksgiving will pour out of our mouths constantly.

When the bottom seems to be falling out of our lives, we should wait patiently upon the Lord. "My soul, wait only upon God and silently submit to Him; for my hope and expectation are from Him. He only is my Rock and my Salvation; He is my Defense and my Fortress, I shall not be moved" (Psalm 62:5-6).

We should "silently submit" to the Lord when we face seemingly insurmountable problems. We have learned that our precious Lord wants us to give our problems to Him and leave them with Him, absolutely refusing to take them back. We should place all of our hope and expectation on the Lord. We should fully expect Him to bring us safely through the challenges we face.

The psalmist David said, "He only is my Rock and my Salvation." The word "only" in this passage of Scripture means that we should place all of our trust in the Lord. Our faith in the Lord should be rock-solid and unwavering. He should be our Defense. He should be our Fortress. Our faith in Him should be so strong, so absolute and so unwavering that nothing will be able to deter us.

We should trust God completely to take care of every one of our needs. We should trust Him so much that we will step out in faith into situations that are far above and beyond what we can handle with our limited human abilities. All of our security should come from God. We should trust our Father completely to take care of every one of our needs.

Our Father has provided all of the security we will need. Our security should come from the inside out, not from the outside in. Instead of trusting in worldly sources of security, all of our security should come from God.

When we go through seasons of difficulty in our lives, our mouths should open continually to boldly speak the Word of God. We should not talk about the problems we face except when we pray to God with faith to answer a specific prayer request. Instead, we should boldly and repeatedly speak promises from the Word of God because we are absolutely certain that our Father is faithful to His promises. We should personalize these promises.

Our faith in God will increase steadily and we continually speak His promises with bold and confident faith in Him. If we want our faith in God to increase, our ears need to *hear* the Word of God continually. "…faith comes by hearing [what is told], and what is heard comes by the preaching [of the message that came from the lips] of Christ (the Messiah Himself)" (Romans 10:17).

Most Christians experience an increase in their faith in God when they hear an anointed speaker boldly speaking words of faith that are solidly anchored upon the Word of God. We cannot receive faith in God from external sources throughout every day of our lives. Our faith in God will increase significantly when *our ears continually hear our mouths* speaking the Word of God as we obey our Father's instructions to habitually meditate throughout the day and night on His Word.

We can be certain that God's promises will be manifested in our lives if we keep on speaking the Word of God continually with unwavering faith in God over a period of time. Speaking the Word of God continually ultimately will break any hold that Satan's demons try to get on us. Our words of faith will prevail. "…the mouth of the upright shall deliver them…" (Proverbs 12:6).

When we face a crisis situation, the worst thing we can do is to panic. The words that continually come out of our mouths should clearly indicate our total, complete and absolute trust in Almighty God. We should be like the psalmist who said, "I believed (trusted in, relied on, and clung to my God), and therefore have I spoken…" (Psalm 116:10).

When we face a crisis situation, we release the power of God by continually speaking words of faith from our innermost being. These words of faith are the same spirit of faith that the human authors of the Bible received from God. The apostle Paul said,

"…we have the same spirit of faith as he had who wrote, I have believed, and therefore have I spoken…" (II Corinthians 4:13).

Paul was referring to the words from the psalmist that we just read in Psalm 116:10. Paul knew that he was experiencing the same spirit of faith that the psalmist experienced many years before when he spoke of his faith in God.

The Word of God is filled with the immense power of Almighty God. If our hearts are filled with the Word of God, we will speak God's Word faithfully. We will release the enormous power of God when our mouths continually speak His Word faithfully. "…he who has My word, let him speak My word faithfully…Is not My word like fire [that consumes all that cannot endure the test]? says the Lord, and like a hammer that breaks in pieces the rock [of most stubborn resistance]?" (Jeremiah 23:28-29).

The Word of God is so powerful that it is like a raging fire that consumes everything in its path. The Word of God is so powerful that it is like a large hammer that is able to break a rock into small pieces. The problems we face cannot stand up against a constant outpouring of God's Word being faithfully released by our mouths because our hearts have been filled to overflowing with the supernatural power of the Word of God.

Many Christians have little or no comprehension of the enormous spiritual power of the words they speak. If we meditate continually on the Word of God, we will boldly speak the promises of God that we are meditating upon. As this process continues over a period of time, we will constantly release the wonderful supernatural power of God with our mouths.

Our faith in God will steadily increase as this process continues over a period of weeks, months and years. Our peace from

God will not be shaken. We will experience God's perfect peace because we are obeying our Father's instruction to keep our minds stayed on Him and to commit ourselves totally to Him as we place all of our hope and confidence in Him.

Peace is a choice. We constantly choose whether we will live in the perfect peace our Father has provided for us or whether we will allow the circumstances in our lives to rob us of this peace. Our Father has made provision for each of His children to enjoy perfect, lasting and permanent peace. He has told us exactly what He wants us to do to enjoy this perfect peace. The perfect peace of God will be with us always if we obey these instructions from God throughout every day of our lives.

Now that we have carefully studied God's perfect peace, we are ready to learn additional facts about the peace of God. We will look into the Bible to see what our Father has instructed us to do to experience His peace that is *so great and so magnificent that it completely surpasses the limitations of our human understanding.*

Chapter 38

The Peace of God Surpasses
Human Understanding

If we truly desire to receive God's peace which is so wonderful that it surpasses the limits of our human understanding, we should obey the following specific instructions from God. "Do not fret or have any anxiety about anything, but in every circumstance and in everything, by prayer and petition (definite requests), with thanksgiving, continue to make your wants known to God. And God's peace [shall be yours, that tranquil state of a soul assured of its salvation through Christ, and so fearing nothing from God and being content with its earthly lot of whatever sort that is, that peace] which transcends all understanding shall garrison and mount guard over your hearts and minds in Christ Jesus" (Philippians 4:6-7).

This passage of Scripture is *so meaningful* that we will devote the next two chapters to examining the spiritual principles contained in this one passage of Scripture. Our Father has given each of His beloved children the opportunity to be calm, quiet, peaceful and confident in the face of a crisis situation even though we cannot logically explain why we are able to react to difficult circumstances in this way.

The peace of God is indescribable and immeasurable. God's wonderful peace will enable us to face extremely difficult problems with quiet confidence in Him even when the circumstances we face are so severe that most people would panic. We may not be able to explain this peace, but we will know this peace when we experience it.

We only need to experience God's supernatural peace one time to know it is real. We then should have a deep and sincere desire to learn exactly what our Father has instructed us to do so that we can continue to receive His wonderful peace throughout the remainder of our lives.

You may have seen an example of God's peace that surpasses human understanding as you have observed Christians who were able to remain calm, quiet and confident when they faced circumstances that would have driven most people to despair. These Christians have spent so much time developing a close personal relationship with the Lord and continually filling their minds and their hearts with His Word that they will not be worried or anxious at any time regardless of the circumstances they face.

Philippians 4:7 begins by telling us that we should not fret or be anxious about *anything*. We are instructed to bring *everything* to God in prayer. Instead of worrying, we should make "definite requests" to God.

We then are instructed to "continue to make our wants known to God." We should pray to God with faith every time we are tempted to worry. Why would we ever worry when we can pray?

If we obey these instructions, we are told that God's peace will be ours. *Why* would any thinking person ever miss out on the opportunity to receive God's supernatural peace when our Father's instructions are so clear and so obvious? He simply tells us to pray continually instead of worrying.

All Christians are assured of their eternal salvation if they believe in the their hearts and confess with their mouths that Jesus Christ has paid the full price for their sins. We are told that we also can be content with whatever we experience here on earth because God's peace which is so great that it "transcends all understanding" will "garrison and mount guard over our hearts and minds in Christ Jesus."

The word "garrison" is a military word that refers to a group of soldiers who are stationed in a fortified place. The words "mount guard" in this context refer to climbing up to an elevated position that will provide maximum protection. God's peace is so great that it is able to completely protect our minds and our hearts regardless of the severity of the circumstances we face.

Many Christians do not experience God's wonderful peace because they worry instead of praying to God. Their failure to ask God for help often blocks them from receiving the help their loving Father has provided for them. "…You do not have, because you do not ask …" (James 4:2).

We should pray to God continually from a pure and humble heart. Our Father will answer our prayers when we pray with humble, sincere, unwavering and persevering faith in Him. Our Father is absolutely delighted when His beloved children come to Him in prayer. "…the prayer of the upright is His delight!" (Proverbs 15:8).

Prayer is *not* coming to God with a list of personal desires such as little children have on a list they give to Santa Claus. Our prayers should be based upon the will of God. We can be absolutely certain that our Father hears *all* of our prayers when we pray according to His will for our lives. "...this is the confidence (the assurance, the privilege of boldness) which we have in Him: [we are sure] that if we ask anything (make any request) according to His will (in agreement with His own plan), He listens to and hears us" (I John 5:14).

Please check each of your prayer requests against this passage of Scripture. Ask yourself, "Is my request part of God's will for my life? Does this prayer request line up with the Word of God?"

We can be absolutely certain that God will answer *all* prayers of persevering faith that are made according to His will. "And if (since) we [positively] know that He listens to us in whatever we ask, we also know [with settled and absolute knowledge] that we have [granted us as our present possessions] the requests made of Him" (I John 5:15).

The amplification of this passage of Scripture includes the words "our present possessions." These words imply that God immediately answers our prayers of faith. I believe that God answers our prayers of faith immediately in the spiritual realm. However, sometimes we must persevere with unwavering faith for a period of time before we see God's plan for this situation come to pass in the natural realm.

The peace of God that surpasses human understanding only can be experienced by Christians who have a strong prayer life. Philippians 4:6 tells us to continually pray to God if we want to experience His peace that surpasses human understanding. Our Father wants us to pray to Him throughout every day of our lives. "Be unceasing in prayer [praying perseveringly]..." (I Thessalonians 5:17).

When we pray to God, we shouldn't pray "mechanical prayers" where we just "mouth words" to God that do not come from our hearts. Our prayers should be sincere and heartfelt. The Pharisees often prayed the same prayer over and over mechanically. They did not pray from hearts that were filled to overflowing with faith in God. Jesus Christ told the Pharisees, "…when you pray, do not heap up phrases (multiply words, repeating the same ones over and over)…" (Matthew 6:7).

Our Father wants us to pray to Him from hearts that are filled with fervent passion. He wants us to be absolutely certain that our fervent prayers will release His supernatural power. "…The earnest (heartfelt, continued) prayer of a righteous man makes tremendous power available [dynamic in its working]" (James 5:16).

Please go back and meditate carefully on this passage of Scripture. Know that your Father wants you to pray earnestly and continually from your heart. When we pray earnestly, we are very intent. We are extremely focused as we pray.

We should treasure the privilege of praying to God that Jesus Christ provided for us through His sacrifice on the Cross. Jesus made everyone who asked Him to be their Savior righteous before God and able to approach the throne of God.

If we can even begin to comprehend the immense power that will be released when we pray in this way, we will pray continually from early in the morning until late at night. This passage of Scripture tells us that *the dynamic power of Almighty God* will be released when we pray continually from hearts that are filled with faith in God. Jesus said, "…whatever you ask for in prayer, believe (trust and be confident) that it is granted to you, and you will [get it]" (Mark 11:24).

We actually are able to approach the throne of God when we pray. We should understand that prayer is our direct line to God. We shouldn't be worried before we pray. We shouldn't be worried while we pray. We shouldn't be worried after we pray.

People who worry while they pray usually negate their prayers. The doubt and unbelief that causes us to worry while we pray often blocks us from receiving the answers to our prayers that our Father has provided for us.

We will *not* pray doubting and hesitant prayers *if* we have obeyed our Father's instructions to constantly fill our minds and our hearts with His Word. We *will* pray prayers of faith when we trust God completely.

We should try to find specific promises in the Word of God that apply to the circumstances we face. The fifteen Christian books and the ten sets of Scripture cards we have written are filled with thousands of these promises. The holy Scriptures are filled with many additional promises from God that apply to specific needs in our lives.

The Word of God also is filled with many all-inclusive promises that we can stand upon with unwavering faith whenever we pray. I believe we should pray the Word of God when we pray. We also must be certain that we do the part of each conditional promise that God requires us to do.

Our Father honors the prayers of His beloved children who absolutely refuse to be worried and anxious about anything as they pray fervently from their hearts with absolute faith that their Father will answer their prayers. Our Father is looking for simple childlike trust when we pray. Many little children here on earth trust their parents completely. How much more can we trust our heavenly Father?

When we pray, we should understand the importance of praying to God with absolute faith in the mighty power of the name of Jesus Christ. When we pray to God with faith in the name of Jesus Christ we are praying to Him in "…the name that is above every name, that in (at) the name of Jesus every knee should (must) bow, in heaven and on earth and under the earth, and every tongue [frankly and openly] confess and acknowledge that Jesus Christ is Lord, to the glory of God the Father" (Philippians 2:9 -11).

We have just seen that the day will come when everyone in heaven, on the earth and under the earth will bow before His name. Jesus said, "…I assure you, most solemnly I tell you, that My Father will grant you whatever you ask in My name [as presenting all that I AM]" (John 16:23).

I read an article about an evangelist from India the day before I was writing the current draft of this chapter. The article said that this evangelist, Su John, survived the attack by terrorists on the World Trade Center in New York City on September 11, 2001.

Su John was on the eighty-first floor of the north tower after it was struck by a plane. The impact was so close that the wing of the plane came into the floor where Su John was located. As he descended, he prayed continually.

When Su John reached ground level, he heard a tremendous noise. The building began to collapse. A shower of concrete and steel fell upon him and the people who were next to him.

Su John prayed for the blood of Jesus Christ to cover him. He cried out the name of Jesus Christ. He told the people around him who did not know Jesus to call out His name. These people did not comply. They died. Su John lived. He said, "It wasn't my time to go."

When we come to God with absolute faith in the mighty and powerful name of Jesus Christ, I believe our prayers are the same to God as they would be if Jesus Himself prayed to Him. Jesus actually is approaching God when we pray with faith in His name because Jesus intercedes for us when we pray with faith. "…He is always living to make petition to God and intercede with Him and intervene for them" (Hebrews 7:25).

Please highlight or underline the word "always" in this passage of Scripture. When we pray to God with faith in the name of Jesus Christ, we can be certain that Jesus *always* petitions God on our behalf. We can be certain that Jesus is interceding and intervening for us. We must not miss out on the privilege we have been given to pray continually with deep faith in the mighty power of the name of Jesus Christ.

In this chapter we have carefully examined the peace of God that passes all understanding. We have learned many specific facts about praying effectively to God. There are two key words in Philippians 4:6 that we have not yet covered. These words are "with thanksgiving." These two words are so important that we will devote the next chapter to a careful study of being thankful to God and thanking our Father continually when we pray.

Chapter 39

Thank the Lord and Praise Him

We have seen that God often uses repetition for purpose of emphasis. The following passage of Scripture shows us that our Father definitely wants us to thank Him. "O give thanks to the Lord, for He is good; for His mercy and loving-kindness endure forever. O give thanks to the God of gods, for His mercy and loving-kindness endure forever. O give thanks to the Lord of lords, for His mercy and loving-kindness endure forever…" (Psalm 136:1-3).

We are so blessed that our Father has given us His mercy, His love and His kindness forever. We have not done anything to earn these wonderful blessings. We should thank our Father again and again and again for all He has done for us. Unfortunately, some Christians seldom, if ever, thank their Father even though we all have countless reasons to be thankful.

On one occasion during His earthly ministry, Jesus healed ten lepers. Only one of these men returned to thank Jesus for being healed from this horrible condition. "Then Jesus asked, Were not [all] ten cleansed? Where are the nine? Was there no one found to return and to recognize and give thanks and praise to God except this alien?" (Luke 17:17-18).

We should not make the mistake these nine men made. We should thank the Lord continually. All Christians should have a constant attitude of gratitude. If we can even begin to comprehend all that the Lord has done for us, our mouths will open continually throughout every day to thank the Lord constantly.

We saw in Philippians 4:6 that we should thank God when we pray. Thanking God when we pray should not be some contrived action on our part because we are trying to follow a "formula" to get God to answer our prayers. Words of praise and thanksgiving should pour out of our mouths spontaneously.

Thanking God when we pray should merely be part of a continual flow of thanksgiving that comes from our mouths because of our deep and continuing gratitude to our loving and gracious Father and His Son, Jesus Christ. God has given us innumerable blessings that we have not earned and do not deserve.

All Christians have many reasons to be grateful to God. Above all else, we should thank our Father continually for making the greatest sacrifice that could be made by sending His beloved Son to earth to pay the full price for all of our sins. We should thank Jesus continually for being our substitute and paying the ultimate price for us that we could not possibly have paid for ourselves. "…thanks be to God for His Gift, [precious] beyond telling [His indescribable, inexpressible, free Gift]!" (II Corinthians 9:15).

The gift of Jesus Christ is so "precious, indescribable and inexpressible" that we cannot even begin to put into words how wonderful this gift is. We should speak from our hearts constantly to say again and again and again, "Thank You, Jesus. Thank You, Jesus. Thank You, Jesus. Thank You, Jesus. Thank You, Jesus. Thank You, Jesus. Thank You, Jesus."

We will thank Jesus continually if we can even begin to grasp what He did for us when He came down from heaven to actually *become sin* for us and to die a horrible death for us on a cross at Calvary. The magnitude of what Jesus did when He left the glory of heaven to come down to earth to pay the price for our sins is indescribable.

We must understand that we are absolutely nothing without Jesus Christ (see John 15:5) and that we can do all things through Jesus Christ (see Philippians 4:13). We owe everything we are, everything we have and everything we ever hope to be to our Lord Jesus Christ.

Instead of being concerned about the problems we face, we should focus continually on the many blessings God has provided for us. Some of us take too many blessings for granted. We always should express our gratitude that we will live eternally in the glory of heaven. We should thank our Father constantly for His Word which is filled with thousands of His promises to us and with thousands of specific instructions telling us how He wants us to live our lives.

We should thank God constantly for the Holy Spirit Who lives in our hearts. The Holy Spirit will comfort us and help us continually if we will yield control of our lives to Him because we trust Him completely.

We should be very grateful for the wonderful opportunity we have been given to approach the throne of God whenever we pray. We should be very grateful that we have been given the glorious privilege to enter into and remain in God's presence.

We should be very grateful for the members of our families – our wives or husbands, our children, our grandchildren, our parents and other relatives. We should be very grateful for our Christian brothers and sisters and for our friends.

We should thank God for the church we attend. We should thank Him continually for whatever ministry He has given to us. We should thank Him constantly for His wonderful anointing and the opportunity He has given us to serve.

If we have health needs, we should thank God for the healing He has provided for us through Jesus Christ. We should thank Him that we can take responsibility for our health to provide conditions for our bodies to heal themselves.

We should thank God continually for the abundance of fresh fruit and vegetables He created for us to enjoy. We should thank Him for fresh air, for pure water and for any exercise we are able to do.

If we live in a free country, we should thank God for this freedom. We should pray continually for people who do not live in free countries. We should thank God every day for the leaders of our country. We should pray for these leaders as well as all other world leaders.

We should thank God for the vocational skills He has given us and the opportunity we have been given to earn an income to provide for the needs of our families. We should be very grateful for the homes we live in, the automobiles we drive and the food we eat. We should be grateful for the recreation God has made available to us so that we can rest from our labors (see Mark 6:30-32).

The Bible teaches us that we should even thank God and rejoice when we face adversity because of the opportunity we have been given to grow and mature as a result of the problems we go through (see James 1:2-4). We should thank God that He is with us and that He is willing to help us when we are in trouble (see Psalm 46:1).

This brief list could go on and on. One of the best things any of us can do is to write down our blessings and to keep adding to this list. Pray and ask the Lord to reveal your blessings to you. Keep your constantly expanding list of blessings in a place where it is readily accessible. Get out your list of blessings from the Lord and focus on them whenever you are tempted to be worried, fearful or discouraged.

Have you ever known a continually grateful and thankful person who was an unhappy person? Happiness and gratitude go together. Have you ever known an ungrateful person who was truly happy? Unhappiness and ingratitude go together.

Our Father promises wonderful blessings to His children who constantly thank Him. "Offer to God the sacrifice of thanksgiving, and pay your vows to the Most High, and call on Me in the day of trouble; I will deliver you, and you shall honor and glorify Me" (Psalm 50:14-15).

This passage of Scripture tells us that thanking God sometimes is a sacrifice. We actually give God an offering when we thank Him. We offer a special sacrifice of praise and thanksgiving when we thank God when we are hurting. The peace of God will fill our hearts when we consistently make this obedient sacrifice with absolute faith in God.

The holy Scriptures contain marvelous spiritual keys that unlock the once-hidden mysteries of God. Constant offerings of praise and thanksgiving are a key to dwelling in the presence of God. A heart that is constantly grateful to God will experience God's wonderful peace and joy.

This passage of Scripture goes on to tell us that we should call on God when we are in trouble. Our Father promises to deliver us from trouble. We should give all honor and glory to Him.

Instead of thanking God, some of us do just the opposite. We complain about the problems we face. Our Father does *not* want to hear us grumbling and complaining when we face difficult problems. "...the people grumbled and deplored their hardships, which was evil in the ears of the Lord..." (Numbers 11:1).

Our Father wants us to grow and mature to the point at which we are able to deal with the circumstances in our lives without grumbling and complaining. We must understand that we actually are complaining against God when we complain. "Do all things without grumbling and faultfinding and complaining [against God]..." (Philippians 2:14).

I have found that the Holy Spirit often nudges me if I complain. When I realize that I have complained, I immediately go to God. I admit my sin of complaining and I ask my Father to forgive me.

The Bible gives us another illustration of complaining when the Israelites complained even though God had provided them with the food they needed. "...when the Lord gives you in the evening flesh to eat and in the morning bread to the full, because the Lord has heard your grumblings which you murmur against Him; what are we? Your murmurings are not against us, but against the Lord" (Exodus 16:8).

There is no question that we are complaining against the Lord whenever we complain. We cannot in any way justify complaining with all of the blessings our Father has provided for us that we have not earned and do not deserve.

Words of complaint actually are words of doubt and unbelief. We must understand that words of complaint that come out of our mouths often block us from receiving the help our Father wants to give us and would give us if we prayed with faith and thanked Him when we prayed instead of complaining.

When we face difficult problems, we can be certain that our Father is able to make every problem work out as a part of His plan for our lives. "We are assured and know that [God being a partner in their labor] all things work together and are [fitting into a plan] for good to and for those who love God and are called according to [His] design and purpose" (Romans 8:28).

Do you love God? Do you seek His will for your life? Do you want to be His partner in everything you do? Any Christian who meets these qualifications can be absolutely assured that God in His wisdom can and will cause everything to work together to fit into His plan for good.

We never should look at the problems we face without looking beyond these problems. Our Father wants us to have absolute faith that He can and will solve the problems we face if we know what His Word says He will do and if we have absolute faith that He always will do exactly what He has planned and promised to do.

Continual thanksgiving should be a way of life for every child of God. We should thank our Father in good times. We should thank Him in bad times. Thanking God at all times is not easy, normal or natural to us. We must learn to thank God regardless of the circumstances we face.

Our Father has instructed us to thank Him in the midst of *every* circumstance. "Thank [God] in everything [no matter what the circumstances may be, be thankful and give thanks], for this is the will of God for you [who are] in Christ Jesus [the Revealer and Mediator of that will]" (I Thessalonians 5:18).

Please highlight or underline the words "in everything" in this passage of Scripture. We are not always thanking God *for* what has happened to us. We thank Him because we have absolute trust that He will bring us safely through whatever problems we face (see Isaiah 43:2).

Our Father wants us to turn away from the limitations of our human understanding. He wants us to react to the circumstances in our lives based upon the instructions He has given us in His marvelous Book of Instructions, the holy Bible. We have clearly seen in this chapter that we should do something that does not make sense to most people. We should thank God and keep on thanking Him regardless of the circumstances in our lives.

We saw in Philippians 4:6-7 that, instead of worrying, we are instructed by God to pray, thanking Him continually, so that we will be able to receive His magnificent supernatural peace that surpasses the limitations of human understanding. We now are ready to go on to Philippians 4:8 to learn what our Father has instructed us to think about. "For the rest, brethren, whatever is true, whatever is worthy of reverence and is honorable and seemly, whatever is just, whatever is pure, whatever is lovely and lovable, whatever is kind and winsome and gracious, if there is any virtue and excellence, if there is anything worthy of praise, think on and weigh and take account of these things [fix your minds on them]" (Philippians 4:8).

Our Father does not want us to allow worried and anxious thoughts to enter our minds. Right after we are told about His peace that passes all understanding, He tells us where our thoughts should rest. We have seen again and again that our Father wants us to fix our minds on Him instead of dwelling upon the problems we face.

The various things we are instructed to fix our minds on in Philippians 4:8 do not describe the problems of life. These words describe the character of Jesus Christ. We should focus on Jesus and thank Him, regardless of the circumstances in our lives.

All Christians would like to receive the peace of God that is so great that it surpasses human understanding. Only a small percentage of Christians actually know what the Word of God tells them to do in order to receive this peace. An even smaller percentage of Christians actually *do* what God has told them to do in Philippians 4:6-8. We cannot expect to reap the harvest of God's peace that surpasses human understanding unless we are willing to sow the seeds our loving Father has instructed us to sow.

You have been given complete scriptural instructions in the past two chapters pertaining to God's peace that surpasses human understanding. If you sincerely desire to experience this peace, I encourage you to go back to carefully study and meditate on the passages of Scripture in these chapters.

Chapter 40

Receive Peace from the Holy Spirit

We already have learned a great deal about receiving God's peace. We now are ready to learn about receiving the peace of God from yielding to the Holy Spirit. "…the fruit of the [Holy] Spirit [the work which His presence within accomplishes] is love, joy (gladness), **peace**, patience (an even temper, forbearance), kindness, goodness (benevolence), faithfulness, gentleness (meekness, humility), self-control (self-restraint, continence)…" (Galatians 5:22-23).

This passage of Scripture describes all of the fruit of the Holy Spirit. We will see this fruit produced in us and through us *if* we will give up our God-given right to do what we want to do to allow the Holy Spirit to empower our lives.

At this time we will focus our study only on the fruit of peace which we have indicated by bold print. Some Christians allow the problems they face to block themselves from receiving the peace of the Holy Spirit that resides in their hearts. We must not allow worry and anxiety to rob us of the peace of God that is available to us if we will learn to yield to the Holy Spirit.

We can clearly see whether we are in control of our lives or whether we are yielding to the Holy Spirit by the way we react to the problems we face. When we face a severe crisis, we often will be worried and anxious if we are in control of our lives. If we truly have yielded to the Holy Spirit, we will be calm, quiet and confident in the face of adversity.

The peace of the Holy Spirit can be compared to the depth of an ocean in the midst of a severe storm. Although the winds at the surface of the ocean may be strong and the waves may be high, the ocean is very calm and still several feet below the surface. The Holy Spirit is calm and still regardless of the circumstances in our lives. He always is at peace. "...the mind of the [Holy] Spirit is life and [soul] peace [both now and forever]" (Romans 8:6).

The supernatural peace of the Holy Spirit lives inside of every Christian. This wonderful peace lives in *your* heart if you have received Jesus Christ as your Savior. Many Christians need to learn how to yield to the wonderful peace of the Holy Spirit.

We must understand that the peace of God does not come from any external source. The peace of God comes from the inside out, not from the outside in. Some of us will experience a great deal of misery and frustration that could have been avoided if we had yielded to the Holy Spirit.

There are no problems that the Holy Spirit cannot solve. He is never alarmed by any problems we face, no matter how difficult these problems might seem to us. We must not block ourselves from receiving His help because of our doubt and unbelief.

The peace and joy of the Holy Spirit only will be manifested in us and through us if we yield to Him. "...the kingdom of God is not a matter of [getting the] food and drink [one likes], but instead it is righteousness (that state which makes a person acceptable to God) and [heart] peace and joy in the Holy Spirit" (Romans 14:17).

We should not look for peace from the same sources where unbelievers search for peace. Many unbelievers pursue pleasure because they believe they will experience peace from this pleasure. They may experience temporary peace, but they cannot experience lasting peace if they constantly pursue pleasure from the food and drinks they like or from other external sources of pleasure. God gave us various things on earth to enjoy, but our focus always should be on Him.

This passage of Scripture tells us that the kingdom of God is the righteousness we receive when we ask Jesus Christ to be our Savior. The shed blood of Jesus Christ enables us to be children of God who can experience the fruit of righteousness through the presence and power of the Holy Spirit. We will experience the fruit of "heart peace and joy in the Holy Spirit" if we yield to the Holy Spirit and allow Him to live in us and through us.

The peace of the Holy Spirit does not come from entertainment, parties, food, drink and a constant search for pleasure. We only will experience the peace of the Holy Spirit if we are humble, submissive and trusting. "…the meek [in the end] shall inherit the earth and shall delight themselves in the abundance of peace" (Psalm 37:11).

Sometimes unbelievers seem to experience peace. They ultimately will come to the point at which their search for peace from external sources will fail. We will experience an "abundance of peace" from the Holy Spirit if we gladly yield to Him because we are meek, humble and trusting.

Jesus Christ gave His disciples instruction on the Holy Spirit just before He was crucified. The instructions that Jesus gave to

His disciples at that time apply to all Christians today. At the Last Supper Jesus began to prepare His disciples for what their lives would be like after He ascended into heaven. Jesus said, "...I will ask the Father, and He will give you another Comforter (Counselor, Helper, Intercessor, Advocate, Strengthener, and Standby), that He may remain with you forever..." (John 14:16).

Jesus told His disciples that He no longer would be with them in the flesh after He ascended into heaven. He told them that God would provide "another Comforter" for them even though He no longer would be there to comfort them and help them. This Comforter is the Holy Spirit. The amplification of this passage of Scripture tells us many things that the Holy Spirit will do to help us.

The Holy Spirit is our Counselor. If we yield control of our lives to Him, He will give us counsel when we need advice. We must understand that we are not alone. Wisdom and guidance from the Holy Spirit are available to each of us throughout every hour of every day of our lives.

The Holy Spirit is our Helper. If we yield to Him, He will help us with the problems we face. He wants us to have absolute faith that He will help us whenever we need help.

The Holy Spirit is our Intercessor. He represents each of us to Almighty God. He always is on our side. He intercedes for us when we pray to God.

The Holy Spirit is our Advocate. An advocate is someone who pleads for another person. A lawyer is an example of an advocate. The Holy Spirit pleads to God on our behalf.

The Holy Spirit will strengthen us when we are weak. His strength, power and ability are available to every one of God's children who learn to live in the Spirit, trusting completely in Him.

The Holy Spirit is our Standby. He is with every believer throughout every minute of every hour of every day of our lives. He wants us to know that He is standing by no matter what problems we face.

As believers in Jesus Christ, we have the Holy Spirit living inside of us. He is our silent partner Who will help us twenty-four hours a day. Jesus referred to the Holy Spirit as "…the Spirit of Truth, Whom the world cannot receive (welcome, take to its heart), because it does not see Him or know and recognize Him. But you know and recognize Him, for He lives with you [constantly] and will be in you" (John 14:17).

Our Father does not want us to live the way unbelievers live. They have not recognized Jesus Christ as their Savior. They have not received the Holy Spirit. We pray that they will. Unfortunately, many Christians know little or nothing about the Holy Spirit.

We cannot see the Holy Spirit with our human eyesight or hear His voice the way we hear other voices speaking to us externally. However, Jesus told us that we can "know and recognize" the Holy Spirit Who is "with us constantly." We will become increasingly aware of the presence of the Holy Spirit as we grow and mature as Christians and continually draw closer to the Lord. We will trust the Holy Spirit more and more to do in us and through us what we know we cannot do apart from God.

The disciples of Jesus Christ could not understand how they could benefit if Jesus left them. Jesus said, "…I am telling you nothing but the truth when I say it is profitable (good, expedient, advantageous) for you that I go away. Because if I do not go away, the Comforter (Counselor, Helper, Advocate, Intercessor, Strengthener, Standby) will not come to you [into close fellowship with you]; but if I go away, I will send Him to you [to be in close fellowship with you]" (John 16:7).

Christians today are able to receive the same blessings from the Holy Spirit that Jesus promised to His disciples many years ago. We should have a constant awareness of the indwelling presence of the Holy Spirit. We should enjoy a close relationship with the Holy Spirit. We should turn to the Holy Spirit constantly with absolute trust that He can and will help us.

Many Christians have a distant relationship at best with the Holy Spirit. They may acknowledge His indwelling presence with their lips and believe in Him with their minds, but we must do more. We should know that the Holy Spirit will guide us into the entire truth of God. Jesus said, "…when He, the Spirit of Truth (the Truth-giving Spirit) comes, He will guide you into all the Truth (the whole full truth)…" (John 16:13).

I believe that one of the primary keys to receiving assistance from the Holy Spirit is to obey our Father's instructions to constantly fill our minds and our hearts with His Word. Jesus told us that the Word of God is the Truth. He said, "…Your Word is Truth" (John 17:17).

We will be able to "tune in" to the Spirit of Truth if we obey our Father's instructions to renew our minds each day in His Word and to meditate constantly on His Word. I often have said that the Holy Spirit speaks to us over "spiritual radio station WORD." We are able to hear a specific radio station when we turn to the proper AM or FM frequency. We are able to hear the Holy Spirit if we "tune in" to Him through minds and hearts that are filled to overflowing with the Word of God.

In this chapter we have established a foundation for the peace we will receive if we yield to the Holy Spirit Who lives in us instead of attempting to control our lives with our fleshly nature. In subsequent chapters we will learn much more about the Holy Spirit and how to live in close relationship with Him.

Chapter 41

Our Father Has Given the Holy Spirit to Us

In the last chapter we learned about peace being produced in our lives as a fruit of the Holy Spirit. In this chapter we will look into the Word of God for additional instruction pertaining to the Holy Spirit. Our Father loves us so much that He has made provision for each of His children to receive constant help and guidance from the Holy Spirit. "…because you [really] are [His] sons, God has sent the [Holy] Spirit of His Son into our hearts, crying, Abba (Father)! Father!" (Galatians 4:6).

The Holy Spirit is the third person of the holy trinity - Father, Son and Holy Spirit. He has been sent to us to let us know that Almighty God really is our loving Father. We become children of God when we ask Jesus Christ to be our Savior. Our Father has sent the Holy Spirit to live in our hearts because we are His children. The Greek word "Abba" that is used in this passage of Scripture is similar to the word "Daddy" that children use today

We should yearn from the depths of our hearts to have a close and intimate relationship with our loving Father. He has given us the opportunity to receive the Holy Spirit so that the Holy Spirit can reveal to us many of the gifts and blessings our Father has provided for each His beloved children. "…we have not received the spirit [that belongs to] the world, but the [Holy] Spirit Who is from God, [given to us] that we might realize and comprehend and appreciate the gifts [of divine favor and blessing so freely and lavishly] bestowed on us by God" (I Corinthians 2:12).

We will turn away from the things of the world when we constantly turn to the Holy Spirit Who makes His permanent residence in the hearts of each of God's children. "…God's Spirit has His permanent dwelling in you [to be at home in you, collectively as a church and also individually]…" (I Corinthians 3:16).

Our Father wants each of His children to have a continual awareness of the indwelling presence of the Holy Spirit. "Do you not know that your body is the temple (the very sanctuary) of the Holy Spirit Who lives within you, Whom you have received [as a Gift] from God?…" (I Corinthians 6:19).

We make a big mistake if we fail to receive the fullness of the marvelous gift of the Holy Spirit Who lives inside of every child of God. Nothing any of us can possess or pursue here on earth can even remotely approach the tremendous value of the Holy Spirit. "…to each one is given the manifestation of the [Holy] Spirit [the evidence, the spiritual illumination of the Spirit] for good and profit" (I Corinthians 12:7).

Please highlight or underline the words "each one" in this passage of Scripture. If you have trusted Jesus Christ for your eternal salvation, you can be certain that these words refer to *you*. Your loving Father has given you the manifestation of the Holy Spirit "for good and profit." Be determined that you will not fail to receive the wonderful blessings of the Holy Spirit that have been made available to you.

Some Christians are completely unaware of the presence of the Holy Spirit Who lives in their hearts. Other Christians look at the Holy Spirit as an "it." They do not look at Him as a "He." The Holy Spirit is a real person. Every aspect of our lives should revolve around our constant awareness of the magnificence of His indwelling presence.

Some Christians seldom, if ever, speak of the indwelling presence of the Holy Spirit. Their words and their actions do not indicate that they are absolutely certain that the Holy Spirit Who lives in their hearts is much greater and much more powerful than any problem they will face.

Our Father wants us to always be aware of the Holy Spirit Who lives in our hearts. Every day of our lives brings us fresh new opportunities to yield to the Holy Spirit so that His peace and all of the other fruit of the Holy Spirit will continue to grow deep down inside of us.

Satan tries to engulf us in his darkness. The Holy Spirit is our light in the midst of darkness. Nothing in the world can quench the light of the Holy Spirit Who is with us twenty-four hours a day. The Holy Spirit is with us when we are awake. He is with us when we are asleep. He is with us when are on the mountaintops of the good times in our lives. He is with us when we are in the valleys of difficult seasons in our lives.

The Holy Spirit lives inside of us to give us a preview of the glorious lives we will live in heaven. "In Him you also who have heard the Word of Truth, the glad tidings (Gospel) of your salvation, and have believed in and adhered to and relied on Him, were stamped with the seal of the long-promised Holy Spirit. That [Spirit] is the guarantee of our inheritance [the firstfruits, the pledge and foretaste, the down payment on our heritage], in anticipation of its full redemption and our acquiring [complete] possession of it - to the praise of His glory" (Ephesians 1:13-14).

This passage of Scripture tells us that the Holy Spirit "is the guarantee of our inheritance." He gives us a "foretaste" of heaven. Everything the Holy Spirit does is related to our salvation in Christ Jesus. The Holy Spirit equips us to carry out our Father's plan and purpose. We are set apart from the world, redeemed, forgiven and empowered by the Holy Spirit to be living vessels for the glory of God.

We have learned that our Father has instructed us to renew our minds in His Word each day and to habitually meditate on His Word throughout the day and night. The Holy Spirit often will remind us of the Scripture that lives in our hearts. You may be speaking and suddenly hear the Word of God coming out of your mouth.

The Holy Spirit gives us the Scripture we need to bless others. This Scripture speaks to the hearts of people who are listening to us. Our part is to fill our hearts with the Word of God so that the Holy Spirit can do His part with the Word of God that lives in our hearts. The more of God's Word that lives in our hearts, the more gloriously the Holy Spirit can bring the Word of God to our remembrance and cause it to bring life to those who hear it.

The Holy Spirit came to us the moment we became a child of God through receiving His Son Jesus Christ as our Savior, our Messiah. The Holy Spirit is so wonderful. He does so many things for us. We are so blessed to have Him reside inside of us. We can know the heart of our Father through the Holy

Spirit. We can know the Son of God through the Holy Spirit. The Holy Spirit is the Breath of Life.

Jesus Christ gave His disciples additional information on the Holy Spirit when He revealed Himself to His disciples after He was raised from the dead. "Then on that first day of the week, when it was evening, though the disciples were behind closed doors for fear of the Jews, Jesus came and stood among them and said, Peace to you! So saying, He showed them His hands and His side. And when the disciples saw the Lord, they were filled with joy (delight, exultation, ecstasy, rapture)" (John 20:19-20).

Stop and think how you would feel if you were a disciple of Jesus Christ and the risen Christ suddenly appeared to you and allowed you to look at the wounds in His hands and His side. The disciples were overwhelmed. They were "filled with joy, delight, exultation, ecstasy, rapture." We can be filled with this same joy and ecstasy when we are able to enter into the presence of the Lord.

At that moment Jesus told His disciples to receive the Holy Spirit. "Then Jesus said to them again, Peace to you! [Just] as the Father has sent Me forth, so I am sending you. And having said this, He breathed on them and said to them, Receive (admit) the Holy Spirit!" (John 20:21-22).

We know that there are different interpretations of the work of the Holy Spirit. We know that there is agreement that the Holy Spirit enters a believer upon receiving Jesus Christ as Savior and Lord. There is agreement that every one must live in a state of being filled with the Holy Spirit. We invite all believers to come together agreeing that the power of the Holy Spirit is needed for every believer to be victorious in these last days before Jesus Christ returns.

We cannot live under the control of the flesh. We will be defeated if we do. We must learn to yield control of our lives to the Holy Spirit. Jesus said, "...you shall receive power (ability, efficiency, and might) when the Holy Spirit has come upon you, and you shall be My witnesses in Jerusalem and all Judea and Samaria and to the ends (the very bounds) of the earth" (Acts 1:8).

We will "receive power, ability, efficiency and might" when the Holy Spirit comes upon us. The Holy Spirit will empower us to carry out our Father's plan to draw all nations unto Himself. We know that some people from every people group on earth will receive Jesus Christ as their Savior before the world as we know it will end (see Matthew 24:14). All people deserve to hear the wondrous message of God's sacrifice of His Son.

The world will experience a mighty outpouring of the Holy Spirit in these last days before Jesus Christ returns. "And it shall come to pass in the last days, God declares, that I will pour out of My Spirit upon all mankind, and your sons and your daughters shall prophesy [telling forth the divine counsels] and your young men shall see visions (divinely granted appearances), and your old men shall dream [divinely suggested] dreams" (Acts 2:17).

If there ever was one generation in the history of the world that needs the Holy Spirit, we live in this generation. We must be filled with the Holy Spirit as we live our lives daily. We cannot possibly receive the power and wisdom we need to live in today's world without the Holy Spirit. All Christians should live in the Spirit, not in the flesh.

Too many of God's children think they have to do everything for themselves. We must know that the Holy Spirit is ready, willing and able to help us. "...be strengthened and reinforced with mighty power in the inner man by the [Holy] Spirit [Himself indwelling your innermost being and personality]" (Ephesians 3:16).

The same Holy Spirit Who lived in Jesus Christ throughout His earthly ministry lives in you today. His mighty power is available to you by faith to provide the strength and reinforcement you need. Refuse to be worried, anxious or discouraged because you face seemingly difficult problems. We can be absolutely certain that the Holy Spirit has the strength, power and ability to lead us and direct us.

We must understand that the Holy Spirit Who lives in our hearts will not help us automatically when we are faced with difficult problems. Our yielding to the Holy Spirit releases His power. We only can live victorious lives in these last days before Jesus Christ returns through the power of the Holy Spirit.

Everything comes together beautifully when the Holy Spirit is in charge of our lives. He knows exactly how to coordinate even the smallest details that have to be coordinated to solve the problems we face. He will work everything out if we will just let go and allow Him to control our lives.

We should focus on the mighty power of the Holy Spirit Who lives in our hearts instead of buying into the worried and anxious thoughts that Satan's demons attempt to put into our minds. We should be in constant peace because the Holy Spirit is peace within us.

In this chapter we have seen many additional scriptural facts pertaining to the peace and power of the Holy Spirit. Please go back and study and meditate repeatedly on God's marvelous truths pertaining to the Holy Spirit. Refuse to allow your consciousness to be filled with anything except the indwelling presence of the Holy Spirit. Surrender control of your life more and more to the Holy Spirit as you study and meditate on these Scripture references pertaining to the Holy Spirit.

In the next chapter we will see what the Bible says will happen to us if our lives are motivated by selfishness, self-centeredness and self-confidence. We will clearly see the problems we will face if we attempt to control our lives instead of allowing the Holy Spirit to control our lives.

Chapter 42

Failure Is Inevitable If We Continue to Control of Our Lives

We cannot experience the peace of God if we insist on controlling our lives. When Adam and Eve turned away from God, they had become self-centered instead of God-centered. They turned away from God because they gave in to the influence of Satan. "…God made man upright, but they [men and women] have sought out many devices [for evil]" (Ecclesiastes 7:29).

Every human being is a descendant of Adam. We have inherited Adam's sinful nature. We all have a tendency to pursue selfish goals instead of fervently seeking God's will for our lives. "…all seek [to advance] their own interests, not those of Jesus Christ (the Messiah)" (Philippians 2:21).

Please highlight or underline the word "all" in this passage of Scripture. Know that this word includes *you*. Know that you have inherited from Adam a tendency to pursue selfish goals instead of cheerfully yielding control of your life to the Lord. Too many of us are independent when our Father wants us to be dependent.

Independence is glorified in the world today. Many people yearn to "do their own thing." Our Father wants us to turn away from this tendency toward independence. He wants us to cheerfully yield control of our lives to the Holy Spirit. He wants us to seek His plan for our lives instead of pursing selfish goals.

Some Christians never have even considered yielding control of their lives to the Holy Spirit. They may go to church each week and spend a few minutes each day in prayer and possibly even study the Bible occasionally, but they still are firmly in control of their lives. They do not understand the tremendous mistake they are making.

The more we yield to our selfish desires, the further we are from God. When our primary goal is to pursue selfish desires, we live the way unbelievers live. Our Father does not want us to make this mistake. Our Father wants us to turn away from the influence of the world to spend precious quiet time alone with Him each day as we constantly draw closer to Him.

Our carnal nature is independent. Our carnal nature insists on controlling our lives. We will realize the joy and freedom of dependence on the Lord as we grow more and more in the Lord. We will yield control of our lives to the Holy Spirit. If He truly is in control of our lives, we will experience His precious fruit of peace.

God placed the Holy Spirit in us when we were saved. The Holy Spirit has lived inside of us from that moment. He will help us continually if we constantly acknowledge His presence and if we place all of our trust and confidence in Him.

Satan wants us to be selfish and self-centered. Satan's demons do everything they can to influence us to pursue carnal desires. God wants us to do just the opposite. "…walk and live [habitually] in the [Holy] Spirit [responsive to and controlled and guided by the Spirit]; then you will certainly not gratify the cravings and desires of the flesh (of human nature without God). For the desires of the flesh are opposed to the [Holy] Spirit, and the [desires of the] Spirit are opposed to the flesh (godless human nature); for these are antagonistic to each other [continually withstanding and in conflict with each other], so that you are not free but are prevented from doing what you desire to do" (Galatians 5:16-17).

This passage of Scripture says that we should "habitually" yield control of our lives to the Holy Spirit. We are instructed to be "responsive to and controlled and guided by the Spirit." If we allow the Holy Spirit to control our lives, we will not allow our carnal desires that are antagonistic to the Holy Spirit to control our lives.

If we *really believe* that the Holy Spirit lives in our hearts, *why* would we ever make the mistake of attempting to control our lives? We should gladly give up our God-given right to control our lives. Yielding control of our lives to the Holy Spirit should be the constant focus of our lives.

Carnal Christians are Christians whose old nature still has a large degree of control in their lives. Christians who allow the new nature of Christ to predominate will gladly relinquish control of their lives to the Holy Spirit.

All believers knowingly or unknowingly make a continual decision. Will they control all or most aspects of their lives or will they constantly yield control of their lives to the Holy Spirit? This decision is influenced by the spiritual food we are fed with on a daily basis. We do not need to feed and exercise our old nature. The carnal part of us is fed automatically by the ways of the world we live in, by the influence of Satan's demons and by the desire for independence we inherited from our ancestor, Adam.

We do not have to study the Word of God to learn how to be proud, selfish and critical. Anger, bitterness and jealousy come naturally to all of us. Hardness of heart and impatience do not require any special study. No training courses are needed to tell us how to be discouraged, doubting, worried, anxious and fearful.

The examples I have given are just a few of the ways our old nature can dominate our lives. We all are weaker in some of these areas than we are in others. Satan's demons continually try to influence each of us in the areas where we are weakest.

If we sincerely want to turn away from the desires of our carnal nature to allow the Holy Spirit to control our lives, we must feed ourselves each day with the exceedingly magnificent and very nutritious spiritual food of the Word of God. We must obey our Father's instructions to renew our minds daily in His Word and to meditate on His Word continually throughout the day and night.

If we faithfully obey these instructions, carnality will not be able to control our lives. The hardest battle any of us ever will fight is the battle with ourselves. The greatest victory any of us ever will win is to continually override our selfish desires to freely and cheerfully yield control of our lives to the Holy Spirit.

We must understand that *every* sin is rooted in selfishness. Please stop and think about this statement for a moment. Can you think of any sin that is not rooted in selfishness? Most of the misery in the world today is caused by selfishness. If you agree with this premise, doesn't it make sense that we only can overcome sin and the misery that comes from sin through selflessness?

Remarkably, the more the Holy Spirit governs our lives, the more all of our gifts and talents and who we are as an individual are enhanced and expressed. As we give up our lives, we receive back a person touched by God and anointed for His glory.

Sin is not complicated. Sin simply is doing things our way instead of God's way. Sin separates us from God. We must understand that pride and selfishness block us from receiving God's peace and all of the other blessings He has provided for us.

Our Father wants to bless each of His children just as parents here on earth want to bless their children. However, when God created us, He gave each of us freedom of choice. We all would be mere robots if God did not give us the freedom to choose. Unfortunately, far too many of us are unable to receive the blessings our Father has provided for us because of pride, disobedience, doubt or unbelief (see I Corinthians 8:9).

Christians who obey God's instructions to continually study His Word will come to the realization that our Father does not want us to have confidence in ourselves. They will learn that self-confidence, self-centeredness and selfishness block us from receiving God's blessings.

When we love God wholeheartedly, our passion will be to seek, find and carry out His will for our lives. We are here on earth to serve God and to help others, not to pursue selfish desires. We should continually yield control of our lives to the Holy Spirit as we gladly allow Him to reveal God's plan for our lives and to empower us to complete this plan. If we truly do yield to the Holy Spirit to the fullest degree, we will experience total satisfaction and fulfillment.

Much of the pain in our lives is caused by giving in to our selfish desires. Young children in the natural realm who think they know more about life than their parents are headed for trouble. This same principle applies in the spiritual realm. We inevitably will encounter severe problems if we insist on doing things our way.

Anything that is rooted in "self" inevitably will cause problems. The only question is *when* these problems will occur, not *if* they will occur. Our Father still loves us when we are proud, selfish, stubborn and self-reliant. However, in spite of His great love for us, we inevitably will reap an undesirable harvest from the seeds we sow with these ungodly traits.

If Satan's demons cannot get at us one way, they will try to get at us another way. If they cannot influence us to be worried, anxious and fearful, they will attempt to pump up our pride when and if we experience success in our lives.

Many people think that all of their problems would be solved if they were successful (from a worldly perspective of success). We ultimately will experience significant problems when we are successful unless we succeed by following God's instructions and unless we continue to follow God's instructions. We will pay a severe price if we allow ourselves to become proud because of worldly success. "When swelling and pride come, then emptiness and shame come also..." (Proverbs 11:2).

Satan wants us to indulge in our God-given opportunity to control our lives. He knows that we will block the enormous power of the Holy Spirit whenever we attempt to control our lives. "Do not quench (suppress or subdue) the [Holy] Spirit..." (I Thessalonians 5:19).

Many Christians quench the power of the Holy Spirit as a result of self-will. We make a tremendous mistake if we fail to allow the power, wisdom and ability of the Holy Spirit to continually flow in us and through us.

We must not subdue the Holy Spirit. God gave us the Holy Spirit to guide us throughout our lives. We were created to be submitted to Him. We must understand the tremendous mistake we make if our thoughts, words and actions suppress the power and ability of the Holy Spirit.

We grieve the Holy Spirit when our words and our actions clearly indicate that we are in control of our lives. "Let no foul or polluting language, nor evil word nor unwholesome or worthless talk [ever] come out of your mouth, but only such [speech] as is good and beneficial to the spiritual progress of others, as is fitting to the need and the occasion, that it may be a blessing and give grace (God's favor) to those who hear it. And do not grieve the Holy Spirit of God [do not offend or vex or sadden Him]…" (Ephesians 4:29-30).

We grieve the Holy Spirit when the words that come out of our mouths do not line up with God's Word. Our Father intended for us to fill our hearts continually with His Word so that the words we speak always will be in accordance with His Word that should fill our hearts abundantly as a result of constant study and meditation on the holy Scriptures (see Matthew 12:34).

In this chapter we have established a spiritual foundation that clearly shows us that we will inevitably face severe problems if we allow self-centeredness to rule our lives. We have seen that our Father does not want us to control our lives. In the next three chapters we will learn more about yielding control of our lives to God. If we obey these instructions, we will experience the joy of anointed living in the center of God's will and plan for our lives.

Chapter 43

Our Lives Belong to Jesus Christ

Jesus Christ paid a tremendous price at Calvary for each of us. If Jesus Christ is our Savior, we should have a deep and continuing desire to serve Him because of our overwhelming gratitude for the price He paid for us. "You were bought with a price [purchased with a preciousness and paid for, made His own]. So then, honor God and bring glory to Him in your body" (I Corinthians 6:20).

The amplification of this passage of Scripture says that Jesus Christ purchased us "with a preciousness." The precious price that Jesus paid for our salvation was a price of the highest value. No higher price could have been paid. Because of the price Jesus paid, we each were "made His own." We should honor God at all times because our lives actually belong to Jesus Christ. Every aspect of our lives should be devoted to glorifying God and serving Him continually.

We receive eternal salvation when we ask Jesus Christ to become our Savior. Jesus must be more than our Savior if we want to experience His peace throughout our lives on earth. Jesus also must be the Lord of our lives.

If Jesus truly is our Lord, we cheerfully will surrender every area of our lives to Him. We consciously will yield our thoughts, words and actions to Him. We will give all of our burdens to Him because we trust Him completely. If Jesus truly is the Lord of our lives, we will let go of every aspect of our lives.

When we live an anointed life, our lives are focused upon an eternal perspective. We are not continually occupied with worldly goals and desires. The touch of God permeates every aspect of our lives. Living for God is total joy.

Many Christians who have asked Jesus Christ to be their Savior have not yielded to Him as their Lord. They will live eternally in heaven, but they do not live in the anointing of Jesus Christ during their lives on earth. These Christians do not understand the vital importance of staying under the anointing of Jesus Christ. This anointing is the awesome touch of God that makes all things fresh and new.

Jesus does not want us to live selfish lives. When He gave His life for us, He died so that we could live for Him. "...He died for all, so that all those who live might live no longer to and for themselves, but to and for Him Who died and was raised again for their sake" (II Corinthians 5:15).

Please highlight or underline the two times the word "all" is used in this passage of Scripture. Know that this word includes *you*. Jesus Christ died for you so that you would "live *no* longer to and for *yourself* but to and for Him Who died and was raised again *for your sake.*"

We cannot possibly live in the peace of God unless Jesus Christ is the Lord of our lives. We must understand that our lives belong to Jesus Christ. We will find that our faith in Jesus will increase when we grasp this spiritual truth and live our lives accordingly.

I believe the primary purpose of our lives here on earth is to get ourselves off the throne of our lives to allow Jesus Christ to take His rightful place on the throne of our lives. God has a plan for each of us to complete. Great new spiritual horizons will open to us to the degree that we are able to turn away from ourselves and turn toward Jesus.

We will live the way Jesus wants us to live if we yield to Him. He will take who we are and anoint us for service beyond what we ever imagined. We won't just say that Jesus is the Lord of our lives. We will show that Jesus truly is our Lord by living our lives anointed by and in obedience to Him.

Jesus wants each of us to have a deep desire to learn exactly how He wants us to live. He wants us to obey His instructions. He said, "Why do you call Me, Lord, Lord, and do not [practice] what I tell you?" (Luke 6:46).

The Word of God is filled with thousands of specific instructions that tell us exactly how our Father wants us to live our lives. Jesus said, "…If anyone intends to come after Me, let him deny himself [forget, ignore, disown, and lose sight of himself and his own interests] and take up his cross, and [joining Me as a disciple and siding with My party] follow with Me [continually, cleaving steadfastly to Me]" (Mark 8:34).

This passage of Scripture tells us that Jesus Christ only can be the Lord of our lives if we ompletely turn caway from selfish goals. Jesus wants us to die to our selfish desires just as He died for us on the cross at Calvary. Jesus wants us to follow Him continually. He will take what we are and create an ambassador for the kingdom of God.

We are instructed to "cleave steadfastly" to Jesus. The word "cleave" in this context means to separate ourselves from the way we used to live. When we do something "steadfastly," we stick to whatever we are doing. We do not change or waver in any way. Jesus wants us to turn completely away from the way we used to live as we follow Him to the exclusion of everything else. We should be like the apostle Paul who said, "...I, Paul, [am] the prisoner of Jesus the Christ..." (Ephesians 3:1).

Paul referred to himself as a prisoner because he gladly relinquished control of his life to Jesus Christ. Paul was a broken and humble man who had finally connected with the eternal plan and principle for his life. He gladly yielded his life to God through Jesus Christ. At one time Paul was a proud and angry Hebrew named Saul who hated Jesus Christ. He went from that extreme to willingly yield control of every aspect of his life to the Lord Jesus Christ (see Acts 9:1-29).

At one time the psalmist David was a proud and sinful man. David ultimately became a humble and broken man who yielded his life to God. David said, "My sacrifice [the sacrifice acceptable] to God is a broken spirit; a broken and a contrite heart [broken down with sorrow for sin and humbly and thoroughly penitent]..." (Psalm 51:17).

Our Father wants each of us to have a broken and contrite heart. He wants us to be sorry for our sins. He wants us to be humble before Him at all times. He wants us to understand that we must be broken before He can use us. Brokenness requires us to give up our God-given right to control our lives by willingly yielding control of our lives to the Holy Spirit Who lives in our hearts.

Some people need to face severe adversity in their lives before they can be broken. Some of us are so proud and self-centered that God cannot even begin to get our attention unless He allows us to be knocked down to such a degree that we turn to Him because our confidence in ourselves has been shattered. Some of us need to face severe adversity before King Ego can be taken off the throne of our lives to be replaced by King Jesus.

Our carnal and selfish old nature must die before we can live our lives the way Jesus wants us to live. Our new nature in Christ must rise within us. We only can live in this way if we can clearly see how much self is in control of our lives.

We must take ourselves off the throne before we can enthrone our precious Lord. Only then will we be able to experience the peace of God and the other blessings our Father has made available to each of His beloved children who have stepped down from the throne of their lives.

Any vessel that the Lord uses must be broken. In the natural realm things that are broken and repaired usually do not have as much value as they had before they were broken. In the spiritual realm we must be broken before we can be made whole.

Some Christians are turned off when they are told that they must surrender control of their lives. Self-centered people do not want to yield their independence. They do not understand that they should turn to the Holy Spirit throughout each day of their lives, continually asking Him to mold them, shape them and guide them any way He chooses.

Our Father has given each of us complete freedom of choice. He has given us an invaluable Book of Instructions, but He does not force us to obey these instructions. He has given us the Holy Spirit to guide us at all times, but He does not force us to yield to the Holy Spirit.

Some Christians do not want to give up what they perceive to be their freedom. They do not understand that true freedom comes only from surrender. They do not understand that they only can receive the blessings their loving Father wants to give them if they freely, willingly and cheerfully yield control of their lives to the Holy Spirit.

The greatest life that was ever lived was a completely surrendered life. Anyone who carefully studies the four gospels of Matthew, Mark, Luke and John will read continually of the total submission of Jesus Christ to His Father as He always sought God's will for His life instead of pursuing selfish desires. Jesus said, "...I do not seek or consult My own will [I have no desire to do what is pleasing to Myself, My own aim, My own purpose] but only the will and pleasure of the Father Who sent Me" (John 5:30).

Jesus wants us to follow His example. We only can become something of value in the spiritual realm if we will stop deceiving ourselves and gladly yield control of our lives to the Holy Spirit. The life of every Christian should be a constant example of selflessness. "Let all men know and perceive and recognize your unselfishness (your considerateness, your forbearing spirit)..." (Philippians 4:5).

We have seen that all sin is caused by selfishness. Our Father wants us to be completely unselfish. He wants us to put our lives under new management. Some Christians say that the Holy Spirit lives in their hearts, but their words and their actions often indicate that they do not really believe the Holy Spirit lives within them. They do not know that He is completely able to make their lives much better and much more successful than they can do by themselves. More importantly, they do not comprehend the eternal plan and purpose of God and their place in it, the specific assignment that God has for each of us.

Some Christians have become dry and stale. Christianity is a routine to them. They try to live a Christian life through self-effort. They fail to understand that our lives should be a continual process of dying to ourselves. The more we die to ourselves, the more vibrant and alive we will become.

We should yield more control of our lives to the Holy Spirit throughout every day of our lives. We should trust the Holy Spirit more. We will become more and more the way our Father wants us to become as this process continues over a period of weeks, months and years. Our love and passion for God will grow exponentially if we constantly yield control of our lives to God. "...offer and yield yourselves to God..." (Romans 6:13).

We must understand that dying to self is a joy, not a penalty. Carnal Christians do not even begin to comprehend this magnificent spiritual principle. They do not understand that, the more we give up control of our lives, the more we will blessed by the Holy Spirit. The Holy Spirit is waiting to do wonderful things in us and through us if we will gladly surrender control of our lives to Him because we trust Him completely.

The death of Jesus Christ on the cross at Calvary was the greatest act this world has ever known. Nothing else can come close to the magnitude of the glorious price that Jesus paid for us at Calvary. We should live our lives like the apostle Paul. He said, "...I die daily [I face death every day and die to self]" (I Corinthians 15:31).

We cannot come alive spiritually without first dying. Jesus Christ had to die before He could be resurrected. We also must die to our selfish desires before we can be resurrected. We must understand the spiritual principle that says that life comes out of death. Anything of significance in the spiritual realm comes out of death.

We gave up all of our so-called "rights" when we asked Jesus Christ to be our Savior. Our lives should be His to do with as He wishes. Jesus wants each of us to willingly, cheerfully and deliberately become His obedient servant.

We never should glorify anything or anyone except our Lord Jesus Christ. We should be like the apostle Paul who said, "...far be it from me to glory [in anything or anyone] except in the cross of our Lord Jesus Christ (the Messiah) through Whom the world has been crucified to me, and I to the world!" (Galatians 6:14).

In this chapter we have looked into the Word of God to see that our Father tells us repeatedly that He has equipped us to live in victory by surrendering our lives to Him. In the next chapter we will study additional scriptural instructions that tell us how to yield control of our lives to the Holy Spirit. We will learn how to become everything He wants us to become so that we can successfully complete the assignment we have been given for the glory of God.

Chapter 44

Be Continually Filled with the Holy Spirit

We only can live our lives the way our Father wants us to live if we continually yield control of our lives to the Holy Spirit. "...if you live according to [the dictates of] the flesh, you will surely die. But if through the power of the [Holy] Spirit you are [habitually] putting to death (making extinct, deadening) the [evil] deeds prompted by the body, you shall [really and genuinely] live forever. For all who are led by the Spirit of God are sons of God" (Romans 8:13-14).

I believe that many people who insist on controlling their own lives will experience premature physical death. We will live the way our Father wants us to live if we habitually put our fleshly desires to death through the power of the Holy Spirit. If we allow the Holy Spirit to control our lives, He will change us over a period of time to become what He wants us to become. We "...are constantly being transfigured into His very own image in ever increasing splendor and from one degree of glory to another; [for this comes] from the Lord [Who is] the Spirit" (II Corinthians 3:18).

We will experience constantly increasing splendor and glory if the Holy Spirit is in control of our lives. We only can live the glorious lives our Father wants us to live if we willingly and cheerfully yield control of our lives to the Holy Spirit.

People who are self-centered often are neurotic and unhappy. We only can become what our Father wants us to become by becoming more and more God-centered as we devote our lives to serving Him and helping others.

Our Father wants each of us to constantly get out of the valley of "me first" to get up on top of the mountain of "God first." If we live in the Spirit, we continually will see new horizons that we were completely unaware of. Life is exciting and full of adventure when the Holy Spirit leads us and guides us. God's plan for our lives is much richer, fuller and more satisfying than anything we could ever imagine.

Satan's demons attempt to influence us to be selfish. As we grow and mature in the Lord, we will see that we constantly will be engulfed in spiritual darkness if we block the Holy Spirit. We only can live in God's light when we yield to the Holy Spirit.

The transfer from self to God is a gradual process. We need to "reprogram" our minds continually with the Word of God so that we can yield our lives more and more to the Holy Spirit Who lives in our hearts. As weeks, months and years go by and we die more and more to ourselves, we will experience new degrees of spiritual maturity that were completely inaccessible when we pursued selfish goals. "...be aglow and burning with the Spirit, serving the Lord" (Romans 12:11).

We should be on fire spiritually because we should have a deep and fervent desire to allow the Holy Spirit to guide us to serve the Lord. We cannot yield control of our lives to the Holy Spirit unless we constantly turn our backs on the ways of the world and renew our minds in the Word of God so that we will draw closer to God on a daily basis.

Our Father wants us to consecrate every area of our lives to Him. He does not want us to be influenced by the ways of the world and by the carnal and selfish nature we inherited from Adam. The precious Holy Spirit is our constant source of power and strength to carry out God's plan and purpose.

A holy life is a surrendered life. The word "holy" is part of the name of the Holy Spirit. We only can become holy if He is in control of our lives. We should "...live and move not in the ways of the flesh but in the ways of the Spirit [our lives governed not by the standards and according to the dictates of the flesh, but controlled by the Holy Spirit]" (Romans 8:4).

We each have been given complete freedom to decide whether we want to control our lives or whether we want the Holy Spirit to control our lives. The Holy Spirit will only control our lives to the degree that we gladly yield this control to Him. "...you are living the life of the Spirit, if the [Holy] Spirit of God [really] dwells within you [directs and controls you]..." (Romans 8:9).

We only can live the way our Father wants us to live if the Holy Spirit directs us and controls us. "If we live by the [Holy] Spirit, let us also walk by the Spirit. [If by the Holy Spirit we have our life in God, let us go forward walking in line, our conduct controlled by the Spirit.] Let us not become vainglorious and self-conceited, competitive and challenging and provoking and irritating to one another, envying and being jealous of one another" (Galatians 5:25-26).

The first part of this passage of Scripture urges us to yield control of our lives to the Holy Spirit. The last part of this passage of Scripture identifies the negative characteristics that will be manifested in the lives of people who do not yield their lives to the Holy Spirit.

Our Father does not want us to be vain. He doesn't want us to be so caught up with ourselves that we continually try to prove ourselves to be superior through competition with other people. "...all painful effort in labor and all skill in work comes from man's rivalry with his neighbor. This is also vanity, a vain striving after the wind and a feeding on it." (Ecclesiastes 4:4).

Our Father does not want us to constantly challenge other people, to provoke others and to irritate others. He doesn't want us to be envious and jealous. Instead, our Father wants us to constantly be filled with the Holy Spirit. "...do not get drunk with wine, for that is debauchery; but ever be filled and stimulated with the [Holy] Spirit" (Ephesians 5:18).

This passage of Scripture compares being filled with the Holy Spirit with people in the world who attempt to find happiness by partaking of Satan's substitutes such as drinking alcoholic beverages. Did you ever stop to think that alcoholic beverages are sometimes referred to as "spirits?" Satan isn't very subtle, is he?

The Bible tells us that we should "not get drunk with wine." Our Father does not want us to settle for second best. He wants us to understand that being in an alcoholic stupor is "debauchery." The word "debauch" means to be separated or to be led astray morally.

Many people who are drunk experience a temporary high that is followed the next day by a tremendous low. Our Father wants us to be "high" continually because we are filled with the Holy Spirit. We only can be filled with the Holy Spirit to the degree that we are empty of self.

What exactly should we do to be filled with the Holy Spirit? The next two verses of Scripture tell us how to be filled with the Holy Spirit. "Speak out to one another in psalms and hymns and spiritual songs, offering praise with voices [and instruments] and making melody with all your heart to the Lord, at all times and for everything giving thanks in the name of our Lord Jesus Christ to God the Father" (Ephesians 5:19-20).

We will be filled with the Holy Spirit and stimulated by Him when words of praise continually flow out of our mouths and when we constantly sing songs of praise, worship and thanksgiving. Our hearts will sing with joy when we constantly express our gratitude for what Jesus Christ has done for us.

The words "at all times and for everything giving thanks in the name of the Lord Jesus Christ to God the Father" tell us that we should have a continual attitude of gratitude. Our mouths should open constantly to speak and sing words of praise and thanksgiving.

We must understand that being filled with the Spirit is not a one-time occurrence. We saw in Ephesians 5:18 that we should "*ever* be filled and stimulated with the Holy Spirit." The word "ever" shows us that being filled with the Holy Spirit is an ongoing process. Our Father wants us to praise Him and worship Him continually. We always will be aware of the presence of the Holy Spirit when our lives are centered around a constant attitude of gratitude.

Some Christians are in control of their lives part of the time and the Holy Spirit is in control of their lives part of the time. I cannot honestly say that the Holy Spirit is in control of every hour of my life. I can say that I yearn for the Holy Spirit to be more and more in control of my life. I have seen great changes when I have yielded to Him.

We all are empty vessels that need to be filled. The more we empty our lives of ourselves, the more our lives can be filled by the Holy Spirit. The highest goal any of us ever can attain to is to yield every aspect of our lives to the Holy Spirit. He can and will do a much better job with our lives than we can do ourselves.

In the last five chapters we have carefully studied the holy Scriptures to learn about the Holy Spirit. We began by studying the fruit of the Spirit which includes peace. We have learned that we only can experience this peace and the other fruit of the Holy Spirit by dying to ourselves continually. We now are ready to look into the Word of God to see what it says about the relationship between experiencing the peace of God and obeying the specific instructions our Father has given us in His Book of Instructions. These instructions tell us exactly how He wants us to live our lives.

Chapter 45

Our Father Gives Peace
to His Obedient Children

A definite relationship exists between the Holy Spirit controlling our lives and our obedience to the Word of God. "...I will put My Spirit within you and cause you to walk in My statutes, and you shall heed My ordinances and do them" (Ezekiel 36:27).

The word "you" is used three different times in this short passage of Scripture. Please personalize this passage of Scripture. Know that God is speaking to *you* each time the word "you" is used here. Pray continually to God asking for the Holy Spirit to help you to progressively understand more and more about the instructions your Father has given you in His wonderful Book of Instructions. Pray for guidance to help you to live your life in obedience to your Father's instructions.

If we will obey our Father's instructions to study and meditate continually on His Word, the Holy Spirit will progressively remove the spiritual "veil" that stops many of His children from learning His ways. Our Father has provided tremendous benefits for each of His children who obey His instructions. "...to us God has unveiled and revealed them by and through His Spirit, for the [Holy] Spirit searches diligently, exploring and examining everything, even sounding the profound and bottomless things of God [the divine counsels and things hidden and beyond man's scrutiny]" (I Corinthians 2:10).

The Holy Spirit can and will show us exactly what our Father wants us to do with our lives. He is able to explain "the profound and bottomless things of God" to us that we cannot possibly understand by ourselves.

When we yield control of our lives to the Holy Spirit, He will cause the Word of God to come alive in our hearts. If we continually obey the instructions in the Word of God that the Holy Spirit reveals to us, our hearts will be purified and cleansed. "…by your obedience to the Truth through the [Holy] Spirit you have purified your hearts…" (I Peter 1:22).

Our Father wants us to love His Word so much that we will fill our minds and our hearts with His Word throughout every day and night of our lives. If we truly love the Word of God so much that we cannot get enough of it, we will experience wonderful peace. "Great peace have they who love Your law; nothing shall offend them or make them stumble" (Psalm 119:165).

I have had a love affair with the Word of God ever since I was saved almost twenty-nine years ago at the age of forty-three. The most exciting thing I do is to study and meditate constantly on the Word of God. Any Christian who continually fills his or her mind and heart with the Word of God over a period of time will become a blessing to others.

Our faith in God will increase as the weeks turn into months and the months turn into years and we continue to faithfully obey our Father's instructions to renew our minds in His Word each day and to meditate on His Word throughout the day and night.

We will experience more and more of God's peace if we have continually increasing faith in the reliability of God's promises and if we consistently obey the specific instructions our Father has given to us.

Psalm 119:165 doesn't merely say we will experience God's peace if we love His Word. We are told that we will experience *"great peace"* when we love God's Word. If we grow and mature as Christians by continually immersing ourselves in the Word of God, we are told that nothing that happens in our lives will offend us or make us stumble. The circumstances in our lives will not be able to overwhelm us. We will not allow Satan, any person or any circumstance to steal the wonderful peace that our Father has provided for His children who love His Word.

If we consistently live our lives in obedience to God's instructions, His peace will flow in us and through us. "Oh, that you had hearkened to My commandments! Then your peace and prosperity would have been like a flowing river…" (Isaiah 48:18).

This passage of Scripture shows us the relationship that exists between obeying God's instructions and experiencing God's peace and prosperity. Unfortunately, some of us block ourselves from receiving the peace and prosperity our Father has provided for us because we fail to obey His instructions to continually fill our minds and our hearts with His Word. *How* can we obey God's instructions if we don't know what they are?

Isaiah 48:18 refers to the Israelites who failed to experience the peace and prosperity God had provided for them because they did not learn and obey the instructions God had given to them. This same spiritual principle applies to each of us today.

If we consistently obey our Father's instructions, peace and prosperity will flow in our lives. Our lives will be a symphony with

Jesus Christ as the conductor. Jesus simply wants us to play our part. He has completed the work. We connect with His finished work by our obedience.

Our Father wants us to study and meditate on His Word over and over again. The Holy Spirit will give us greater revelation over a period of time. We clearly will see that disobedience results in catastrophe and obedience results in blessings.

When we face a crisis situation, we always will react to the crisis based upon what we truly believe deep down in our hearts. Can you imagine having *so much peace inside of you* that your sense of well-being in the face of adversity is so strong that it is like a flowing river?

We will experience this peace and prosperity from God when we put into practice in our daily lives the instructions and principles we learn from the Bible. The presence and power of God will permeate every fiber of our being. We will receive God's peace if we obey the following instructions that the apostle Paul gave to the Philippians. "Practice what you have learned and received and heard and seen in me, and model your way of living on it, and the God of peace (of untroubled, undisturbed well-being) will be with you" (Philippians 4:9).

Paul urged the Philippians to obey the Word of God in every area of their lives just as they saw him obeying God's instructions. This passage of Scripture promises us that "the God of peace" will be with us if we consistently obey His instructions. The amplification of this passage of Scripture tells us that we will not be disturbed by the circumstances we face. We always will have a sense of well being that cannot be disturbed by any problem we face, no matter how severe this obstacle might seem to be. The God of peace is with us. God is much greater than any circumstances we will face.

The prophet Isaiah explained to the Israelites the relationship between learning from the Lord, obeying the Lord's instructions and experiencing His peace. "...all your [spiritual] children shall be disciples [taught by the Lord and obedient to His will], and great shall be the peace and undisturbed composure of your children" (Isaiah 54:13).

Would you like to experience *so much* of God's peace that *nothing* can disturb your composure? This promise that was made to the Israelites many years ago applies to every child of God today. Great blessings are available to all of God's children who faithfully obey their Father's instructions. "My son, forget not my law or teaching, but let your heart keep my commandments; for length of days and years of a life [worth living] and tranquility [inward and outward and continuing through old age till death], these shall they add to you" (Proverbs 3:1-2).

If we obey our Father's instructions, this promise that King Solomon made to his son applies to each of us today. Our Father promises that we will enjoy a long and full life if we consistently obey His instructions. He promises that we will experience wonderful peace and tranquility throughout our final years on earth right up to the time we die and go to be with Him in heaven.

Are you a senior citizen? If you are, please meditate even more carefully on Proverbs 3:1-2. This promise of God is especially meaningful to those of us who are in the twilight years of our lives.

How can any person read these wonderful blessings our Father has promised to us and not make the decision to continually study and meditate on the Word of God? The relationship between learning God's instructions, obeying God's instructions and experiencing God's supernatural peace is very clear.

The peace of God is valuable to us at all times, but I believe that it is especially valuable to us during the final years of our lives. Some Christians lose their peace when they experience health problems and other problems as they grow older. The following passage of Scripture applies to all of God's children, but it is especially pertinent to those of us who are senior citizens. "The [uncompromisingly] righteous shall flourish like the palm tree [be long-lived, stately, upright, useful, and fruitful]; they shall grow like a cedar in Lebanon [majestic, stable, durable, and incorruptible]. Planted in the house of the Lord, they shall flourish in the courts of our God. [Growing in grace] they shall still bring forth fruit in old age; they shall be full of sap [of spiritual vitality] and [rich in the] verdure [of trust, love, and contentment]" (Psalm 92:12-14).

This passage of Scripture begins with the words "uncompromisingly righteous." We will flourish throughout our lives if we refuse to compromise our lives and if we do our very best at all times to obey God's instructions and to yield to the Holy Spirit.

We will live long, full, meaningful and fruitful lives. We will continue to "bring forth fruit in our old age." We will be filled with spiritual energy and vitality. We will trust God. We will be secure in our Father's love. We will be calm, quiet and content.

We will experience God's peace if we have a deep and continuing desire to know Him more intimately. We will enjoy a wonderful personal relationship with our Father if we have spent many hours in His presence over a period of years.

We will have a deep and continuing desire to seek, find and carry out God's will for our lives if we live our lives in obedience to God's instructions and if we yield control of our lives to the Holy Spirit. "Acquaint now yourself with Him [agree with God and show yourself to be conformed to His will] and be at peace; by that [you shall prosper and great] good shall come to you.

Receive, I pray you, the law and instruction from His mouth and lay up His words in your heart. If you return to the Almighty [and submit and humble yourself before Him], you will be built up..." (Job 22:21-23).

These magnificent words of instruction were birthed in the suffering of Job many years ago. We must not ignore the spiritual truth that Job learned as a result of the adversity he experienced. Let us examine very carefully what Eliphaz, a friend of Job, speaking under the anointing of the Holy Spirit, instructed Job to do. These same instructions apply to us today.

We should constantly become better acquainted with God. We should do our very best to come into agreement with God. We should have a deep and sincere desire to conform to God's will. We can accomplish these goals by continually "programming" the Word of God into our minds and our hearts.

God's children who obey these instructions will experience God's wonderful peace. They will prosper and great blessings will come to them. We will humble ourselves before God if we constantly fill our minds and our hearts with the Word of God. We will trust God. Our faith in God "will be built up."

Our Father can and will do wonderful things in the lives of His children who faithfully obey His instructions. God will even cause our enemies to be at peace with us if He is pleased with the way we live. "When a man's ways please the Lord, He makes even his enemies to be at peace with him" (Proverbs 16:7).

We have seen again and again that a definite relationship exists between experiencing the peace of God, learning how our Father wants us to live and consistently obeying His instructions. We will experience severe problems in our lives as a result of any disobedience that is caused by our failure to learn and obey God's instructions. "Streams of water run down my eyes, because men do not keep Your law [they hear it not, nor receive it, love it, or obey it]" (Psalm 119:136).

The psalmist tells us that his observation of people who do not love the Word of God, receive the Word of God and obey the Word of God brought tears to his eyes. We must understand the tremendous mistake we will make if we disobey God's instructions. We must comprehend the awesome results of consistently learning and obeying God's instructions. "Keep the charge of the Lord your God, walk in His ways, keep His statues, His commandments, His precepts, and His testimonies, as it is written in the Law of Moses, that you may do wisely and prosper in all that you do and wherever you turn" (I Kings 2:3).

This Old Testament principle applies to each of us today. Would you like to receive God's wisdom and to prosper in every area of your life? These blessings are available to each of us if we will continually learn our Father's instructions and live our lives to the best of our ability in obedience to the instructions He has given to us. The New Testament gives us several similar promises. "…we receive from Him whatever we ask, because we [watchfully] obey His orders [observe His suggestions and injunctions, follow His plan for us], and [habitually] practice what is pleasing to Him" (I John 3:22).

Would you like to receive an answer to all of your prayers? This passage of Scripture tells us exactly what our Father wants us to do to receive *"whatever we ask"* Him for. We should obey God's instructions, we should seek and carry out His plan for our lives and we should live our lives the way He has instructed us to live.

Our Father promises to bless His children who persevere in studying and meditating on His Word and doing what He tells them to do. "…he who looks carefully into the faultless law, the

[law] of liberty, and is faithful to it and perseveres in looking into it, being not a heedless listener who forgets but an active doer [who obeys], he shall be blessed in his doing (his life of obedience)" (James 1:25).

Our Father refers to His Word as "the faultless law, the law of liberty." God's Word is absolutely perfect – there are no faults in it. We will experience wonderful liberty and freedom if we persevere in our study and meditation of God's Word so that we faithfully will obey God's instructions.

We must not make the mistake of being a "heedless listener who forgets" God's instructions. Our Father wants us to be "active doers who obey" His instructions. He promises to bless our obedience. Jesus Christ said, "…Blessed (happy and to be envied) rather are those who hear the Word of God and obey and practice it!" (Luke 11:28).

We have seen in this chapter the definite and unquestionable relationship that exists between obeying our Father's instructions and receiving manifestation of His wonderful peace and the other blessings He has provided for us. Please go back and study and meditate on the promises and instructions from the Word of God in this chapter.

I pray that this study and meditation will cause you to be determined to fill your mind and your heart with God's Word constantly throughout every day of your life. Christians who continually immerse themselves in the Word of God, obey God's instructions and yield control of their lives to the Holy Spirit cannot fail to experience God's wonderful peace.

In the remaining chapters of this book we will study the third type of peace our Father has provided for us. First, we learned that we must be at *peace with God* before we can experience the fulfilled life our Father has provided for us. Then, we carefully studied about *the peace of God* that can and should be manifested in our lives. Now we are ready to learn from the holy Scriptures how to live at peace with other human beings, regardless of the way they treat us.

Chapter 46

Our Father Wants Us to Have a Peaceful Relationship with Everyone

Our Father does not want us to think that a peaceful relationship with other people is just a "nice to have." He wants us to place a high priority on doing whatever is necessary to live at peace with all people. "Strive to live in peace with everybody and pursue that consecration and holiness without which no one will [ever] see the Lord" (Hebrews 12:14).

We are instructed to "strive" for a peaceful relationship with everyone. Whenever we strive to do something, we try very hard to achieve that specific goal. Our Father will bless us when we strive diligently to live at peace with others and to pursue a consecrated and holy life. Jesus said, "Blessed (enjoying enviable happiness, spiritually prosperous – with life-joy and satisfaction in God's favor and salvation, regardless of their outward conditions) are the makers and maintainers of peace, for they shall be called the sons of God!" (Matthew 5:9).

Would you like to be so happy that other people will envy you because of your happiness? Would you like to be "spiritually prosperous" and filled with "life-joy and satisfaction?" Our Father promises these blessings to us when we do everything we can to maintain a peaceful relationship with other people. We should "…definitely aim for and eagerly pursue what makes for harmony and for mutual upbuilding (edification and development) of one another" (Romans 14:19).

Our Father instructs us to "definitely aim for and eagerly pursue" whatever is required to live harmoniously with others. He wants us to do everything we can to encourage other people and build them up.

Our primary goal on earth should be to serve the Lord by doing whatever He wants us to do with our lives. We cannot serve the Lord effectively if we habitually argue and fight with other people. "…the servant of the Lord must not be quarrelsome (fighting and contending). Instead, he must be kindly to everyone and mild-tempered [preserving the bond of peace]…" (II Timothy 2:24).

As we study these passages of Scripture, there cannot be any doubt that our Father wants each of His children to learn how to live at peace with others. Now that we know how important it is to our Father for us to live at peace with one another, we are ready to study His Word to learn how to achieve this goal. We will learn exactly what we should do to enjoy peace with other people, regardless of how these people treat us.

We have learned that the peace of God is manifested in our lives as a fruit of the Holy Spirit. This fruit is produced when we yield control of or lives to the Holy Spirit. We only give up a peaceful relationship with other people when we are in control of our lives. If the Holy Spirit truly is in control of our lives, we will not allow negative emotions to stop us from living at peace with others.

Our Father wants us to continually yield our emotions to the Holy Spirit. The peace of Jesus Christ that has been given to us (see John 14:27) can be stolen from us if we do not learn how to be Spirit-controlled instead of being emotion-controlled. No person or circumstance can steal our peace if we make a quality decision that we will not give up our precious God-given peace and if we learn how to remain at peace with other people regardless of how they treat us.

When someone says or does something to us that would seem to warrant an angry reaction from us, we should look at that person and say quietly to ourselves, "Holy Spirit, I ask You to handle this situation. I feel angry inside, but I yield to You. I will not allow this person to steal the peace Jesus Christ has given to me. Keeping His wonderful peace is *much more important* to me than giving this person a piece of my mind."

Some of us lose our peace because of the way other people treat us. We make it possible for Satan and his demons to steal our peace whenever negative emotions prevail in our lives. We should not make the mistake of doing anything that will enable Satan and his demons to get a foothold in our lives.

Satan wants to steal from us (see John 10:10). Satan and his demons always will do everything they can to influence us to react to other people in a way that is not consistent with the way the Word of God instructs us to react. We will not allow Satan and his demons to obtain a foothold in our lives if our minds and our hearts are filled with the Word of God and if our lives truly are yielded to the Holy Spirit.

We *must* understand that many times the way we are treated by other people actually is caused by the ability that Satan's demons have to successfully influence that person. "…we are not wrestling with flesh and blood [contending only with physical opponents], but against the despotisms, against the powers, against [the master spirits who are] the world rulers of this present darkness, against the spirit forces of wickedness in the heavenly (supernatural) sphere" (Ephesians 6:12).

Most people do not understand that many of the problems they have in their relationships with other people do *not* come directly from that person. This passage of Scripture tells us that "we are *not* wrestling with flesh and blood." Many negative actions of other human beings actually have their root in the influence that Satan's demons have been able to obtain upon these people.

We must not allow Satan's demons to steal the wonderful peace Jesus Christ gave to us just because they have been able to influence another person. We always should respond with the love of God that lives in our hearts (see Romans 5:5) instead of retaliating in kind when someone treats us unfairly because of the influence Satan has obtained on him or her. "See that none of you repays another with evil for evil, but always aim to show kindness and seek to do good to one another and to everybody" (I Thessalonians 5:15).

The words "none of you" in this passage of Scripture are all-inclusive. God is speaking to *you.* Our Father wants every one of His children to respond to the evil influence of Satan with His wisdom that is available to us (see James 1:5). When we are confronted by people who are controlled by evil, we should pray for God's wisdom. We should follow the Holy Spirit's leading.

Pride often causes us to have a poor relationship with other people. If we are humble at all times, Satan's demons cannot get a foothold in our minds and our hearts. "Live in harmony with one another; do not be haughty (snobbish, high-minded, exclusive), but readily adjust yourself to [people, things] and give yourselves to humble tasks. Never overestimate yourself or be wise in your own conceits. Repay no one evil for evil, but take thought for what is honest and proper and noble [aiming to be above reproach] in the sight of everyone. If possible, as far as it depends on you, live at peace with everyone" (Romans 12:16-18).

This passage of Scripture is filled with specific information telling us exactly what our Father wants us to do to live at peace with other people. We should not be proud or haughty. Pride always gives Satan an opportunity to obtain a foothold in our lives.

Our Father wants us to be humble at all times. We should not overestimate ourselves. Once again, we are instructed to "repay no one evil for evil." We should not respond to Satan's evil influence on another person with an evil response. We always should respond based upon the specific instructions we are given in the Word of God. We should do what is "honest and proper and noble." We should have a deep and sincere desire to maintain peaceful relationships with other people.

We should not retaliate when someone strikes out at us. "Never return evil for evil or insult for insult (scolding, tongue-lashing, berating), but on the contrary blessing [praying for their welfare, happiness, and protection, and truly pitying and loving them]. For know that to this you have been called, that you may yourselves inherit a blessing [from God - that you may obtain a blessing as heirs, bringing welfare and happiness and protection]" (I Peter 3:9).

We have seen that the Bible uses repetition to emphasize a particular spiritual principle. For the third time we have seen that we should "*never* return evil for evil." We will not retaliate in fleshly anger if we truly have yielded control of our lives to Jesus Christ.

The Holy Spirit will empower us to stand against the devil. We will be strong enough in Him to face any evil. Our Father has given us specific instructions that tell us exactly how to resist the devil. "…God sets Himself against the proud and haughty, but gives grace [continually] to the lowly (those who are humble enough to receive it). So be subject to God. Resist the devil [stand firm against him], and he will flee from you" (James 4:6-7).

We cannot resist the devil if we are proud because Satan originally fell because of pride. We do exactly what Satan wants us to do whenever we respond to any situation in a proud and haughty manner. We are proud whenever we attempt to return evil for evil.

This passage of Scripture goes on to make an astounding statement. We have discussed this principle in a previous chapter. We must understand that our loving Father *actually will set Himself against us* when we are proud and haughty. *Why* would any of us ever want to do *anything* that would cause *Almighty God to oppose us?*

We may be proud occasionally and repent of our pride and ask forgiveness. However, we can be assured that our Father always will oppose us if we continue to be proud and haughty for a sustained period of time. He goes on to tell us that we *continually* will receive His grace (favor that we have not earned and do not deserve) whenever we are "humble enough to receive it."

We only can resist the influence of the devil when we are "subject to God." When we are subject to God, our lives are humbly yielded to Him. Our Father has given us specific instructions telling us exactly how to react to people who treat us unfairly. "Exercise foresight and be on the watch to look [after one another], to see that no one falls back from and fails to secure God's grace (His unmerited favor and spiritual blessing), in order that no root of resentment (rancor, bitterness, or hatred) shoots forth and causes trouble and bitter torment, and many become contaminated and defiled by it…" (Hebrews 12:15).

Our Father wants us to have foresight whenever we are tempted to react proudly to another person. He wants us to understand that our proud reaction could cause Him to oppose us. Our Father does not want us to fail to receive His wonderful grace because we are proud.

Our Father instructs us to be watchful and to check ourselves for any root of bitterness that has planted itself in our hearts. We can pull out a root when it is small. Have you ever tried to pull out the root of even a small tree that has started to put down its roots? The roots are strong and deep. We cannot allow bitterness to become deeply rooted in our hearts.

If we do have a root of bitterness that has planted itself deep in our hearts, we must ask God to remove it. We may need to spend time in prayer and fasting. We must persevere in the Holy Spirit until the bitterness is gone. One touch of God can remove the bitterness. Just ask Him to do it.

If we have been deeply hurt by someone, we continue to enable that person to control our lives if we live in bitterness toward that person. God promises to handle any vengeance that is due (see Romans 12:19). When we release the bitterness, we are set free.

We must resist the temptation to react resentfully because we believe we have been treated unfairly. Continuing bitterness actually can cause our body chemistry to become toxic. If this body chemistry continues, degenerative diseases often will form in our bodies.

A proud reaction often will cause us to be "contaminated and defiled" by Satan's demons. Satan and his demons *cannot* have any influence on us if we refuse to give up the peace that Jesus has given to us. We always should react in the humble and loving manner that will predominate whenever we truly have yielded to the Holy Spirit.

We will experience much less strife and contention and much more peace and joy if we build our relationships with other people upon these principles from the Word of God. We should have a deep and sincere desire to look at every relationship with another person through the eyes of Jesus Christ Who lives inside of us. We must listen to Him when we are in a crisis situation. He will reveal to us exactly what we should do in any situation.

In this chapter we have established a spiritual foundation that will help us to react in a humble and loving way, no matter how other people treat us. In the next chapter we will look into the Word of God to see exactly *how* to react with love and humility at all times.

Chapter 47

Peace and Love Are Fruit of the Holy Spirit

We have seen that our Father definitely wants us to have peaceful relationships with other human beings. We also have learned that peace is a fruit of the Holy Spirit. Peace is a fruit that the Holy Spirit will produce in us and through us to the degree that we truly yield control of our lives to Him.

Galatians 5:22 also tells us that love is a fruit of the Holy Spirit. When we are dealing with people who are very difficult to love, we only can love these people with the love of God that has been given to us through the Holy Spirit Who lives inside of us. "…God's love has been poured out in our hearts through the Holy Spirit Who has been given to us" (Romans 5:5).

The same Holy Spirit Who will produce the fruit of peace in us also will produce the fruit of love in us if we will surrender to Him because we trust Him completely. We *only* can enjoy peaceful relationships with other people who are difficult to love when the love of God flows in us and through us to these people. This love will flow to them because we have voluntarily surrendered our lives to the Holy Spirit Who lives in our hearts.

Our Father does not want us to pick and choose which people we will love and which people we will not love. He wants every aspect of our lives to be centered around His love flowing to us, in us and through us to others. "Let everything you do be done in love (true love to God and man as inspired by God's love for us)" (I Corinthians 16:14).

Loving everyone may seem to be absolutely impossible. If loving everyone was impossible, our Father would not have told us to let *everything* we do to be done in love. A direct correlation exists between the closeness of our relationship with God and our ability to love people who are difficult to love. "He who does not love has not become acquainted with God [does not and never did know Him], for God is love" (I John 4:8).

The key words in this passage of Scripture are the words "God is love." *Love and God are one and the same.* If we are unable to love all other people, we "have not become acquainted with God." We will be able to love everyone regardless of how these people treat us if we constantly draw closer to God. (Please refer to our Scripture cards and cassette tapes titled *A Closer Relationship With the Lord* and *Our Father's Wonderful Love* for additional scriptural information).

Jesus Christ urged us to love our enemies. He said, "You have heard that it was said, You shall love your neighbor and hate your enemy; but I tell you, Love your enemies and pray for those who persecute you, to show that you are the children of your Father Who is in heaven; for He makes His sun rise on the wicked and on the good, and makes the rain fall upon the upright and the wrongdoers [alike]. For if you love those who love you, what reward can you have? Do not even the tax collectors do that? And if you greet only your brethren, what more than others are you doing? Do not even the Gentiles (the heathen) do that? You, therefore, must be perfect [growing into complete maturity of godliness in mind and character, having reached the proper height of virtue and integrity], as your heavenly Father is perfect" (Matthew 5:43-48).

Jesus would not have instructed us to love our enemies and to pray for them if this goal was impossible to achieve. We easily can love people who love us. Christians should go one step beyond this human love. Our Father wants us to constantly grow and mature to the point at which we really are able to love people who are very difficult to love.

Some of these people know they are difficult to love. They have been rejected by many other people. When we love these people regardless of the way they treat us, our unconditional love clearly indicates that we are children of God. Some of these people will have a deep desire to have the godly love they see in us.

Some immature people would rather fight then reason. Their lives are not peaceful. They are continually squabbling with someone. Our Father wants us to say, "There must be some way we can work this out. Let's try to work our way through this problem."

When other people are cruel toward us and we respond to them with the love of God that is in our hearts, our loving response often removes opposition. This loving response differentiates us from the people who were cruel to us. These people can only affect us if we come down to their level by failing to obey our Father's instructions to love them unconditionally regardless of what they do to us.

Our Father does not want us to just act like we love people who are difficult to love – He wants us to *really love them* with His deep and sincere love that lives in our hearts. "[Let your] love be sincere (a real thing); hate what is evil [loathe all ungodliness, turn in horror from wickedness], but hold fast to that which is good. Love one another with brotherly affection [as members of one family], giving precedence and showing honor to one another" (Romans 12:9-10).

Our love for others should be sincere and real. Even though we are commanded to hate the evil influence that Satan has upon some people, we still should love them with the love of God that lives in our hearts. God hates sin, but He loves sinners. He wants us to love people who sin against us. We should pray for wisdom because dealing with irrational people requires the wisdom of God.

We have seen that the Word of God teaches that we often are not "wrestling with flesh and blood" when we have problems with other people. When people treat us unfairly, we should have enough spiritual maturity to realize that the way these people are treating us often is caused by Satan's ability to influence them. Some of these people will see God in us if we turn from Satan's wicked influence and reach out to them with the unfeigned and unconditional love of God.

The love of the world is conditional. God's love is unconditional. Our Father wants us to love others unconditionally just as He loves each of us unconditionally. Love is "...not conceited (arrogant and inflated with pride); it is not rude (unmannerly) and does not act unbecomingly. Love (God's love in us) does not insist on its own rights or its own way, for it is not self-seeking; it is not touchy or fretful or resentful; it takes no account of the evil done to it [it pays no attention to a suffered wrong]" (I Corinthians 13:5).

We have seen that love and peace are fruit that are produced when we have yielded our lives to the Holy Spirit. We only can love people who are difficult to love *when we love them with God's love* that the Holy Spirit continually places in our hearts. If we have yielded to the Holy Spirit, we will not be conceited, proud and rude. When God's love is flowing through us, we will not be selfish. We will not be resentful because someone has treated us unfairly.

We have seen that our Father does not want us to be proud. We cannot love unconditionally if we are proud. Unconditional love only can come out of a humble heart. The apostle Paul said, "I therefore, the prisoner for the Lord, appeal to and beg you to walk (lead a life) worthy of the [divine] calling to which you have been called [with behavior that is a credit to the summons to God's service, living as becomes you] with complete lowliness of mind (humility) and meekness (unselfishness, gentleness, mildness), with patience, bearing with one another and making allowances because you love one another. Be eager and strive earnestly to guard and keep the harmony and oneness of [and produced by] the Spirit in the binding power of peace" (Ephesians 4:1-3).

Paul urged the Ephesians to seek God's will for their lives. He explained that all of God's children have a divine calling. Our Father has a specific plan for each of our lives. We should have a deep and sincere desire to seek, find and carry out God's will for our lives (see our Scripture cards and the cassette tape that are titled *Find God's Will for Your Life).

We only can achieve this goal if we are humble and unselfish. Proud and selfish people cannot carry out God's will for their lives. Proud and selfish people are not patient with people who are difficult to love.

This passage of Scripture goes on to tell us that we should be flexible with people who are difficult to love. We are instructed to "strive earnestly" for harmony with other people. This harmony only can be acquired when it is produced by the Holy Spirit.

This passage of Scripture beautifully ties together peace, humility, love and the guidance of the Holy Spirit. We *can* love people who are difficult to love when we really do yield control of our lives to the Holy Spirit. "Love bears up under anything and everything that comes, is ever ready to believe the best of every person, its hopes are fadeless under all circumstances, and it endures everything [without weakening]. Love never fails [never fades out or becomes obsolete or comes to an end]..." (I Corinthians 13:7-8).

This passage of Scripture tells us that we should love at all times and under every circumstance. We always should look for the good qualities in other people instead of focusing on their faults. Our love should not weaken or fail. We have seen that God is love. *The reason that love never fails is because God never fails.*

In this chapter we have studied several Scripture references that show us the relationship between love, humility and being able to live at peace with other people because we have humbly surrendered our lives to the Holy Spirit Who continually pours the love of God into our hearts. In the next chapter we will study the Word of God to learn how to maintain the peace of God by overcoming the temptation to be angry with other people when we believe they have treated us unfairly.

Chapter 48

Peace Instead of Anger

If we truly are at peace with God, we will not allow ourselves to be easily provoked to anger. When anger starts to rise up on the inside of us, our Father wants us to turn to the Holy Spirit, trusting Him to help us as we yield to Him. Some of us need to learn more about managing anger than others. Some people who are extremely intense also are intense in conveying their anger. Other people are calm by nature. They do not become angry easily.

In addition to inherent individual personality characteristics, a definite relationship also exists between the degree of our surrender to God and how quickly we become angry. "A fool's wrath is quickly and openly known, but a prudent man ignores an insult" (Proverbs 12:16).

Immature people often respond very quickly with anger. As we grow and mature as Christians, the love of God should permeate our hearts. We will not respond angrily as we did before. "Good sense makes a man restrain his anger, and it is his glory to overlook a transgression or an offense" (Proverbs 19:11).

Some people feel that they have to respond when they believe they are being treated unfairly. They are so upset about the way they have been treated that they immediately respond. Our Father wants us to grow and mature to the point at which we will not automatically respond in anger. We should avoid senseless arguments with irrational people. Instead, we should pray for these people. "It is an honor for a man to cease from strife and keep aloof from it, but every fool will quarrel" (Proverbs 20:3).

Some of us are provoked to anger much too easily. Anyone can quarrel, but Christians who are yielded to the Holy Spirit will obey God's instructions to refuse to give in to anger. They will not allow their emotions to control them. "Let all bitterness and indignation and wrath (passion, rage, bad temper) and resentment (anger, animosity) and quarreling (brawling, clamor, contention) and slander (evil–speaking, abusive or blasphemous language) be banished from you, with all malice (spite, ill will, or baseness of any kind). And become useful and helpful and kind to one another, tenderhearted (compassionate, understanding, loving-hearted), forgiving one another [readily and freely], as God in Christ forgave you" (Ephesians 4:31-32).

This comprehensive passage of Scripture gives us many specific instructions pertaining to anger management. Please highlight or underline the word "all" in this passage of Scripture. Our Father wants each of us to grow and mature to the point where *all* bitterness, anger and resentment disappear from our lives. He wants us to be kind, compassionate and forgiving.

We should make the sacrifice of forgiving others just as we have been forgiven for our sins by the sacrifice of Jesus Christ. Anger and unforgiveness allow the person who caused us to be angry to control us. Kindness and forgiveness in spite of being treated unfairly clearly indicate that we have yielded to the Holy Spirit.

I believe that quiet, determined anger often can be justified when we see something wrong being done to someone else. We can be angry against the evil that is so rampant in the world today. Healthy anger against evil should be surrendered to the Holy Spirit for wisdom and counsel.

Selfish people allow anger to rise up quickly within them. Our Father wants us to be slow to anger. People who have a "short fuse" become angry very quickly. These people make a big mistake. "He who foams up quickly and flies into a passion deals foolishly…" (Proverbs 14:17).

Proud people often strike back at others immediately. Christians who truly are humble are able to restrain their anger and remain calm. "A [self-confident] fool utters all his anger, but a wise man holds it back and stills it" (Proverbs 29:11).

Christians who are living in the peace of God do not fly off the handle at the slightest provocation. Immature people show their immaturity by becoming angry quickly. "He who is slow to anger has great understanding, but he who is hasty of spirit exposes and exalts his folly" (Proverbs 14:29).

We have seen that repetition often is used in the Bible for purposes of emphasis. The Word of God repeatedly emphasizes that we should not become angry quickly. "A hot-tempered man stirs up strife, but he who is slow to anger appeases contention" (Proverbs 15:18).

Our Father is pleased when we refuse to give in to anger quickly. If we are slow to anger, we often will be able to stop problems before they start. "He who is slow to anger is better than the mighty, he who rules his [own] spirit than he who takes a city" (Proverbs 16:32).

When the Book of Proverbs was written, military commanders who took control of a city received great honor. This passage of Scripture tells us that being slow to anger is more honorable before God than taking control of a city in battle.

Our Father wants us to "rule our own spirits." He does not want us to be ruled by the circumstances in our lives, by our emotions or by the influence of Satan. Our Father wants us to stop contention before it becomes worse. "The beginning of strife is as when water first trickles [from a crack in a dam]; therefore stop contention before it becomes worse and quarreling breaks out" (Proverbs 17:14).

Sometimes disaster can be averted if a crack in a dam can be repaired quickly. The dam will burst if the power of the water builds up. This same principle applies to anger. Our Father wants us to immediately stop being angry before our anger becomes worse.

We have learned that the Holy Spirit must be in control of our lives if we want to experience the peace of God. We will not "fly off the handle" quickly if the Holy Spirit truly is in control of our lives. We will not allow anger to fester and build up deep down inside of ourselves. "Do not be quick in spirit to be angry or vexed, for anger and vexation lodge in the bosom of fools" (Ecclesiastes 7:9).

This passage of Scripture refers to "vexation." People who are vexed are easily irritated. They allow petty things to bother them. The Bible says that these people are fools.

Instead of opening our mouths immediately to vent our anger, we should think before we speak. Christians who are quickly angered are not living the way our Father wants us to live. "Understand [this], my beloved brethren. Let every man be quick to hear [a ready listener], slow to speak, slow to take offense and to get angry. For man's anger does not promote the righteousness God [wishes and requires]" (James 1:19-20).

We have seen that the Word of God repeatedly instructs us to be slow to anger. We now will see that the Word of God also repeatedly tells us to respond in a soft voice whenever we are tempted to be angry. Many arguments can be controlled solely by the tone of a person's voice. The first angry words will cause problems only *if* they are followed by an angry retort from the person these angry words were spoken to.

We face a test whenever other people raise their voices against us. How will we respond? Will we fail the test by responding with a raised voice or will we be wise enough to realize that we must not respond with anger just because angry words are spoken to us? Proud people respond angrily. Humble Christians respond softly or not at all.

If we respond quietly to angry words, we often will be able to stop a potentially volatile situation from developing. We "pour fuel on the fire" if we respond to anger with more anger. "A soft answer turns away wrath, but grievous words stir up anger" (Proverbs 15:1).

We will respond quietly if we have yielded to the Holy Spirit. This quiet response often stops the situation from becoming worse. "…soft speech breaks down the most bonelike resistance" (Proverbs 25:15).

"The most bonelike resistance" (very strong resistance) often can be broken down by speaking softly. We do not have to get the last word just because we have been wronged. Arguments always are prolonged when a proud person has to get in the last word. Many times an argument quiets down only to have one person suddenly say another angry word and the argument becomes heated again.

God's ways are very different from the ways of the world (see Isaiah 55:8-9). We must not respond the way that many worldly people respond if we want to experience the peace of God in our relationship with other people. "Say not, I will do to him as he has done to me; I will pay the man back for his deed" (Proverbs 24:29).

Some people think they can respond indignantly just because they obviously have been treated unfairly. Instead of retaliating in kind, we can trust the Lord to take care of the situation whenever we are treated unfairly. "Beloved, never avenge yourselves, but leave the way open for [God's] wrath; for it is written, Vengeance is Mine, I will repay (requite), says the Lord" (Romans 12:19).

Please highlight or underline the word "never" in this passage of Scripture. We should never seek revenge by taking things into our own hands. When we are treated unfairly, we always should give the problem to the Lord. We should let go of the problem and leave it with the Lord because we trust Him completely.

CONCLUSION

This book contains 441 Scripture references that give specific instructions on overcoming worry and anxiety and walking in the peace of God. The first twenty-eight chapters are filled with instructions and promises from the Word of God that will help you to overcome worry and anxiety. The next twenty chapters thoroughly explain scriptural principles pertaining to peace with God, the peace of God and peace with other human beings.

No reader can comprehend everything in this book in just one reading. This comprehensive book is meant to be studied, not just read. I believe you will find that you will learn much more from this book the second time you read it. Those readers who decide to study and meditate on the scriptural contents of this book three or more times will learn even more great truths from the Word of God.

I hope that you are as blessed after reading this book as Judy and I have been as we have written this book. I cannot explain the blessings I have experienced by receiving all of these magnificent revelations from the Holy Spirit and working with the many additions and corrections my wife has made. We are very fulfilled to see all of these spiritual truths between the covers of one book. We give all of the glory to the Lord. Praise the Lord.

We pray that the scriptural instructions and our explanation of these scriptural principles will be a practical help to you. We pray that you will be able to overcome worry, anxiety and fear as a result of applying the scriptural principles that are explained in this book. We pray that you will experience the peace of God to the fullest as you obey our Father's instructions and believe His promises pertaining to His peace.

We invite you to share this book with others. We all have a sphere of influence with a certain group of people who know us and trust us. Every person reading this book knows *many other people who need to learn how to overcome worry and anxiety.* We all know many people who need to learn how to be at peace with God, how to walk in the peace of God and how to live in peace with other human beings.

Do *not* hesitate to give this book to unbelievers. Many people have asked Jesus Christ to be their Savior as a result of the salvation message that is contained in each of our books.

If you will refer to the order forms at the end of this book, you will see that we offer a substantial quantity discount. We have offered this discount from the beginning of our ministry because we want our readers to be able to share the scriptural contents of our publications with as many people as possible.

Please look at the following list to see if you are interested in any of our other publications. All of our books and Scripture Meditation Cards are solidly anchored upon the Word of God.

Overcome worry and fear
Book: *Conquering Fear*
Scripture cards and cassette tape: *Freedom from Worry and Fear*

Increase your faith in God
Scripture cards and cassette tape: *Continually Increasing Faith in God*

Find God's will for your life
Book: *God's Will for Your Life*
Scripture cards and cassette tape: *Finding God's Will for Your Life*

Receive healing from sickness
Scripture cards and cassette tape: *Receive Healing from the Lord.*

Improved health
Book: *Increased Energy and Vitality.*

Financial success
Book: *Trust God for Your Finances*
Scripture cards and cassette tape: *Financial Instructions from God*

Assurance of God's indwelling presence
Scripture cards and cassette tape: *God is Always with You.*

Experience peace with God and the peace of God
Book: *Exchange Your Worries for God's Perfect Peace*
Scripture cards and cassette tape: *Enjoy God's Wonderful Peace*

Calm confidence in a crisis
Book: *Quiet Confidence in the Lord*

Your Father's love for you
Scripture cards and cassette tape: *Our Father's Wonderful Love*

A closer relationship with the Lord
Scripture cards and cassette tape: *A Closer Relationship with the Lord*

Increased patience and perseverance
Book: *Never, Never Give Up*

Your eternal home in heaven
Book: *What Will Heaven be Like?*

Overcoming adversity
Book: *Soaring Above the Problems of Life*

Scripture cards and cassette tape: *Receive God's Blessing in Adversity*

Effective Bible study

Book: *How to Study the Bible*

Eternal salvation

Book: *100 Years from Today*

Each of these topics is covered in scriptural detail in our books, Scripture Meditation Cards and cassette tapes. I also have recorded 35 individual cassette tapes to provide additional teaching on these and other subjects. We pray that many of our publications and cassette tapes will be a blessing to you and, through you, to several other people.

You might want to take a few moments to read comments from people all over the world whose lives have been changed by our books and Scripture Meditation Cards. As you read these comments, please ask yourself if the publication that is commented upon contains topical material that could help you or someone you know.

We pray that this book on the peace of God has blessed you abundantly. We pray that you will live in the peace of God and carry out in peace and joy your part in God's plan. We would be so pleased to hear from you.

Comments on our Books

The following are just a few of the hundreds of comments we have received on our books. Please take a few minutes to read these comments to see if any of these books can be a benefit to you.

- "I originally made a goal to read one chapter of the book on wisdom every day as part of my daily meditation and fellowship with God. However, sometimes I get to the point where even one page is more than enough for me. Sometimes even just one Scripture is enough. I stop and meditate on that Scripture throughout the day. This book is tremendous. It is just overwhelming. Sometimes I can only take very small bites of it because it is way too much if I try to read it too quickly." (Wisconsin)

- "You did a fantastic job on *God's Wisdom is Available to You*. This book is an encyclopedia on God's wisdom. The writing style is just great. Many books don't bring the reader through the subject the way this book does. I'm very impressed with that. You have made it a real joy for me to study and re-digest Scripture. This book has been very good for me." (North Carolina)

- "As I write, I am in a prison cell in South Africa awaiting trial. I want to thank Mr. Jack Hartman for his book *Soaring Above the Problems of Life*. I really do not know what I would have done without it. As I read through the pages, light dawned on me and I got comforted and understood why it is necessary that we go through a season of adversity." (Zimbabwe)

- "The free books and Scripture cards you sent me were so much more than I expected. I was moved almost to tears. May our Lord bless you one thousand times over for your generosity. I now have four of your books in my library. I dedicated my life to the Lord in part to your book *100 Years From Today*. I have loaned this book to five other men here in prison. Four of these men also have turned their lives over to the Lord. Hallelujah!" (Florida)

- "I am incarcerated at this time in a prison in Georgia. I thank you very much for your book *How to Study the Bible*. I fell in love with this book. I read it over three times before I put it down. This book has been such a positive factor in my spiritual life that I really feel super close to my God and my Lord Jesus Christ." (Georgia)

- "God sent me your book *Never, Never Give Up*. I praise God for using you to write and publish that book. Doing time in prison, especially here because I'm locked down 23 hours a day, 5 days a week and 24 hours on the weekend, has really taught me patience, endurance and perseverance living as a Christian and an inmate. I'm giving this book to the chaplain to put in the Chaplain's prison library so that it will be a blessing to other inmates." (Oklahoma)

- "When I received your book, *Never, Never Give Up*, all was well in my life. I was suppose to be married when I graduated from the Higher Institution of Learning, but this marriage never materialized. The lady I loved so much suffered from migraine headaches and eye pain. She suffered in great pain for almost a year and then she died. In all of this journey of suffering I read your book three times. The contents were meaningful to me and built a good strong character in me. Though my fiance died and went to be with the Lord, God saw me through that problem. *Never, Never Give Up* was a timely book. It is written simply and is easy to understand. I pray that the Lord will continue to use your ministry to help people who are going through tough times." (Zambia)

♦ "I would like permission to translate *Trust God for Your Finances*. This book is badly needed by the people of Turkey. Your books and your Scripture cards have been very helpful to my wife and myself. Thank you for your help." (Turkey)

♦ "We find your material to be so readable and upbuilding. Your writing communicates a clear and fatherly concern for the edification of the believer. *Trust God for Your Finances* is a tremendous book. Your book by far is the most thorough and systematic work I have read to date. The church here in Greece has a great need for this book." (Greece)

♦ "Thank you for the free books you sent me. I read *What Will Heaven be Like?* and I became a Christian immediately. Jesus Christ is now my Savior. I have started preaching to others who need Christ. God bless you and your family and all of your ministry workers." (Ghana)

♦ "I have just finished your book, *Soaring Above the Problems of Life*, and I am so excited. Each chapter ministered to me so much. My husband is an alcoholic. This book has prepared me for what I am struggling with now. It could not have come at a better time. God bless you." (Colorado)

- "It's a miracle. I read your book *Soaring Above the Problems of Life* with the idea of underlining all the good parts. I have underlined it all! It is wonderful that you went through all of that trouble to be a blessing to others." (Florida)

- "I've looked at several books on heaven and bought some, but none had the depth of the Holy Spirit in them as your book on heaven. I want to express my appreciation for the way the Spirit wrote through you." (Kentucky)

- "Your book, *What Will Heaven be Like?*, moved me deeply and made me even more anxious to join my husband in that wonderful eternal home. You will rejoice with me that one person to whom I gave your book has been saved as a result of reading it. The Holy Spirit is working through you." (New York)

- "I lost my brother, father-in-law, brother-in-law and our family dog of fifteen years in six months. Two years later, I lost my Mom. I suffered deep depression. Your book on heaven was a lifesaver. It lifted my spirits so much. It meant so much in my life that I ordered several to have on hand for friends. Thank you for writing it." (Missouri)

- "I am the Youth Director of our church and I'm leading a group of high school students in a Bible study of your book on heaven. We all respect your opinions and have found your book to be an excellent springboard for discussion. It is thought provoking and informative. This book has much substance and is well organized." (California)

- "Your book *How to Study the Bible* is terrific. At last we have a method to help on this important task. My wife and I just love it." (Nebraska)

- "My wife and I are utilizing the Bible study method that you explained in *How to Study the Bible*. We are really growing spiritually as a result. Our old methods of study were not nearly as fruitful. Thanks for writing about your method." (Idaho)

♦ "Thank you for pioneering into God's Word. Your book *How to Study the Bible* has somehow caused my rebelliousness, confusion and resistance to God's grace to dissipate. I am now able to quit arguing and confidently agree that 'all Scripture is given by inspiration of God' and build upon that. I am growing in my relationship with God. Thank you." (Alabama)

♦ "Your book, *How to Study the Bible*, has helped me and opened my eyes. Because of this book I accepted the Lord Jesus Christ as my personal Lord and Savior. Now I am a Baptist preacher. Please help me to help others. Bless you in His Name." (Ghana)

♦ "I must tell you how much your book, *Trust God for Your Finances*, has meant to me. I wish I had read it ten years ago when I first began my dental practice. It would have saved me much financial woe." (Mississippi)

♦ "Your book *Trust God for Your Finances* is absolutely terrific!!! You wrote it so clearly and in such a relaxed manner that anyone at any level can certainly understand it. Praise God!" (Minnesota)

♦ "My wife and I feel that *Trust God for Your Finances* is one of the most significant books of the last few decades. It is balanced, scriptural and corrective. Many will be encouraged to step out now that a mature word has been spoken in the midst of some confusion and imbalance. I predict an astonishing fruitfulness from this book." (Washington)

♦ "Your book *Trust God for Your Finances* is tremendous and has helped me very, very much. I found your book so interesting and knowledgeable and it excited me so that I found myself reading too fast just to find out what was ahead. The second reading of your wonderful book has helped me tremendously. Jack Hartman, you are gifted from God. I think that every Christian should have a copy of this book. God bless you." (Illinois)

♦ "Your book Trust *God for Your Finances* is so 'loaded' that it takes awhile to digest. God is opening my eyes to truths I haven't understood in the past. This book gives me fresh courage and faith." (Virginia)

♦ "I do not even have my G.E.D., but *Trust God for Your Finances* is so simple in detail that I am excited about understanding it." (Texas)

Comments on our Scripture Meditation Cards

If you haven't used our Scripture Meditation Cards, we hope that the following comments will cause you to use these valuable tools for Bible study and Scripture meditation.

♦ "Out of everything I have ever seen or read, your Scripture cards are the most simple but inspirational tools of God. As I'm visiting friends here in Florida, each morning we walk on the beach and take a set of Scripture cards with us and read them. We read them throughout the day and before we go to bed at night. I rang my sister in Australia and shared with her how inspirational the cards are. I am so excited about finding something so simple and easily shared with everyone I meet." (Australia)

♦ "I received the Lord just two months before I came to Bible school. My life is 180 degrees from what it was. I was bound by fear. I began to go over the *Freedom from Worry and Fear* Scripture Meditation Cards in the daytime and I listen to the tape at night. The verses jumped off the cards and into me! They became part of me. It was awesome. It was really a blessing!" (Florida)

♦ "My back was hurting so badly that I couldn't get comfortable. I was miserable whether I sat or stood or laid down. I didn't know what to do. Suddenly, I thought of the Scripture cards on healing that my husband had purchased. I decided to meditate on the Scripture in these cards. I was only on the second card when, all of a sudden, I felt heat go from my neck down through my body. The Lord had healed me. I never knew it could happen so fast. The pain has not come back." (Idaho)

♦ "I was recently involved in an automobile accident that was so severe that my car spun 360 degrees. While this was happening, I was amazed at how calm I was because I had just been meditating on one of the cards from *Freedom from Worry and Fear* with the Scripture reference, 'Fear not, I am with you always.' I wasn't afraid. I *knew* the Lord was with me." (Haiti)

♦ "I am very enthusiastic about your Scripture cards and your tapes titled, *Receive Healing from the Lord.* I love your tape. The clarity of your voice, your sincerity and compassion will encourage sick people. They can listen to this tape throughout the day, before they go to sleep at night, while they're driving to the doctor, in the hospital, etc. The tape is filled with Scripture and many good comments on Scripture. This cassette tape and your Scripture cards on healing are powerful tools that will help many sick people." (Tennessee)

♦ "Your cards and tapes on the subject of *Freedom From Worry and Fear* constantly remind me of God's great mercy, love, blessings and protection. I carry the cards in my shirt or jacket pocket where I can reach them easily. I have been greatly encouraged." (New Hampshire)

♦ "My husband is incarcerated in prison. I can't tell how much your Scripture cards and cassette tapes have helped me. I meditate on them continually. I gave the cards and tapes on healing to a friend of mine. She was very pleased. She said it was like I had given her a million dollar gift." (Florida)

♦ "I had no idea when you sent me these Scripture cards on *Freedom From Worry and Fear* that I would be using them every day. We have to get these out to the world. Thank you again for the cards. They're absolutely incredible." (Utah)

♦ "The result of meditating on these cards is amazing. I accomplished several times as much work as usual. In addition to increased energy, I was accurate and made no mistakes. My employer has noticed and favorably commented. These cards are also resulting in peaceful sleep each night. This is only the first week!" (Florida)

♦ "I have been in excellent health throughout my life and I was discouraged to learn recently that I had Hodgkin's disease. I often have trouble sleeping at night because of my concern because of this illness. I have found that meditating continually on the *Freedom From Worry and Fear* Scripture Meditation Cards has comforted me and helped me to sleep." (Illinois)

♦ "Your meditation cards have been so much rich food and an inspiration to me. I give them away for gifts. Now others are asking me where to send for them. They too would like to send them to their friends. These cards are a blessing to me and food for my soul. I enjoy giving them to others. God bless you richly for your work." (Pennsylvania)

♦ "I recently received a packet of cards titled *Freedom From Worry and Fear*. I have concluded that they would be ideal gifts for the members of my senior citizens Sunday school class. I'm enclosing my check to order 16 packets. I sincerely thank you for your thoughtful and unique distribution of Scripture." (Ohio)

♦ "I meditate constantly on the healing cards and listen to your tape on healing over and over. Your voice is so soothing. You are a wonderful teacher. My faith is increasing constantly." (New Hampshire)

♦ "A friend of mine recently gave me a pack of your financial meditation cards. They have changed my life. My relationship with my husband has even improved. Please send me ten packs of *Financial Instructions From God.* I would like to give them to my friends." (Maryland)

♦ "My friend gave me your Scripture Meditation Cards and the tape that goes with them. I have been in such bondage to negative thinking and speaking. I knew that I needed to renew my mind but I was unable to do so until I received this material. I decided to just read the cards and listen to the tape. Something broke and I was able to actually get the Word of God into my heart. I am finally 'getting it.' The anointing is setting me free. I want to thank you for being obedient to your heavenly Father to help others. Your material has helped me so much. I would like to send the enclosed publications to my friends. God bless you." (Florida)

♦ "I have truly enjoyed and found much peace from your meditation cards titled *Enjoy God's Wonderful Peace.* My work involves high pressure sales. Between phone calls I read these cards. They help to keep me focused on what is really important and what is not important. These meditation cards are an awesome idea to spread God's Word. They bring much hope, clarity and happiness in any trying time I run into." (Florida)

♦ "I was very pleased with the tape and cards on healing. My wife and I both love them. We are old and have several health problems. The cards and tape are going to help us." (Maine)

♦ "I cannot tell you how much interest your Scripture Meditation Cards have generated. I keep them at my desk and several people have borrowed them. They are truly a great teaching tool." (California)

♦ "I meditate over and over on a daily basis on God's promises from your Scripture cards. I want these promises to be a part of my makeup so that I will always respond with faith whenever I am tempted to be upset. The tapes that go with these cards are excellent. I have given the cards and the tapes to many people. One friend of mine who was suffering from Hodgkin's disease told me that meditation on these Scripture cards brought him through his most difficult time. Thank you for the Scripture cards." (Iowa)

♦ "Thank you very much for the many dynamic blessings that come from your meditation cards. They are very unique, very rich, full of life and very real." (Zambia)

Appendix

This book contains comprehensive biblical instructions that explain how to be set free from worry and anxiety, how to experience peace with God, how to receive the peace of God and how to be at peace with other human beings. These instructions are given to God's children - those human beings who have entered into His kingdom. We ask each person reading this book, "Have *you* entered into the kingdom of God?"

We do not enter into the kingdom of God by church attendance, baptism, confirmation, teaching Sunday school or living a good life. We *only* can enter into the kingdom of God if we have been "born again." Jesus said, "...I assure you, most solemnly I tell you, that unless a person is born again (anew, from above), he cannot ever see (know, be acquainted with, and experience) the kingdom of God" (John 3:3).

Some people are so caught up with their religious denomination and their personal beliefs that they completely miss God's instructions on how to enter His kingdom. We each were born physically when our mother delivered us from her womb. We also must be born spiritually. This process begins by admitting that we are sinners. We then must repent of these sins. Jesus said,"...unless you repent (change your mind for the better and heartily amend your ways, with abhorrence of your past sins), you will all likewise perish and be lost eternally" (Luke 13:5).

Many people miss out on eternal life in heaven because they are trusting in the goodness of their lives to get them to heaven. With the exception of Jesus Christ, *every* person who has ever lived is a sinner. "...None is righteous, just and truthful and upright and conscientious, no, not one" (Romans 3:10). We *all* are sinners. "...all have sinned and are falling short of the honor and glory which God bestows and receives" (Romans 3:23).

God does not have degrees of sin. If we have committed one sin, we are just as guilty before God as someone who has committed many sins. "For whosoever keeps the Law [as a] whole but stumbles and offends in one [single instance] has become guilty of [breaking] all of it" (James 2:10).

In addition to acknowledging our sins and repenting of them, we must take one additional step. "...if you acknowledge and confess with your lips that Jesus is Lord and in your heart believe (adhere to, trust in, and rely on the truth) that God raised Him from the dead, you will be saved. For with the heart a person believes (adheres to, trusts in, and relies on Christ) and so is justified (declared righteous, acceptable to God), and with the mouth he confesses (declares openly and speaks out freely his faith) and confirms [his] salvation" (Romans 10:9-10).

We must do more than just pay mental assent to the crucifixion of Jesus Christ to receive eternal salvation. We must admit that we are sinners. We must repent of our sins. We must believe deep down in our *hearts* that Jesus Christ has paid the full price for all of our sins by taking our place on the cross at Calvary. We must believe that Jesus died for us and that He has risen from the dead. We must believe totally, completely and absolutely that we will live eternally in heaven *only* because of the price that Jesus Christ paid for us.

If we really believe these spiritual truths in our hearts, we will speak them with our *mouths*. We may feel timid about doing this at first, but speaking of Jesus increases our faith and draws others to Him. We should tell other people that we have been born again, that we are Christians and that we trust completely in Jesus Christ for our eternal salvation.

All of us were born physically on the day our mothers gave birth to us. We must have a *second birth* to be born spiritually. "You have been regenerated (born again), not from a mortal origin (seed, sperm), but from one that is immortal by the ever living and lasting Word of God" (I Peter 1:23).

Why do we have to be born of the Spirit? We are born into the world with a body and a mind. The spirit of man was separated from God when Adam and Eve sinned. We live our lives only in the body and mind until the Spirit of God plants Himself in our hearts. At that moment, we are born of the Spirit. We are born again.

Jesus Christ became a man and lived a sinless life to become the required sacrifice for our sins. Jesus Christ is our bridge back to God. God sees us as righteous not because we are good, but because we are in Christ Jesus. The blood of Jesus Christ, the sinless sacrifice, was required to enable us to come into God's holy presence.

God does not reveal Himself to us through our intellects. He reveals Himself through our hearts. We may be adults in the natural realm, but we need to start all over again as children in the spiritual realm. We must have childlike faith. Jesus said,

"...unless you repent (change, turn about) and become like little children [trusting, lowly, loving, forgiving], you can never enter the kingdom of heaven [at all]" (Matthew 18:3).

The following prayer will result in your spiritual birth if you truly believe these words in your heart and if you boldly confess them to others with your mouth. "Dear Father God, I come to You in the name of Jesus Christ. I admit that I am a sinner. I am genuinely sorry for my sins. I believe in my heart that Jesus Christ is Your Son and that He died on the cross to pay for my sins. I believe that You raised Him from the dead and that He is alive today, sitting at Your right hand. I trust completely in Jesus Christ as my only way of receiving eternal salvation. Thank You, dear Lord Jesus. Thank You, dear Father. Amen."

You have been "born again" if you prayed this prayer from your heart and if you confessed these heartfelt beliefs with your mouth. You have been given a fresh new start "...if any person is [ingrafted] in Christ (the Messiah) he is a new creation (a new creature altogether); the old [previous moral and spiritual condition] has passed away. Behold, the fresh and new has come!" (II Corinthians 5:17).

You now have entered into the most precious relationship of all. Your previous spiritual condition changed when you were born into Christ Jesus. You are not the same person you were before. You are a child of Father God.

Begin to talk with your Father each day. Pray to Him continually. Study the Bible daily. Find other Christians who love God. Fellowship with them. Speak to others of your relationship with God. This new relationship that began when you asked Jesus Christ to be your Savior will grow and grow and your new life will be a very wonderful life where you will constantly draw closer to God.

Please contact us and let us know that you have become a child of God. We would like to pray for you and welcome you as our new brother or sister in Christ Jesus. We love you and bless you in the name of our Lord Jesus Christ. We would be so pleased to hear from you.

Study Guide

What Did You Learn
From This Book?

Many individuals, Bible study groups, Sunday school classes and home fellowship groups have carefully studied the Scripture references in our books and Scripture Meditation Cards to learn from the Word of God. The following questions have been designed as a study guide to help individuals and groups to receive maximum retention from the 441 Scripture references contained in this book.

This book can help you only if you are persuaded by the Word of God and by the Holy Spirit to obey the specific instructions from the holy Scriptures that are contained in this book. We believe the following questions will provide you with a thorough overview of the contents of this book:

Page Ref.

1. What did Jesus Christ tell us to do so that our hearts would not be overburdened with worry? (Luke 21:34) 1 1

187. When Jesus Christ walked on the water to approach a boat containing His disciples, they reacted with fear. What did Jesus say to them? How did Peter respond to these words from Jesus? Why did Peter ultimately

Spirit in his or her life. Have you received the Holy Spirit by faith in your life? Are you receiving the power and ability of the Holy Spirit? Are you experiencing the mighty outpouring of the Holy Spirit that is taking place in these last days before Jesus Christ returns? (John 20:21-22, Acts 1:8 and Acts 2:17) 321-322

A few words about
Lamplight Ministries

Lamplight Ministries, Inc. originally began in 1983 as Lamplight Publications. After ten years as a publishing firm with a goal of selling Christian books, Lamplight Ministries was founded in 1993. Jack and Judy Hartman founded Lamplight Ministries with a mission of continuing to sell their publications and also to give large numbers of these publications free of charge to needy people all over the world.

Lamplight Ministries was created to allow people who have been blessed by our publications to share in financing the translation, printing and distribution of our books into other languages and also to distribute our publications free of charge to jails and prisons. Over the years many partners of Lamplight Ministries have shared Jack and Judy's vision. As the years have gone by Lamplight Ministries' giving has increased with each passing year. Tens of thousands of people in jails and prisons and in Third World countries have received our publications free of charge.

Our books and Scripture Meditation Cards have been translated into eleven foreign languages – Armenian, Danish, Greek, Hebrew, German, Korean, Norwegian, Portuguese, Russian, Spanish and the Tamil dialect in India. The translations in these languages are not available from Lamplight Ministries in the United States. These translations can only be obtained in the countries where they have been printed.

The pastors of many churches in Third World countries have written to say that they consistently preach sermons in their churches based upon the scriptural contents of our publications. We believe that, on any given Sunday, people in several churches in many different countries hear sermons that are based upon the scriptural contents of our publications. Praise the Lord!

Jack Hartman was the sole author of twelve Christian books. After co-authoring one book with Judy, Jack and Judy co-authored ten sets of Scripture Meditation Cards. Judy's contributions to *God's Wisdom Is Available To You* and *Exchange Your Worries for God's Perfect Peace* were so significant that she is the co-author of these books. Jack and Judy currently are working on several other books that they believe the Lord is leading them to write as co-authors.

We invite you to request our newsletter to stay in touch with us, to learn of our latest publications and to read comments from people all over the world. Please write, fax, call or email us. You are very special to us. We love you and thank God for you. Our heart is to take the gospel to the world and for our books to be available in every known language. Hallelujah!

Lamplight Ministries, Inc.,
PO Box 1307, Dunedin, Florida, 34697. USA
Phone: 1-800-540-1597 • Fax: 1-727-784-2980 • website: lamplight.net • email: gospel@tampabay.rr.com

We offer you a substantial quantity discount

From the beginning of our ministry we have been led of the Lord to offer the same quantity discount to individuals that we offer to Christian bookstores. Each individual has a sphere of influence with a specific group of people. We believe that you know many people who need to learn the scriptural contents of our publications.

The Word of God encourages us to give freely to others. We encourage you to give selected copies of these publications to people you know who need help in the specific areas that are covered by our publications. See our order form for specific information on the quantity discounts of 40% to 50% that we make available to you so that you can share our books and cassette tapes with others.

A request to our readers

If this book has helped you, we would like to receive your comments so that we can share them with others. Your comments can encourage other people to study our publications to learn from the scriptural contents of these publications.

When we receive a letter containing comments on any of our books, cassette tapes or Scripture Meditation Cards, we prayerfully take out excerpts from these letters. These selected excerpts are included in our newsletters and occasionally in our advertising and promotional materials.

If any of our publications have been a blessing to you, please share your comments with us so that we can share them with others. Tell us in your own words what a specific publication has meant to you and why you would recommend it to others. Please give as much specific information as possible.

We will need your written permission to use all or any part of your comments. We will never print your name or street address. We simply use the initials of your first and last name and the state or country you live in (E.G., Illinois).

Thank you for taking a few minutes of your time to encourage other people to learn from the scripture references in our publications.

Books by Jack and Judy Hartman

Exchange Your Worries for God's Perfect Peace — Our Father does not want His children to worry. He wants each of us to be absolutely certain that He has provided for all of our needs, that He lives in our hearts, that He is with us at all times and that He will help us if we have faith in Him. This books contains over 400 Scripture references that explain exactly what we should do to be set free from worry and fear and exactly what we should do to receive God's perfect peace that has been provided for us.

God's Wisdom Is Available To You explains from more than 500 Scripture references how to receive the wisdom our Father has promised to give to us. God looks at the wisdom of the world as "foolishness" (see I Corinthians 3:19). You will learn how to receive the revelation knowledge, guidance and wisdom from God that bypasses sense knowledge.

Trust God for Your Finances is currently in its nineteenth printing with more than 150,000 copies in print. This book which has been translated into nine foreign languages contains over 200 Scripture references that explain in a simple, straightforward and easy-to-understand style what the Word of God says about our Father's instructions and promises pertaining to our finances.

Never, Never Give Up devotes the first five chapters to a scriptural explanation of patience and the remaining thirteen chapters to scriptural instruction pertaining to the subject of perseverance. This book is based upon almost 300 Scripture references that will help you to learn exactly what our loving Father instructs us to do to increase our patience and perseverance.

Quiet Confidence in the Lord is solidly anchored upon more than 400 Scripture references that explain how to remain calm and quiet in a crisis situation. You will learn from the Word of God how to control your emotions when you are faced with severe problems and how to increase your confidence in the Lord by spending precious quiet time alone with Him each day.

What Will Heaven Be Like? explains from more than 200 Scripture references what the Bible tells us about what heaven will be like. Many people have written to tell us how much this book comforted them after they lost a loved one. We have received many other letters from terminally ill Christians who were comforted by scriptural facts about where they would be going in the near future.

Soaring Above the Problems of Life has helped many people who were going through severe trials. This practical "hands on" book is filled with facts from the Word of God. Our Father has given each of us specific and exact instructions telling us how He wants us to deal with adversity. This book is written in a clear and easy-to-understand style that will help you to learn to deal with the adversity that we all must face in our lives.

How to Study the Bible. Many Christians attempt to study the Bible and give up because they are unable to find a fruitful method of Bible study. This book explains in detail the method that Jack Hartman uses to study the Bible. This practical, step-by-step technique will give you a definite, specific and precise system for studying the Word of God. Any person who sincerely wants to study the Bible effectively can be helped by this book and our two cassette tapes on this subject.

Increased Energy and Vitality. Jack and Judy Hartman are senior citizens who are determined to be in the best possible physical condition to serve the Lord during the remainder of their lives. They have spent many hours of study and practical trial and error to learn how to increase their energy and vitality. This book is based upon more than 200 Scripture references that will help you to increase your energy and vitality so that you can serve the Lord more effectively.

Nuggets of Faith – Jack Hartman has written over 100,000 spiritual meditations. This book contains some of his early meditations on the subject of increasing our faith in God. It contains 78 "nuggets" (average length of three paragraphs) to help you to increase your faith in God.

100 Years from Today tells exactly where each of us will be one hundred years from now if Jesus Christ is our Savior and where we will be if Jesus Christ is not our Savior.

This simple and easy-to-understand book has helped many unbelievers to receive Jesus Christ as their Savior. This book leads the reader through the decision to eternal salvation. The book closes by asking the reader to make a decision for Jesus Christ and to make this decision now.

Conquering Fear – Many people in the world today are afraid because they see that various forms of worldly security are disappearing. Our Father does not want us to be afraid. He has told us 366 times in His Word that we should not be afraid. This book is filled with scriptural references that explain the source of fear and how to overcome fear.

God's Will For Our Lives teaches from the holy Scriptures why we are here on earth, what our Father wants us to do with our lives and how to experience the meaning and fulfillment we can only experience when we are carrying out God's will. God had a specific plan for each of our lives before we were born. He has given each of us abilities and talents to carry out the assignment He has given to us.

Scripture Meditation Cards and Cassette Tapes by Jack and Judy Hartman

Each set of Scripture Meditation Cards consists of 52 2-1/2 inch by 3-1/2 inch cards that can easily be carried in a pocket or a purse. Each set of Scripture cards includes approximately 75 Scripture references and is accompanied by an 85-minute cassette tape that explains every passage of Scripture in detail.

Freedom From Worry and Fear

The holy Scriptures tell us repeatedly that our Father does not want us to be worried or afraid. There is no question that God doesn't want us to be worried or afraid, but what exactly should we do if we have a sincere desire to overcome worry and fear? You will learn to overcome worry and fear from specific factual instructions from the Word of God. You will learn how to have a peaceful mind that is free from fear. You'll learn to live one day at a time forgetting the past and not worrying about the future. You'll learn how to trust God completely instead of allowing worry and fear to get into your mind and into your heart.

Enjoy God's Wonderful Peace

Peace with God is available to us because of the sacrifice that Jesus Christ made for us at Calvary. In addition to peace with God, Jesus also has given us the opportunity to enjoy the peace of God. You will learn how to enter into God's rest to receive God's perfect peace that will enable you to remain calm and quiet deep down inside of yourself regardless of the circumstances you face. You will learn exactly what to do to experience God's peace that is so great that it surpasses human understanding. The Holy Spirit is always calm and peaceful. We can experience His wonderful peace if we learn how to yield control of our lives to Him.

Find God's Will for Your Life

The Bible tells us that God had a specific plan for every day of our lives before we were born. Our Father will not reveal His will for our lives to us if we seek His will passively. He wants us to hunger and thirst with a deep desire to live our lives according to His will. God's plan for our lives is far over and above anything we can comprehend with our limited human comprehension. We cannot experience deep meaning, fulfillment and satisfaction in our lives without seeking, finding and carrying out God's will for our lives.

Receive God's Blessings in Adversity

The Lord is with us when we are in trouble. He wants to help us and He will help us according to our faith in Him. He wants us to focus continually on Him instead of dwelling upon the problems we face. We must not give up hope. Our Father will never let us down. He has made provision to give us His strength in exchange for our weakness. Our Father wants us to learn, grow and mature by facing the problems in our lives according to the instructions He has given us in His Word. We must persevere in faith to walk in the magnificent victory that Jesus Christ won for us.

Financial Instructions from God

Our loving Father wants His children to be financially successful just as loving parents here on earth want their children to be successful. God's ways are much higher and very different from the ways of the world. Our Father doesn't want us to follow the world's system for financial prosperity. He wants us to learn and obey His instructions pertaining to our finances. You will learn how to renew your mind in the Word of God so that you will be able to see your finances in a completely different light than you see them from a worldly perspective. You will be given step-by-step instructions to follow to receive financial prosperity from God.

Receive Healing from the Lord

Many people are confused by the different teachings about whether God heals today. Are you sick? Would you like to see for yourself exactly what the Bible says about divine healing? Study the Word of God on this important subject. Draw your own conclusion based upon facts from the holy Scriptures. You will learn that Jesus Christ has provided for your healing just as surely as He has provided for your eternal salvation. You will learn exactly what the Word of God instructs you to do to increase your faith that God will heal you.

A Closer Relationship with the Lord

Because of the price that Jesus Christ paid at Calvary all Christians have been given the awe-inspiring opportunity to come into the presence of Almighty God. These Scripture cards clearly explain the secret of enjoying a sweet and satisfying relationship with the Lord. Many Christians know about the Lord, but He wants us to know Him personally. We should have a deep desire to enjoy a close personal relationship with our precious Lord. He has promised to come close to us if we sincerely desire a close relationship with Him.

Our Father's Wonderful Love

God showed His love for us by sending His beloved Son to earth to die for our sins. Jesus Christ showed His love for us by taking the sins of the entire world upon Himself on the cross at Calvary. The same love and compassion that was demonstrated during the earthly ministry of Jesus Christ is available to us today. Because of the sacrifice of Jesus Christ all Christians are the beloved sons and daughters of Almighty God. God is our loving Father. Our Father doesn't want us to seek security from external sources. He wants us to be completely secure in His love for us. You will learn from the Word of God exactly how faith works by love and how to overcome fear through love.

God is Always with You

God is not far away. He lives in our hearts. We must not neglect the gift that is in us. We are filled with the Godhead -- Father, Son and Holy Spirit. Why would we ever be afraid of anything or anyone if we are absolutely certain that God is always with us? God's power and might are much greater than we can comprehend. He watches over us at all times. He wants to help us. He wants us to walk in close fellowship with Him. His wisdom and knowledge are available to us. He wants to guide us throughout every day of our lives.

We all are given the same amount of faith to enable us to become children of God. Our Father wants the faith that He gave us to grow continually. We live in the last days before Jesus Christ returns. We must learn how to develop deeply rooted faith in God. You will learn how to walk in the authority and power you have been given over Satan and his demons. You can walk in victory over the circumstances in your life. You will learn exactly what the holy Scriptures tell us to do to receive manifestation of God's mighty strength and power. You will learn the vital importance of the words you speak. You will learn that there is only one way to control the words you speak when you are under severe pressure in a crisis situation.

Why you cannot combine orders for quantity discounts for Scripture Meditation Cards with other products

We desire to make the purchase of our products as *simple* as possible. However, we are unable to combine orders for our Scripture Meditation Cards with orders for our other products.

The reason for this decision is that the cost of printing and packaging Scripture Meditation Cards is much higher in proportion to the purchase price than the price of printing books. If we wanted to offer the same percentage quantity discount that we offer with our books, the cost for one set of Scripture Meditation Cards would have to be $7. This price was unacceptable to us.

We decided to offer each individual set of Scripture Meditation Cards for a reasonable price of $5 including postage. In order to keep this price for individual sets of Scripture Meditation Cards this low we had to develop an entirely different price structure for quantity discounts. Please see the enclosed order form for information on these discounts.

Cassette Tapes
by Jack Hartman

01H How to Study the Bible (Part 1) – 21 scriptural reasons why it's important to study the Bible

02H How to Study the Bible (Part 2) – A detailed explanation of a proven, effective system for studying the Bible

03H Enter Into God's Rest – Don't struggle with loads that are too heavy for you. Learn what God's Word teaches about relaxing under pressure.

04H Freedom From Worry – A comprehensive scriptural explanation of how to become free from worry

05H God's Strength, Our Weakness – God's strength is available if we can admit our human weakness and trust instead in His unlimited strength.

06H How to Transform Our Lives – A scriptural study of how we can change our lives through a spiritual renewal of our minds.

07H The Greatest Power in the Universe (Part 1) – The greatest power in the universe is love. This tape explains our Father's love for us.

08H **The Greatest Power in the Universe** (Part 2) – A scriptural explanation of our love for God and for each other, and how to overcome fear through love.

09H **How Well Do You Know Jesus Christ?** – An Easter Sunday message that will show you Jesus as you never knew Him before.

10H **God's Perfect Peace** – In a world of unrest, many people search for inner peace. Learn from God's Word how to obtain His perfect peace.

11H **Freedom Through Surrender** – Many people try to find freedom by "doing their own thing." God's Word says that freedom comes from surrendering our lives to Jesus Christ.

12H **Overcoming Anger** – When is anger is permissible and when is it a sin? Learn from the Bible how to overcome the sinful effects of anger.

13H **Taking Possession of Our Souls** – God's Word teaches that patience is the key to the possession of our souls. Learn from the Word of God how to increase your patience and endurance.

14H **Staying Young in the Lord** – Some people try to cover up the aging process with makeup, hair coloring and hairpieces. Learn from the Bible how you can offset the aging process.

15H **Two Different Worlds** – Specific instructions from the Word of God to help you enter into and stay in the presence of God.

16H **Trust God For Your Finances** – This tape is a summary of the highlights of Jack's best-selling book, *Trust God For Your Finances.*

17H **The Joy of the Lord** – Learn how to experience the joy of the Lord regardless of the external circumstances in your life.

18H **Let Go and Let God** – Our Father wants us to give our problems to Him and leave them with Him because we have complete faith in Him..

19H **Guidance, Power, Comfort and Wisdom** – Learn the specific work of the Holy Spirit Who will guide us, empower us, comfort us and give us wisdom.

20H **Go With God** – This tape is based on 35 Scripture references that explain why and how to witness to the unsaved.

21H **One Day at a Time** – Our Father doesn't want us to dwell on the past nor worry about the future. Learn how to follow biblical instructions to live your life one day at a time.

22H **Never, Never Give Up** – Endurance and perseverance are often added to our faith as we wait on the Lord, releasing our will to His.

23H **The Christ-Centered Life** – Some Christians are still on the throne of their lives pursuing personal goals. Learn how to center every aspect of your life around the Lord Jesus Christ.

24H **Fear Must Disappear** – The spirit of fear cannot stand up against perfect love. Learn what perfect love is and how to attain it.

25H **Internal Security** – Some Christians look for security from external sources. In this tape, Jack shares his belief that difficult times are ahead of us and the only security in these times will be from the Spirit of God and the Word of God living in our hearts.

26H **Continually Increasing Faith** – Romans 12:3 tells us that all Christians start out with a specific amount of faith. In these last days before Jesus returns, we will all need a stronger faith than just the minimum. This tape offers many specific suggestions on what to do to continually strengthen our faith.

27H **Why Does God Allow Adversity?** – Several Scripture references are used in this tape to explain the development of strong faith through adversity.

28H **Faith Works by Love** – Galatians 5:6 tells us that faith works by love. Christians wondering why their faith doesn't seem to be working may find an answer in this message. A life centered around the love of the Lord for us and our love for others is absolutely necessary to strong faith.

29H **There Are No Hopeless Situations** – Satan wants us to feel hopeless. He wants us to give up hope and quit. This tape explains the difference between hope and faith. It tells how we set our goals through hope and bring them into manifestation through strong, unwavering faith.

30H **Walk By Faith, Not By Sight** – When we're faced with seemingly unsolvable problems, it's easy to focus our attention on the problems instead of upon the Word of God and the Spirit of God. In this tape, Jack gives many personal examples of difficult situations in his life and how the Lord honored his faith and the faith of others who prayed for him.

31H **Stay Close to the Lord** – Our faith is only as strong as its source. A close relationship with the Lord is essential to strong faith. In this tape, Jack explores God's Word to give a thorough explanation of how to develop a closer relationship with the Lord.

32H **Quiet Faith** – When we're faced with very difficult problems, the hardest thing to do is to be still. The Holy Spirit, however, wants us to remain quiet and calm because of our faith in Him. This message carefully examines the Word of God for an explanation of how we can do this.

33H **When Human Logic is Insufficient** – Human logic and reason often miss God. This message explains why some Christians block the Lord because they're unable to bypass their intellects and place their trust completely in Him.

34H **The Good Fight of Faith** – In this message, Jack compares the "good fight of faith" with the "bad" fight of faith. He explains who we fight against, where the battle is fought, and how it is won.

ORDER FORM FOR BOOKS AND CASSETTE TAPES

Book Title	Quantity	Total
Exchange Your Worries for God's Perfect Peace ($12.00)	_____	_____
God's Wisdom is Available to You ($12.00)	_____	_____
Increased Energy and Vitality ($10.00)	_____	_____
Quiet Confidence in the Lord ($9.00)	_____	_____
Never, Never Give Up ($8.00)	_____	_____
Trust God For Your Finances ($8.00)	_____	_____
What Will Heaven Be Like? ($8.00)	_____	_____
Conquering Fear ($8.00)	_____	_____
Soaring Above the Problems of Life ($8.00)	_____	_____
God's Will For Our Lives ($8.00)	_____	_____
How to Study the Bible ($5.00)	_____	_____
Nuggets of Faith ($5.00)	_____	_____
100 Years From Today ($5.00)	_____	_____

Cassette Tapes (please indicate quantity being ordered) • *$5 each*

_____01H _____02H _____03H _____04H _____05H _____06H _____07H
_____08H _____09H _____10H _____11H _____12H _____13H _____14H
_____15H _____16H _____17H _____18H _____19H _____20H _____21H
_____22H _____23H _____24H _____25H _____26H _____27H _____28H
_____29H _____30H _____31H _____32H _____33H _____34H

Price of books and tapes	_____
Minus 40% discount for 5-9 items	_____
Minus 50% discount for 10 or more items	_____
Net price of order	_____
Add 15% **before discount** for shipping and handling	_____
(Maximum of $50 for any size order)	
Florida residents only, add 7% sales tax	_____
Tax deductible contribution to Lamplight Ministries, Inc.	_____
Enclosed check or money order (do not send cash)	_____

(Please make check payable to Lamplight Ministries, Inc. and mail to: PO Box 1307, Dunedin, FL 34697)

MC_____ Visa_____ AmEx_____ Disc._____ Card # _____

Exp Date _____ Signature _____

Name _____

Address _____

City _____

State or Province _____ Zip or Postal Code _____

(Foreign orders must be submitted in U.S. dollars.)

ORDER FORM FOR BOOKS AND CASSETTE TAPES

Book Title	Quantity	Total
Exchange Your Worries for God's Perfect Peace ($12.00)	_____	_____
God's Wisdom is Available to You ($12.00)	_____	_____
Increased Energy and Vitality ($10.00)	_____	_____
Quiet Confidence in the Lord ($9.00)	_____	_____
Never, Never Give Up ($8.00)	_____	_____
Trust God For Your Finances ($8.00)	_____	_____
What Will Heaven Be Like? ($8.00)	_____	_____
Conquering Fear ($8.00)	_____	_____
Soaring Above the Problems of Life ($8.00)	_____	_____
God's Will For Our Lives ($8.00)	_____	_____
How to Study the Bible ($5.00)	_____	_____
Nuggets of Faith ($5.00)	_____	_____
100 Years From Today ($5.00)	_____	_____

Cassette Tapes (please indicate quantity being ordered) • *$5 each*

_____01H _____02H _____03H _____04H _____05H _____06H _____07H
_____08H _____09H _____10H _____11H _____12H _____13H _____14H
_____15H _____16H _____17H _____18H _____19H _____20H _____21H
_____22H _____23H _____24H _____25H _____26H _____27H _____28H
_____29H _____30H _____31H _____32H _____33H _____34H

Price of books and tapes _____
Minus 40% discount for 5-9 items _____
Minus 50% discount for 10 or more items _____
Net price of order _____
Add 15% **before discount** for shipping and handling _____
  (Maximum of $50 for any size order)
Florida residents only, add 7% sales tax _____
Tax deductible contribution to Lamplight Ministries, Inc. _____
Enclosed check or money order (do not send cash) _____

(Please make check payable to Lamplight Ministries, Inc. and mail to: PO Box 1307, Dunedin, FL 34697)

MC_____ Visa_____ AmEx_____ Disc._____ Card # _____
Exp Date _____ Signature _____
Name _____
Address _____
City _____
State or Province _____ Zip or Postal Code _____
(Foreign orders must be submitted in U.S. dollars.)

ORDER FORM FOR SCRIPTURE MEDITATION CARDS AND CASSETTE TAPES

Due to completely different price structure for the production of Scripture Meditation Cards and 85-minute cassette tapes, we offer a different quantity discount which cannot be combined with our other quantity discounts. The following prices *include shipping and handling.* $5 per card deck or cassette tape; $4 for 5-9 card decks or cassette tapes; $3 for 10 or more card decks or cassette tapes.

SCRIPTURE MEDITATION CARDS	QUANTITY	PRICE
Find God's Will for Your Life		
Financial Instructions from God		
Freedom from Worry and Fear		
A Closer Relationship with the Lord		
Our Father's Wonderful Love		
Receive Healing from the Lord		
Receive God's Blessing in Adversity		
Enjoy God's Wonderful Peace		
God is Always with You		
Continually Increasing Faith in God		

CASSETTE TAPES

Find God's Will for Your Life		
Financial Instructions from God		
Freedom from Worry and Fear		
A Closer Relationship with the Lord		
Our Father's Wonderful Love		
Receive Healing from the Lord		
Receive God's Blessing in Adversity		
Enjoy God's Wonderful Peace		
God is Always with You		
Continually Increasing Faith in God		

TOTAL PRICE _____

Florida residents only, add 7% sales tax _____

Tax deductible contribution to Lamplight Ministries, Inc. _____

Enclosed check or money order (do not send cash) _____

Please make check payable to Lamplight Ministries, Inc. and mail to: PO Box 1307, Dunedin, FL 34697

MC____ Visa____ AmEx____ Disc.____ Card # _____

Exp Date _____ Signature _____

Name _____

Address _____

City _____

State or Province _____ Zip or Postal Code _____

(Foreign orders must be submitted in U.S. dollars.)

ORDER FORM FOR SCRIPTURE MEDITATION CARDS AND CASSETTE TAPES

Due to completely different price structure for the production of Scripture Meditation Cards and 85-minute cassette tapes, we offer a different quantity discount which cannot be combined with our other quantity discounts. The following prices *include shipping and handling.* $5 per card deck or cassette tape; $4 for 5-9 card decks or cassette tapes; $3 for 10 or more card decks or cassette tapes.

SCRIPTURE MEDITATION CARDS	QUANTITY	PRICE
Find God's Will for Your Life		
Financial Instructions from God		
Freedom from Worry and Fear		
A Closer Relationship with the Lord		
Our Father's Wonderful Love		
Receive Healing from the Lord		
Receive God's Blessing in Adversity		
Enjoy God's Wonderful Peace		
God is Always with You		
Continually Increasing Faith in God		

CASSETTE TAPES

	QUANTITY	PRICE
Find God's Will for Your Life		
Financial Instructions from God		
Freedom from Worry and Fear		
A Closer Relationship with the Lord		
Our Father's Wonderful Love		
Receive Healing from the Lord		
Receive God's Blessing in Adversity		
Enjoy God's Wonderful Peace		
God is Always with You		
Continually Increasing Faith in God		

TOTAL PRICE _____

Florida residents only, add 7% sales tax _____

Tax deductible contribution to Lamplight Ministries, Inc. _____

Enclosed check or money order (do not send cash) _____

Please make check payable to Lamplight Ministries, Inc. and mail to: PO Box 1307, Dunedin, FL 34697

MC____ Visa____ AmEx____ Disc.____ Card # _____

Exp Date _____ Signature _____

Name _____

Address _____

City _____

State or Province _____ Zip or Postal Code _____

(Foreign orders must be submitted in U.S. dollars.)

The Vision of Lamplight Ministries

Lamplight Ministries, Inc. is founded upon Psalm 119:105 which says, "Your word is a lamp to my feet and a light to my path." We are so grateful to our loving Father for His precious Word that clearly shows us the path He wants us to follow throughout every day of our lives.

From the beginning of our ministry God has used us to reach people in many different countries. Our vision is to share the instructions and promises in the Word of God with multitudes of people in many different countries throughout the world.

We are believing God for the finances to provide the translation of our publications into many different foreign languages. We desire to give our publications free of charge to needy people all over the world who cannot afford to purchase them.

We are believing God for many partners in our ministry who will share our vision of distributing our publications which are solidly anchored upon the Word of God. It is our desire to provide these publications in every foreign language that we possibly can.

We yearn to share the Word of God with large numbers of people in Third World countries. We yearn to share the Word of God with large numbers of people in prisons and jails. These people desperately need to learn and obey God's instructions and to learn and believe in God's promises.

Please pray and ask the Lord if He would have you help us to help needy people all over the world. Thank you and God bless you.